CRICKET
ON
EVEREST

ALAN CURR

To everyone involved in
The Everest Test 2009, thanks for your support.

ABOUT THE AUTHOR

Alan Curr was born in Gibraltar in 1981 and spent two early years living in Hong Kong before returning to the family home in Cornwall aged five. Upon finishing school in 1999 he earned a degree in history from Reading University and during this time began his independent travelling. A career in travel followed, working for Flight Centre on and off between 2004-2010 while also gaining a National Council of Training Journalist qualification from Sportsbeat News Associates in 2008. He also did some freelance writing for the cricket website Cricinfo.com and the football publication The Non-League Paper prior to The Everest Test and was lucky enough to be present at every game of the successful 2003 World Cup campaign in Australia, as well as the 2007 Cricket World Cup Final in Barbados in 2007. After spending much of 2009-10 travelling Alan has currently visited more than 40 countries worldwide, including a three-month stint living in Kathmandu. He returned to London in 2010 where he works as an Operations Manager for the Adventure Travel company Wild Frontiers.

CONTENTS

Authors Note – *viii*
Acknowledgements – *ix*
Cricket Foreword – *xi*
Adventure Foreword – *xiii*

Part One: The Preparation – *1*
Part Two: The Mountain – *95*
Part Three: The Test – *107*
Epilogue – *241*
Everest Test People – *246*

AUTHOR'S NOTE

Although it has taken three years for the full story behind the Everest Test to come to print, the vast majority of what you will read was penned within three months of our return from Kathmandu.

Naturally I have revisited the text many times in the years since, but I have been keen not to make major changes with the benefit of hindsight. When I read the final draft recently I smiled at the insignificance of some things that had annoyed me so much back then, but feel it is important to keep emotion at the surface and not tone things down in fear of upsetting someone.

Of course, with this being an event that involved so many people, it is impossible for me to have been present for every situation mentioned. I was careful to trawl through people's blogs, diaries, and emails, as well as carry out interviews after the event in order to cover as many angles as I possibly could before I sat down to write. Should there be any minor inaccuracies then I apologise.

Writing this book has given me great pleasure, as well as plenty of frustration and many headaches. It has enabled me gain a greater understanding of Nepal, its people and its mountain. Climbers and the adventure community in general are also a new world that I am delighted to have discovered. In finishing this book however, I finally feel that Cricket on Everest is complete. I hope you enjoy reading the story and should you ever be tempted, I can strongly recommend a visit to Nepal and of course, if you need anyone to organise a cricket match....

Alan Curr,

London, 2012

ACKNOWLEDGMENTS

The sheer number of people involved with The Everest Test makes it impossible to acknowledge them all in a space as short as this, but there are a few key people not mentioned in the pages that follow who deserve to be singled out.

The first is unquestionably Jenny Roesler, who has read, re-read, cut, edited and proofed this book from the first draft to the final product. This process has taken the best part of two years, and for which she has asked for nothing in return. Quite simply, this would not have been produced without your support and assistance. I cannot thank you enough.

My immediate family have of course been incredibly supportive, especially my parents Sue and Ralph Curr allowed me to take over their living room for the summer months after the expedition which enabled me to collect my notes and write the first draft of this book. I know they have a sense of pride in what we achieved, and I hope this finished work increases that. Making you guys proud was one of my chief motivations for this entire project.

Next would have to be my good friend Phil Reid, who has designed the cover, the layout, helped choose the pictures and been a constant source of advice and assistance – all while trying to run his own business and again, has asked for nothing more than a few beers in return. Cheers buddy, I owe you.

Jeremy Thompson and his team at Troubadour Publishing were a breath of fresh air at a time when I was ready to give up on the publication altogether. Trying to publish anything is it seems is an incredibly difficult task when you know absolutely nothing about it and have no clue where to start. Jeremy answered every one of my mundane and quite often stupid questions promptly and with good humour. It was a great relief to find a publisher were happy to help.

Lawrence Booth and Oli Broom have provided the forewords you will shortly read. I have met each of these gentlemen just once at the time of writing, but they both agreed to pen a few words as soon as I asked. At a time when players (both past and present) wanted to know how much I'd be willing to pay for a foreword to a book I was self publishing, these two asked for nothing more than a copy of the manuscript before lending their time and effort to endorse it. Thank you both.

Andrew Hill and Marcus Williams are two gentlemen who had sons on the trip and were again happy to lend their time and expertise to me at different times in the creation of this book. Marcus helped in the initial planning and Andrew did the final proof. Thank you both very much.

There are plenty of images throughout these pages, basically because I found it too hard to choose a small selection. This says much about the quality of those taken by Will Wintercross, George POwell and Jamie Zubairi, so thank you all for those.

It would be remiss of me not to thank the guys I worked with at Flight Centre during the organisation period. Becky Greaves, Julie Johnson and Neil Holland certainly had to pick up some of my workload as I rather obviously allowed all things Everest to dominate my thoughts. Likewise Tasha Mason, Jenny Brooke and Matt Johnson who shared our office and had to put up with bags upon bags of cricket equipment (scoreboard and all) stacking up around them as departure loomed.

In the same vein, my flatmates Nick and Marie Newman required a special patience as their crazy tenant told them about this peculiar idea and then took over the living room with planning meetings, kit storage and even the occasional massage table in the injury plagued months leading up to the Berlin Marathon.

To the rest of those involved, I hope what follows is acknowledgement enough to what you all achieved. Everyone on the trip contributed in one way or another and make the story what it is. Those who did not come to Nepal, but helped shape events through media coverage, and especially to those who gave sponsorship and support, are just as significant and I thank you all equally.

Finally, to my buddy Kirt, thanks man – what are we doing next?

Alan Curr,

London, 2012

FOREWORD *by Lawrence Booth, Wisden Editor 2012*

Cricket likes an alpine metaphor. Batsmen scale the heights. Imposing run-chases are steep, not to say mountainous. A cluster of wickets inevitably begets a slippery slope. Top-edged hooks are nothing if they don't come down with snow on them. And, yes, fielders enjoy a sledge.

But in times of crisis, hysteria and hype, the language moves from the Alps to the Himalayas. Specifically, it moves to the highest point on Earth.

When the former New Zealand captain Martin Crowe was dismissed for 299 by the last ball of a Test match against Sri Lanka, he claimed it was "a bit like climbing Everest and pulling a hamstring in the last stride".

India's Virender Sehwag was more fortunate. When he hit a world-record 219 in a one-day international against West Indies last year, his innings was described in some quarters as "the equivalent of scaling Mount Everest" – which may have been slightly overegging the honest seam-up of Ravi Rampaul and Darren Sammy.

And as India impatiently awaited Sachin Tendulkar's 100th international hundred – a landmark he finally ticked off on the day I wrote this – The Times of India declared the impending feat to be a "veritable Mount Everest of cricket records". Presumably the defeat to Bangladesh a few hours later was the K2 of upsets.

I imagine that Team Hillary, Team Tenzing, the Trektators and everyone else who contributed to the amazing story that follows will never again be able to read a glib Everest analogy without a knowing chuckle and a well-deserved self-pat on the back.

For them, Everest can no longer be a mere sporting cliché. It is the venue for a once-in-a-lifetime experience in which they set off into the unknown, learned a despairing amount about acute mountain sickness, oxygen deprivation and each other's bowel movements, and returned with a whole heap of friends and a few more blisters. Oh, and they broke a world record along the way. They are utterly mad and I salute them for it.

This is a story about a remarkable game of cricket, but – at the risk of veering off into territory more suited to the Hollywood blockbuster – it's also a story about the human spirit. (Actually, this book would make a damn good film.)

Plenty of people talk about doing crazy things such as – I dunno – playing the world's most altitudinous game of organised cricket. Few have the guts to carry it out. The feat of shifting a party of 50-plus up to Everest base camp left me exhausted just reading about it. Alan's narrative confirms that, when you were there in person, it was not exactly a picnic either.

More than once as I read his story, I found myself moved by the group's tenacity, passion and moments of despair. I took sides as Alan described the inevitable conflicts that arise when time is short and glory beckons. I pitied the poor souls who failed to make the final XIs. I raged at the mysterious Mr X. And I cheered them all the way back down again.

George Mallory said he climbed Everest "because it was there", but made no mention – as far as we know – of the speed at which a square-cut travels in the Himalayan air, or the difficulty of pouching a catch when your fingers are frozen to the bone. In that sense, Team Hillary and Team Tenzing will always have the edge. I hope they dominate dinner parties for years to come.

It was a pleasure to read the book and an honour to be asked to contribute the foreword. Many congratulations to everyone.

FOREWORD *by Oli Broom*

I remember reading about the Everest Test shortly after the group's launch party in early 2009. The first emotion this wild endeavour stirred in me was envy. How had I not heard about their plans sooner, for surely it was now too late to join them? I had been thinking of a way to escape my desk job for months, if not years, and a barmy game of cricket half way up the world's highest mountain would have provided the perfect opportunity to pack it all in and head for somewhere remote.

But I didn't join them, and the teams left a little while later leaving me to follow their efforts from a computer in London. At the same time I was putting thought into an around-the-world bicycle ride, and as I followed the progress of Teams Hillary and Tenzing a thought struck me - why not cycle to a cricket match somewhere distant and exciting? By the end of May 2009 I had committed to undertaking a trip I called "Cycling To The Ashes". I played cricket in 23 countries on my way to watch The Ashes in Australia in November 2010. I spent 14 months cycling alone through many of the world's wild places, playing cricket as I did so; with the national teams of Serbia, Bulgaria and Turkey, with nomads in Sudan and Google executives in India. Sadly I didn't reach Nepal for a hit on Gorak Shep, as perhaps I should have.

So I have the cricketers of the Everest Test, in part, to thank for inspiring me to embark on a long-haul cricketing expedition of my own. As the two teams will have found out before, during and no doubt after the expedition, cricket means an awful lot to a great number of people in some surprising locations. They will have inspired many people with their extraordinary efforts, both physical and cricketing.

I was delighted to meet Alan on my return. He has, in these pages, provided a hilarious, often moving account of the expedition, from its conception to the moment the teams achieved their goal - the cricket match on Gorak Shep; the highest ever played,.

From one cricket tragic to a group of cricket tragics, I applaud you!

PART ONE

THE PREPARATION

Where the idea came from. Gorak Shep as taken by Kirt: 2006

CHAPTER ONE

———

The world is full of good ideas. Everyone has them and more often than not they are created when people are talking together, exchanging thoughts or opinions and suddenly, bam! There's your idea. People get excited, start making plans and can get exceedingly carried away. Then, the following morning the excitement of this ground breaking idea is replaced by a sore head and empty wallet – well, that had always been my experience anyway. Then an idea came around that was so good, so unique, so mind-blowingly insane that it seemed too good to let go. The idea was to play a cricket match at the Base Camp of Mount Everest.

The idea belonged to my friend Richard Kirtley, or Kirt as everyone knows him, who first floated it to me at the end of 2006. Back then it really was just a figment of his imagination, but with careful nurturing and the help of many it would grow to be bigger than anything any of us could imagine. It would be the world's highest cricket match. It had to be done.

To even trek to Base Camp is fraught with extreme danger, never mind playing cricket and carrying up all of the equipment needed.

The place Kirt had in mind was 5,165 metres (16,945 feet) above sea level, which meant the following risks:

» One third less oxygen - so your heart has to beat one third faster.
» Suppressed appetite - your body won't tell you it needs fuel until it's too late.
» Sleeplessness – your body won't tell you it needs to rest, even after a week of hiking.
» Acute Mountain Sickness - which can lead to cerebral or pulmonary oedema (official names for your brain, and then your lungs, exploding).

Even with those dangers, the trek was an irresistible proposition.

But really we need to go back to the very beginning to understand a little about how and why this idea came about.

It was Saturday 26th July 2003 and the venue was Bowerswaine Farm in Dorset. I was about to open the bowling for a team that would later take the name of the local pub down the road, The Drovers. Being the worst cricketer on either side I was entrusted to open the batting and the bowling that day, and therein lies the ethos of the club.

The match was really suggested as a way for a group of friends to stay in touch after leaving University and dispersing around the UK, and it took another two years for us to start playing other fixtures, but the club became a big part of the lives of many and after several tours of varying success a conversation cropped up one afternoon that was to start the ball rolling on an event that would snowball – almost literally - beyond anything any of us could imagine.

Kirt was not on the field that day back in 2003 as I sent down a string of longhops and half volleys. He was instead working in a bar in London to save up enough money to go travelling the following year. In fact, I did not even meet him until a year later when I moved to London to take up a career in the travel industry. We were introduced by a mutual friend and immediately got along through a shared sense of the absurd. He spent much of his time in the next couple of years doing bits of travelling and trying to find work as an actor and we saw a fair bit of each other.

In 2006 he came to me to book his next trip that included a visit to Nepal, somewhere I knew very little about but it sounded mysterious and exotic and as I sat across the desk I grew increasingly jealous of the places he was going. He bought a ticket into Delhi and out of Bangkok; when I asked how he planned to get between the two he simply said he would figure it out once he got there. While I know this is not exactly revolutionary thinking, to me it was a carefree nature that I had never really encountered before. I am a planner; I like to know where I am going to be, when I am going to be there and most importantly, how I'm going to get there, particularly when it involves covering hundreds of miles between two developing countries.

I had little idea of what his plans were when he set off, and when he returned a few months later with his hair down to his shoulders and a beard that screamed "I've been travelling" he told me about his time in Nepal and his trek to Everest Base Camp. This was something that I was aware was possible but that few people, in the grand scheme of things, actually did. I knew of very few tour operators who offered it and so I was captivated, swearing that I would get there one day.

On his return a group of us caught up over a quiet drink or two: Kirt told us stories of being chased by dogs in Kathmandu and falling ill in India then we somehow started talking about how we could get the Drovers into the record books. This was the first time I heard about a place called Gorak Shep which, as mentioned is situated at 5,165 metres above sea level and is, we believed, the highest plateau of its size on earth, and it just so happened to be oval in shape, just like a cricket pitch. Kirt had done some research and discovered that there was no record in the Guinness Book for the highest game of cricket and some weeks later he emailed me a photo of the place where he wanted us to play. The email read:

"Thought you should see the cricket arena. It's at 5,100m, and will therefore, I think, be an eternally unbreakable record. Let me know what you think."

I was in. Not only did I now have a reason to go to Base Camp, but a reason to start honing my cricket skills as well.

I did a little more research on the record and found out a few bits and pieces about sport at altitude and it appears there is some debate as to which is the world's highest actual cricket ground. The Bogota Sports Ground seems to take the title at 2,600 metres above sea level and has certainly hosted official games, but my personal favourite is the ground at Chali in India, even if it is slightly lower at around 2,400 metres (7,874 ft). This was built in 1893 by the Maharaja of Patiala. Now, he would by no means be the only man to go to the extreme of building his own ground purely for the sake of it - Paul Getty for example built a replica of The Oval in his Buckinghamshire Estate - but when the Maharaja wanted to watch the game in all its splendour from his living room, he simply ordered to have the top of a nearby mountain chopped off.

It was not just cricket we were aiming for however, we soon discovered that our record would also be the highest team sport ever

played. The Mexico Olympics in 1968 took place at around 2,240 metres
(7,350 ft), while FIFA have now banned football matches above 2,750
metres for safety reasons. All of this boded well for our record attempt,
not just at it being a success, but it being unbeatable as well.

In the spring of 2007 Kirt floated the idea to the members of the
Drovers, to gauge interest. He explained some of the practicalities: time
off work, fitness requirement, cost; while laying out the basic principles
of a cricket match at 5,165 metres that would set a world record and be a
charity event. As expected the vast majority were immediately keen, but
as the days moved into weeks a few people did start thinking practically
and realised that other commitments could be problematic, and thus is
the reason so many great ideas are destined to fail. Several months later
I visited Kirt again and we talked at length about the idea and whether
or not it was feasible. To my surprise, this guy who had always been a bit
of a joker and full of slightly off-the-wall ideas that were not necessarily
all that practical, had done a considerable amount of work and when you
listened to him it was clear he knew what he was talking about. He had
already made contact with a trekking company in Nepal and was laying
the foundations for the trip to take place in 2009.

By the end of the 2007 summer it looked to many in the club that
the idea had faded, but two people who were as taken by the idea as I had
been came to Kirt in October and wanted to know what the situation
was: saying if he was not going to get the project moving, they would.
Kirt was living in Cheltenham at the time and suddenly realised that he
was in danger of losing a grip on his dream and that he needed to be
in London and start showing people all the work he had done and the
groundwork that had already been laid. He was slightly taken aback at
the lack of faith some people seemed to have in him and it fired him up,
so he packed his bags and returned to live in London and would work
alongside Gareth Wesley (Wes) and Charlie Campbell in making cricket
on Everest a reality. It was a brave decision, and one that very nearly
backfired just weeks after he made it.

It seemed like he had barely been in London a few hours when I
read the news about a group of people heading up to the exact same

spot that we wanted to go to in order to set the record before us. Of course, they had no idea what we were planning, but this group had four current professional cricketers among them and were raising money for the Professional Cricketers Association Benevolent Fund so had a fair bit of backing and would generate publicity.

We were devastated. There was absolutely nothing we could do and it would take until January for the feeling of genuine despair to lift. That came as I was sat on the Tube one frosty morning and saw a small article in the paper saying that no record had been set by the PCA group because they did not play an official game, merely had a bit of a knockabout with plastic bats and rubber balls. Some months later I was able to speak to Graham Napier, one of the professionals on that trek, and he explained that for them it was really just about trekking to Base Camp rather than playing a game of cricket, that was just something they did while they were there. Napier said:

"It was no more than beach cricket really, and a useful distraction because we were all feeling pretty terrible by that stage. For us the cricket was a small aside, it was all about reaching Base Camp."

Despite Napier wishing us luck and saying how difficult he thought it would be to play a proper game at that height, it was dispiriting that the match played by the PCA group was to hang over our heads throughout our journey with many people questioning what we were doing since it had already been done. We already knew that people had played cricket at Gorak Shep; in fact, in my research into the World Record I had read about Pakistani soldiers playing cricket high up on the Baltoro Glacier, but nobody had ever taken their own wicket, stumps, helmets, umpires and the rest up to such a height. We intended to play a full format game of Twenty Over cricket, with real bats made of willow and balls made of leather.

So it was a setback, but also an incentive. Now the idea was out in the open we knew we needed to get a move on. We felt we had dodged a bullet in terms of missing out on a place in the record books, but with the target having already been set as April 2009 the time for action was now.

A presentation was planned for April 6th 2008 at The Duck in Clapham Junction.

Wes and Charlie were both at Reading University with me, and while Charlie was a founding member of the Drovers back in 2003, Wes came on board a few years later. He played a crucial role in getting the expedition off the ground; as anyone who has tried to take on any serious challenge will tell you, getting started is always the hardest part, once you are on your way everything is easier from there. He was one of the many on the trip who had graduated between 2002 and 2004 and although not directly involved with our larger group of friends back then, ended up playing cricket for the Drovers in 2005 and was part of the group ever since. He is determined, driven, passionate, and will work as hard as anyone if the situation and project are worth it.

Wes was not aware that Kirt was doing research himself and the two of them did not know each other particularly well at that stage: this turned into a useful battle for power in the early days which brought the best out of both of them, although Kirt has admitted that he felt he had to "gain Wes's trust" in those first few months. They remain very different characters, but this served well in the most part when it came to organising the trip. Their respective skills complemented each other and there was rarely a crossover, which enabled them to focus on different aspects and work at a good speed.

Wes was the creative mind, coming up with the phrase 'A Test Above The Rest' – that became the title of the blog - while Kirt knew the practicalities of what we would face on the mountain. Wes used his social media skills to quickly set up a Facebook page and website and even getting himself and Kirt Twitter accounts before a lot of people had even heard of it, but his main role was as a strategist who could turn an idea into a project that would fly at a commercial level and become self-sustaining.

Wes was also looking for something to motivate him; he loved Bear Grylls' book 'Facing the Frozen Ocean' which tells the story of his five-man team's calculated attempt to complete the first unassisted crossing of the frozen north Atlantic in an open rigid inflatable boat. Things did not go quite according to plan and what unfolded served to inspire Wes at a time when he was off work indefinitely with undiagnosed chronic fatigue, something which affected him throughout the planning and expedition itself, and keen to find an adventure of his own.

Wes's beliefs in the project were strong, and while Kirt saw it as a chance to raise some money and set a world record, Wes saw it as a potentially huge expedition that could capture the imagination of people and get a lot of media coverage. He proved to be right on that one. He also wanted to give people a platform to showcase their skills and perhaps benefit in the long run once the trip was over - it should be something people would happily put on their CV and be proud of, but he wanted everyone to contribute, not just leave it to a small handful. He was always on my case, as a wannabe journalist, to write articles and get the story out there, showing people I could string a sentence together, which I did and it was great to have someone pushing you on and believing that he and Kirt were not the only people benefitting from organising an adventure like this.

That first meeting, on April 6th, was almost a year to the day from when we would eventually depart. There were definitely nerves in the build-up and some of the people who did not know what work had gone on behind the scenes questioned if it was too early and suggested we risked blowing the chance of getting this out to a wider audience if we failed to impress. They needn't have worried.

Around 30 people arrived at the Duck, a pub that had hosted many Drovers social events in the previous years, and it seemed only appropriate that there was a huge dump of snow that morning. While this probably detracted from numbers - it certainly prevented the chap who was supposed to bring the projector along - the guys were immediately happy with the initial interest especially as so many of those present were not part of our cricket club. In fact, sitting at the back and not being involved with proceedings almost left me feeling like a bit of a stranger in my own home. I admit to being quite disappointed at not being involved that day. Kirt and I had talked so often during the previous two years or so, and promised each other that no matter what we would make this thing happen, that I really felt like I had missed my chance to be involved and would now have to settle for simply being one of the team. Turns out I was pretty wrong about that.

The boys did a great job from the off. The trip was priced at an incredibly reasonable £1,500 per person and everyone was told they would also have to raise a separate £1,500 for the designated charities, which at this stage were Sport Relief, who raise money for disadvantaged people within the UK, and the Himalayan Trust, which was set up by Sir Edmund Hillary in order to help and educate the mountain people of Nepal.

While talking Wes and Kirt both came across as knowledgeable and passionate, two critically important things in getting people to buy into your project. Without the projector Wes was forced to hold his laptop above his head in a rather comical fashion when trying to illustrate what Kirt was describing and at the end of the talk a total of 17 people handed in application forms immediately and within 10 days the number was more than 50. Before the presentation Kirt was unsure if they would even get 22 players, but by the date applications closed they had more than 80 and numbers for the trip had to be revised, he knew he simply could not take more than 50 and even that was ambitious, but is where he settled. The number had started off at 30.

Another thing that happened at The Duck was the first mention of "Trektators" coming as a support crew. The meeting was by no means a male-only event and several women, including my sister Helen, had come along. The plan at first was that the organisational team would look after the two playing teams while anyone who wanted to join in the fun purely as trekkers could just contact our handlers in Nepal and book themselves a holiday. As it turned out that simply wasn't practical and they essentially became a third team on the trip and helped provide an essential balance to the testosterone-based competitiveness that could easily have boiled over. Not only that, but by and large they proved far better fundraisers and excellent organisers.

With so many applications it became inevitable that some people would be left disappointed, and actually I became rather grateful to not be involved as Kirt would constantly tell me how he felt like the most unpopular man in Britain. I reassured him as best I could by commenting that footballer Ashley Cole still had that in the bag.

It was a genuinely difficult task though, especially for the guys trying to be impartial. I was one of the lucky ones as Kirt told me right away that I was in whether I'd filled out an application or not since I was one of the first to hear about the idea and had always supported it. This was just as well because the form I did fill out in The Duck was a token gesture, no more than putting my name on a sheet of paper. I had paid little attention to the questions about fundraising and contacts that I might be able to contribute.

As the three of them sorted through the applications it became obvious that friendships would have to be put aside as some pretty impressive people were making their case, and we knew none of them. We had one from Venezuela by a guy called Jamo Peterson who had heard about us through the Maladroit Cricket Club, the friendly nemesis of the Drovers, and had to send in his application in four instalments over two days because of the lack of internet access and power where he was – we liked that commitment. Another from someone called Glen Lowis who claimed he had carved a cricket bat out of a tree trunk with a Swiss Army knife while on a volcano, which gave us the impression he was some kind of born survivor, a modern day MacGyver perhaps.

At the same time several friends had done poor applications or simply failed to complete one and as a result were left very disappointed and not a little bitter as time went on. One person who had said that he could not commit to fundraising because he was too busy with work and subsequently was not selected then emailed Kirt with some fairly harsh abuse. This left him feeling quite unpopular for a few weeks and was one of the least enjoyable aspects of the entire 18 months.

While Kirt was adamant that he wanted friends of his who would be worth their weight in gold up the mountain, all three of the guys agreed that they needed outsiders to bring in a breath of fresh air as well as their own skill sets and ideas, plus people who would be around and able get involved as much as possible, which ruled out friends of ours who had moved overseas. Kirt, Wes and Charlie did agree, however, that they would each get two 'wild cards' in selection, people that they were allowed to bring on board with no objections from anyone else just in case any arguments did crop up. This meant we would have some known quantities and were not relying on paper applications alone. Two people who went on to be key members of the trip actually got in this way, Kirt's cousin David Kirtley, and Chris 'Blinky' Beale who Wes wanted for his IT skills.

Kirt and Wes took the lead on selection, while Charlie was busy making contacts at the Himalayan Trust UK, which was established almost immediately as one of our charities. Charlie was able to make direct contact with the Chairman, George Band OBE, who was not only the youngest member of the first ever successful summit team which put Edmund Hillary and Tenzing Norgay on top of Mount Everest in 1953, but two years later he became the first man to summit Mount Kanchenjunga, the third highest peak in the world. He is also a former President of the Alpine Club and the British Mountaineering Council. With a CV as impressive as that we were more than happy to have him lend his name to our trip, now calling itself an expedition. By the end of April the three trip leaders had all met with George and were really taken by how a man with his long list of achievements could be interested in a rabble such as ours, but he remained a staunch supporter throughout and came to several events from curtain up to final bow.

Another thing that happened before the end of April, on the 27th to be exact, was the first meeting of those who had been selected. By this point I had agreed to be the man in charge of taking payment from everyone since there was as yet no official bank account set up and I could organise this relatively easily at work and enter it all into a central account. It was my first step towards the involvement I craved beyond just going along for the ride, so although I knew what a total pain it would be I agreed, on the strict condition that I would have nothing to do with money from fundraisers and sponsorship. My sole responsibility was to get the £1,500 out of everyone on the trip and once we had it I would transfer it over. The theory was that people would set up a direct debit and pay £150 each month so that we would have all travellers' funds by the end of January 2009, three months before departure. Needless to say it did not work that way and I spent countless hours poring over bank statements and ticking off names every week while trying to track who had paid what out of the 50 people travelling, not to mention the countless phone calls I had from people wanting to pay by card every month since setting up a direct debit was evidently too complicated. One person just paid the whole lot in one go come November after I threatened to have him kicked off the trip for not having paid anything to date.

The other issue that came out of volunteering for this task was dealing with the situation when some of the original 50 dropped out. It was inevitable this would happen and the committee had, on my advice, written up a disclaimer that essentially said anyone dropping out by December 4th (which was the day we had to provide names to the airline for our flights) would not be eligible for any kind of refund. It's important to realise that at this stage it was three guys working out of someone's kitchen and we were a long way from being a registered organisation of any form so getting signatures for something like this was essential, and as it turned out, just as well.

The meeting took place on a Sunday and I had to work that day, but thankfully the location was a bar in Parsons Green so given I was working in Fulham I dashed over for the second half. A fairly inauspicious way to introduce myself it must be said. Wes thought it would be a good idea to go around the room and each say a little bit about ourselves by way of an introduction, so feeling like it was our first day at school we did just that. The comments were all fairly standard, and I simply said that I was the guy who would be taking everyone's cash and likely doing a runner; something that had sounded a lot funnier in my head in the moments before I stood up.

The whole thing was just an introduction but a few formalities were laid out and we were also split into groups of four to write down any ideas we had on fund and profile raising while also discussing potential fitness regimes and the fact that we would all have to take regular Bleep

Tests, a minimum of two with the first being right away and the second being before departure. The Bleep Test is a method used by the UK Police Force, Fire Service, British Army, Royal Marines and the UK Prison Service to see if applicants have the right levels of fitness. It's safe to say that barring perhaps five or six people in the room that day, there was zero chance of us turning into Royal Marines in the coming 12 months. What became clear however was that we had better bloody try.

Trim trail: Battersea, December 2008

CHAPTER TWO

A whole host of things started to happen after that meeting which really set the tone for how the majority of us were going to live our lives for the next year. The first one was that my sister Helen, who was part of the Trektators, somehow persuaded me to sign up for a marathon. Yep, a full one, all 26.2 miles of it. This seemed like a good idea in principle when we were sitting in her cosy house and the marathon she was talking about was not scheduled to take place until the final weekend in September in sunny, and flat, Berlin. I began running in May and it quickly became my least favourite part of the trip.

I hate running. Really, I do. When I began training, people were telling me how addictive it can be and how once I start I will want to be out doing it all the time. I wish that were true, I honestly do, but for me running was, and always will be, a chore. Running around Richmond Park, occasionally with Helen or my friend Jules at my side, but mostly alone with only cyclists speeding past for company was genuinely miserable.

Helen kept saying to me: "You know you're training for a marathon when you discover there is more than one five o'clock in the day" - hardly encouraging words. So why did I do it? Because it was necessary. I was overweight and out of shape and in need of a target to set myself. As a salesman I should be immune to someone trying to sell me on an idea that I quite clearly do not want anything to do with; nevertheless, I signed up to run the course in Berlin on September 27th that year.

At first, being typically lazy, I restricted my training to the gym. After all, I had been a member at the Virgin Active in South Wimbledon for a year and been approximately twice in that time, so now it was time for me to get my money's worth and show those evil people running health centres that they could no longer take my money without me getting something in return. At least that was what I told myself. The truth is that gyms are warm, and there is usually music playing, and there is always some sport on the TV. So I could pound the treadmill for hours

(OK, minutes) while watching whatever Sky Sports decided to show me. Often I would hop on and start running while staring at the screen in front of me and go home convincing myself that I had run a certain amount of miles. Yes, it is exercise and yes, it was doing me good, but marathon training it is not. Eventually Helen persuaded me to tackle Richmond Park and that is where it all began to get serious.

This happened largely because we had our first Bleep Test in Parsons Green at the end of June and I was the first to drop out, at a pitiful level 8.9. To put that into some perspective Tom Sharland topped it on that occasion, hitting level 13.8. With the marathon only three months away, it was time to step up a gear. The park is approximately seven miles round and the first time I went with Helen I made it halfway before my right knee seized up so badly I could hardly walk. At the time I thought some invisible creature was trying to rip my knee cap off so he could use it as an ashtray, but it turned out I was just suffering from the appropriately named 'runner's knee.' I will spare you the boring mechanics; suffice to say this problem would plague me for the rest of my training months, as would the lifestyle that comes with living in London during the summer.

The Bleep Test served as a rocket to several people, and so the Trim Trail was born. This was an hour-long workout that Kirt and Miles Nathan were doing long before it became a means of getting fit for the trip, along with two others who were also now coming with us, the Sharland brothers Tom and Neil, and it was these two who generally ran the sessions after Kirt told everyone that it would be a great way to get the right sort of fitness needed for climbing to Gorak Shep. This was a twice-weekly event, after work on a Wednesday (most of the time) and then on Saturday mornings, and it involved the kind of training that most of us had not been subjected to since school. Tom and Neil are two very mild mannered people, almost quiet, but get them in their shorts and trainers and they transform. Star-jumps, burpees, squat-jumps, chin ups, dips, thrusts, lunges and shuttle runs, all finished off with the pleasantly named Circle of Death, would leave those of us who had done nothing more energetic than playing Pro Evolution Soccer on the Playstation 2 wondering what on earth we had got ourselves into, and aching in places we did not even know we had come the following morning. As time wore on the numbers swelled; in late summer it would often be between four and eight, but once 2009 arrived and the trip began to loom large on the horizon more and more people began to turn up and it was not uncommon to have around 20 people at some sessions. It took a while but the girls would come too after the fear was dispelled that it was a bunch of alpha-males all trying to out-do each other while clad in Lycra and beating their chests.

The principle was that you went there to get fit, not because you were fit. One evening Gareth Lewis, who lives in Oxford, had come to stay at my place so I took him along. Gareth of course knew everybody and one could argue was the fittest man on the whole expedition, as he was also training for an Ironman due to take place in June 2009, and even he was surprised at the workout we would do and was clearly impressed with both how everyone coped and how well Tom ran the show that night. It was lost on nobody after the event the role that Tom in particular had played in getting a large group of people fit for the trip and should he decide to move away from his career working for a charity he could most certainly take up a new one pushing people to within an inch of their lives on a Saturday morning.

As it was difficult for everyone to always be able to make certain evenings Chris Palmer (Kiwi – guess where he comes from) also started a 'running club' to take place every Monday night, which basically involved laps of Battersea Park at various speeds. I would give more details on this, but I never went. I am sure I had a very legitimate excuse every time. This is also a good example of guys just setting something up for themselves and offering it to anyone who wanted to join in. These things are easy to do and, most importantly, free, and as much as many of us struggled in some of the sessions and spent a large amount of time swearing, mostly at Tom, we would always go home pleased we made the effort and resenting the £60 a month we were still paying for our gym memberships. These sessions would take place regardless and there were some pretty testing ones in the rain and snow at the start of 2009 that would have been enough to stop most people coming back, but as much as anything it was another opportunity for those on the trip to get together and work towards a common goal. For those of us who generally ended these sessions feeling on the verge of collapse it was summed up quite nicely by Nick Toovey in his blog:

"These sessions have hit a couple of points home, firstly despite me thinking that exercise is impossible for me, it isn't. Secondly, the mountain isn't going to lower itself for me for having shorter legs than the others, nor is the oxygen going to increase for me during the game just because I don't possess any natural fitness or athletic ability."

In the same entry Tooves went on to quote Steve Waugh in his autobiography, talking about how in 1991 he would often be in the gym and stop at 17 or 18 leg-raises thinking 'That'll do' and that 'Nobody will know I didn't make it to 20.' I am pretty sure that this is an attitude that many people can understand, but Waugh goes on to say that these were the little battles that he needed to win in order for things to improve, and most importantly the only person he needed to impress was himself. That blog entry was the inspiration I needed when the marathon training was getting the better of me.

During June and July, Kirt and Wes worked hard on the charity angle of the trip as well as deciding how our groups would be split. They were also facing up to the fact that, although we were taking 50 people, we could still only play 11-a-side. It was decided that we would take two playing squads of 15 each and then a support crew of 20 Trektators which would be made up of umpires, cameramen, photographers, as well as a couple of wives and girlfriends and general well-wishers, all of whom were raising the required £1,500 for charity, and also paying the same amount as everyone else despite the fact that they were not actually playing in the match.

The problem with all of this was that there would be four people on each side who would have to be left out. It was made clear to all involved that this was being done simply because when trekking to 5,000 metres above sea level (nearly 17,000ft) there is no guarantee that everyone will make it. Altitude sickness is something that strikes at random so the team selection would be left down to the captains, who would be appointed in

September after the teams had had time to bed in. The issue of selection was to end up being the most contentious and unpleasant of the whole project - but everyone always knew that would be the case.

By now Charlie Campbell was starting to drift away a little from the other two. He had unfortunately been made redundant as the recession started to bite. The charities were becoming something of a headache; all was fine with the Himalayan Trust as they were very upfront with us right away. Their UK arm is small and everyone there volunteers. They do not have a lot of reach within the UK but should we require they could certainly help us out in Nepal. They do not have a huge database of people that we could contact in order to invite to fundraisers or the like, simply because they are still run in a pretty old-fashioned manner, and that was fine. We knew about the work that they do in Nepal and as Khumjung School, one of their flagship projects, was to be on our route then paying them a visit was going to happen regardless, to teach cricket and give the kids a chance do something different. Another plus the Himalayan Trust has is that often when you donate lump sums you never know quite where that might go. By investing directly in the projects that they run we know that 91% of the donations they receive goes directly to building schools and hospitals in Nepal, and just 9% to administrative costs, a pretty impressive ratio compared to some other charities.

The Himalayan Trust has also made a huge difference to the lifestyles people are leading in Nepal, where once all the teachers and doctors were westerners, now the training courses that are set up mean it is local people doing the teaching and seeing the patients, so now there are career options outside of farming, guiding or being a porter. Sir Edmund Hillary summed it up best when he said:

"I have enjoyed great satisfaction from my climb of Everest and my trips to the poles. But there's no doubt, either, that my most worthwhile things have been the building of schools and medical clinics. That has given me more satisfaction than a footprint on a mountain."

Kirt was always keen to support a Nepali charity so that he too could give back to the area that we were visiting and had given him so much pleasure already. He had originally looked at the Trust and the Porter

Fund as the two he wanted to give to, but was talked out of it by Wes and Charlie who felt that if we were raising funds in the UK then some of it needed to stay here. Kirt was never fully in agreement with this but with the other two adamant he gave in and so the search began for others.

Sport Relief was decided on really as a means to get some publicity and to keep the funds in the UK. Obviously they are an excellent charity who do a lot of good and is something that is in the British consciousness, but we had three major problems with them. Firstly, it was not a Sport Relief year, but a Comic Relief one, which did not really have any logical fit to us. This was exacerbated by the fact that by now their celebrity Kilimanjaro climb was in the planning process, although still very much a secret. Finally, timing was also a problem. Comic Relief actually took place a month before we left for Nepal which would make it difficult for us to get maximum benefit for them.

Before we got into that however, we had the rather important business of choosing who would be in each team. It was vital to spread the cricket ability and also break up cliques. When the trip was first taking shape the idea was to play a Drovers XI versus someone else, but as the event evolved it quickly became clear that was a bad idea as relationships could turn fractious and the two teams not mix.

Instead the teams were named Hillary and Tenzing, to both pay homage to the two men who first reached the 8,848 metre (29,029 ft) summit of Everest and give the teams a strong identity. This also made them more marketable - while this may sound a cold truth, more money could be raised this way for the charities. The Drovers would be evenly split between the two and those who came on board in groups were also split, so the Sharland brothers for example were on opposing teams. This meant that they would be driven to get one over on each other, but not be so competitive that it would cause a rift that might lead to bad feeling or problems. It was also kept in mind that only one team could win, so a little bit of sensitivity and understanding between the players would be a very good thing to have.

The announcement, made on the blog on May 20th, read as follows:
"The Squads:

Team Hillary:

Players: *Will Simmons, David Kirtley, Chris Palmer, Ben Jarman, Chris Martin, Tom Sharland, Jules Staveley, Jonathan Woods, John Richards, Charles Bathurst-Norman, James Peterson, Russell de Beer, Glen Lowis, Charlie Campbell, Richard Kirtley.*

Reserve: *Patrick Dawson*
Umpire: *Alan Curr*
Film Crew: *Miles Nathan*

Team Tenzing:

Players: *Peter Spence, Kinsey Hern, Charlie Meek, Mark Waters, Joe Williams, Neil Sharland, Nick Toovey, James Markby, James Carrington, Charlie Brewer, Chris Beale, Haydn Main, Mike Preston, Gareth Lewis, Gareth Wesley.*

Umpire: *Jonathan Hill*
Film Crew: *Paul Stadden*
Reserve: *David Harrison.*

Now we will look to see who emerges from the crowd to show themselves as potential Team Captains, an honour that will be earned on merit."

Of that list of 36, seven would end up not departing the UK at all, while this was also the day I discovered that I would in fact not be playing in the match after all.

The subject of umpires had come up in conversation with Kirt saying that in order for it to be a world record we would need fully qualified officials to oversee the contest, but that he was not sure how to go about getting them. Would they be willing to pay and fundraise or would they just accept a free trip? Would we even be able to get any since the first class season was due to start the very day we were set to fly from Heathrow airport? I suggested that, since several people were going to end up missing out on selection anyway, why not just get a group of us trained up as umpires. We had a year to do so and since most of us had stood in village matches and knew enough about the game, how hard could it really be to get the required certificate? Well, very as it turned out, but more on that later.

Now, as mentioned in Chapter One, I'm no cricketer and there had always been a nagging thought at the back of my mind questioning whether I'd really want to go all the way there only to suffer from the yips and not be able to bowl, or get out very first ball. But given the Drovers ethos of 'Ability doesn't matter', I was keen to be involved. Then Jonathan Hill (Hillsy), one of my best friends from University who was Chairman of the Drovers at the time, also expressed an interest in umpiring.

Now, he is a formidable sportsman. One of those people who is naturally good at all sports and generally drives people like me insane with jealous rage. I was surprised that he wanted to give up a playing spot in order to stand to wear the white coat. His take on it was that we would be the only people on the field for the duration of the match, and that being in charge of a game like this would be incredibly rewarding. I had agreed he had a point, but never actually said that I definitely wanted to umpire. Now however, the decision was made.

I could have kicked up a fuss, but instead decided to be a team player on this one and throw myself into my increasing organisational responsibilities. The two umpires were attached to a team each, which may seem strange given that we were impartial, but this whole experience was about meeting new people and getting involved in team building events on both a social and a physical front. I was delighted to be part of Team Hillary, as I knew more people associated with that team, and I threw myself into being a "Hillarian" as much as everyone else did, and am supremely glad about that.

The more significant sentence in the general scheme of things however, was the final one. While it was tempting to name two captains from the people we knew, or even for Kirt and Wes to choose themselves, they decided instead to throw it open. There would be a captain and vice for each team and this would be decided by seeing who emerged during the upcoming four months with the next big meeting scheduled for September 27th. The decision would be based on who was visible and had leadership qualities, but also on who brought the most to the trip in terms of helping the organisers.

The front runners were Jules Staveley, who was very quick to get involved with partners and through his contacts managed to secure us a whole load of free kit from Gray-Nicolls including pads, bats and gloves. After that he contacted Flicx Wickets who kindly offered to provide us with a free custom-pitch to take up with us, which was hugely significant and saved us several hundred pounds. Jules' last immediate contribution was to secure a company called Met-Rx, who supply training supplements, and they really did give us a lot of stuff, and on one training weekend in the New Year we almost looked like a Met-Rx convention as about 95% of people were decked out in their T-shirts and hats. Later on Jules persuaded the guys at Addison Lee to provide us with free transport to and from Heathrow airport, which was also extremely useful. These significant contributions at an early stage were also what put Jules in the frame early on for the captaincy of Team Hillary.

Another huge contribution that came early was from James Carrington of Team Tenzing. James has a friend who worked closely with the head people at Qatar Airways and, since our options of flying to Nepal were quite limited (there are no direct flights), the Middle-East was always going to be the most likely route. An approach was made and a meeting was set up between the CEO and our guys. James and Wes went to meet him at the Farnborough Air Show, not somewhere they would usually hang out, and were under the impression they would be having a sit-down meeting. What transpired was quite different, as Wes explains:

"This was our first major corporate meeting. I had spent quite a few of the previous evenings working into the night to create a business document of what the expedition was about, how it was going to be activated and why it was a great investment for Qatar Airways. Vicks and I spent considerable time finalising this because we would then use it as a base document to send to any company. A white label document was then sent out to everyone on the expedition shortly afterwards.

When we went to Farnborough we were armed with this document which laid out the business case for investment. However we were given five minutes with the CEO which made going through the document look unlikely (the CEO of Boeing apparently only got two minutes the previous day). This became even more-so when I was abruptly asked what I wanted and why he should give it to us. This was a setback; it was obvious that I was never going to get the chance to deliver the work we had spent hours on. So I just bit the bullet and went at it hard, basically saying: 'This document details the value and business case for what I am proposing. We are attempting to set a world record altitude for sport by playing cricket officially at 5,165m on Everest. This will categorically be the biggest expedition of next year out of Britain. Our national carrier can't service us directly so by partnering with us you can activate a message that for British people travelling east Qatar Airways and the hub of Doha is the best way to do so.'

This seemed to do the trick; he said 'We will fly your expedition to and from Nepal'. Buoyed by this I proceeded to jump into Jerry Maguire mode saying that they didn't want to just become an official airline but that they should title sponsor etc, which was the spiel I always had in mind.

Shortly after this the Qatari Royal Family turned up and all other business meetings with the CEO were cancelled - we got our deal by the skin of our teeth.

After this we then went with his marketing team to go through the full proposal in depth. During this time the Air Show was continuing. We were engrossed in discussion when we heard a massive roar. The famous Vulcan Bomber was making its first flight since a multi-million pound restoration; it was the highlight of the show. I blurted out that my Godfather was the pilot and this proved to be good timing and the rest of the day went well. We secured the airline partnership and they would consider the full sponsorship proposal'.

So they left the meeting with 50 free flights and almost half a ton of excess baggage allowance. This was an enormous coup as Qatar are a massive corporation and a real name which meant we could finally boast a credible sponsor, even though they had not given us any hard currency. What they had done was supply us with something worth around £25,000. We decided against giving this money back to the guys and thus lowering the price, instead saying we would use that money as a buffer for unexpected costs; anything left would go to charity. It was just as well we did this, otherwise there would have been simply no way we could have kept the price at £1,500.

Next was Charlie Bathurst-Norman (BN), also of Hillary, who through his contacts at work, approached people at Surrey County Cricket Club for help. They were happy to allow us to use their net facilities for an hour once a week which was fantastic and also said that we could use one of their function rooms for an event after we returned and that they would provide some items that we could either auction off or use as raffle tickets to help raise money for charity.

Gareth Lewis, a friend of mine from school, was also being touted as a potential captain despite the fact that he lived outside of London and his job as a policeman meant he worked some pretty unsocial hours which would limit his availability for certain events. He was always on the emails though, offering advice for training schedules and generally enthusing about the whole thing. Likewise Haydn Main was often sending stirring messages on email about the Tenzing spirit would be vital and that a determination to win was actually far more important than the taking part.

For Hillary a similar role was being played by both Glen Lowis and Jamo Peterson, who between them were organising social get-togethers, training sessions and charity runs, so it was clear that we had plenty of people to choose from. The nice thing from the organisers' point of view was that the majority of these people were relative unknowns to them at the start of the summer. Two pretty random groups of 15 people had basically been thrown together and were forming their own identity and team spirit before a step on the mountain was taken.

London 5k

CHAPTER THREE

The summer of 2008 will live long in my memory as the Everest Test gathered momentum. Branded "A Test Above The Rest" we were finally starting to get the attention of a wider audience. A competition was launched to design a suitable logo with all manner of entries coming in that would eventually be voted on.

Wes was working hard on the partner plan and had asked everyone to provide any and every useful contact that they could think of so that we could try to get sponsorship and support. Then, on a Tuesday morning in the middle of June, we got the kick-start we really needed. It was around 8am when Charlie BN called me, telling me he had organised an interview on BBC Radio London for us that night. Kirt, Wes and I would appear at 21:30 that night and so we all headed straight to Wes's place after work to prepare.

This was something of a watershed day as we suddenly realised that Charlie Campbell was struggling with trying to find work and as a result a lot had not been done on the charity side. At the moment the only page we had running was the blog, which from here on in I would take over the running of, while Kirt and Wes would contribute when they felt necessary. We had no donation page and, in fact, did not really have anything official from our charities at all so most of the day was spent getting that sorted. When the time came around the interview went very well and we were left on a real high and believing that we were now on the right track. It's a shame Charlie Campbell wasn't there that night as there was a sensational vibe in the air as the three of us high-fived and whooped before receiving numerous calls and text messages from people who had tuned in.

A couple of days later Wes called me up and asked me if I wanted to take on a greater role alongside him and Kirt. My official title would be Expedition Secretary and while I would be taking on a fair bit of admin work I was more than happy to do that. I had no desire to be a passenger.

The arrival of July also meant the first of our planned publicity stunts.

Nothing major, just a gentle 5k run around the Victoria Embankment on a Sunday morning dressed in full cricket attire. Eight of us met at 07:15 to prepare and don our whites, pads and gloves while Jules Staveley even brought his helmet along and ran the entire course in it. It was the first organised run we did and we all went round pretty quickly before posing for a photo under Nelson's Column. Later on that photo would have Mount Everest Photo-shopped into the background and would be used in a number of publicity photos.

This was also the first time I had spent some proper time with a few of the guys, and the first time I met Joe Williams, one of the younger lads who loves cricket and hates exercise. Joe was to become quite a brother-in-arms on the trip and I think the fact that we both really did not enjoy running a meagre 5k in the July heat said a lot about where we both were physically at that time while acting as a timely wake-up call.

By now I had also managed to pressure a decent amount of the group into setting up blogs. Most of us knew very little about what a blog actually was at the time, and even less about how to set one up. I certainly had no idea but Wes was quite insistent that we all did one as it would help raise the profile of the website on Google, so I found instructions on how to create a simple one and sent them around. By mid-July, 15 people had at least set them up and it was to become something of a target for me to get everyone on the trip to have their own. This was actually achieved, although I would say only about half the people wrote anything in them on anything more than an occasional basis. Those who did however, really got into it and there were some fantastic ones around.

This was also a way to learn about personalities. Mark Waters is a great example. He lives out of town and is a two-time father while also being one of the oldest on the trip. He is quite quiet when you first meet him, but his blog was absolutely hysterical and kept me entertained for months; as a result I made an extra effort to chat with him when he came to meetings – something I might not have done otherwise given the sheer numbers in the group.

The next boost that came was when the English Cricket Board (ECB) gave us their support. With David Kirtley, brother of former

England cricketer James, (and cousin of Kirt) in the team he has some pretty decent connections and managed to get a quote from Managing Director Hugh Morris wishing us all the best and at the same time the Cricket Association of Nepal (CAN) also gave us their backing.

As the summer moved on the chase for sponsors became even more hectic, as did the behind-the-scenes work going into future events. One idea that was floating around was a fundraiser in the form of a black tie auction but we eventually settled on a more fitting launch party.

We had also been getting plenty of coverage in local newspapers both in and out of London. As I had recently completed a journalist qualification at Sportsbeat News Associates in Wimbledon I used my contacts there to help us get stories on our guys into any regional papers possible and it was paying off. On August 25th however, we appeared on Cricinfo for the first time and now felt like the ball was rolling at a real pace. With a readership into the millions this article would get word out to a far wider audience than we could hope to reach ourselves, and it was the start of a publicity bandwagon that was to roll and roll.

The following weekend there was another burst of more local publicity in the form of two 10k runs which our guys once again ran in full pads, this time carrying bats. The first was the Nike 10k which had five runners including David Kirtley who took on the challenge of telling everyone, including Marathon World Record holder Paula Radcliffe, that he was playing cricket on Everest - she apparently accelerated into the distance at quite alarming speed when he did so, not surprising since he was waving a cricket bat in a crowd of thousands.

Then came the Gyro 10k, organised by the company Glen and Neil both worked for, and done around the Chiswick area, where four of us padded up while another three ran carrying an enormous banner with the details of The Everest Test on it, and again managed to hassle a celebrity when they saw Alastair McGowan minding his own business on the other side of the street. He wished us luck and promised to look at our website.

For me these runs were all part of my marathon training, which was due to take place at the end of the month. By September I had given up alcohol for four weeks and was feeling like I might just be able to finish the event, although I certainly wouldn't be breaking any records. I arrived on the start line at Berlin both terrified and feeling terribly under prepared: I had done one 16-mile run three weeks before but other than that I had never done more than nine miles. Still, Helen and I did indeed both complete the course. She beat me, naturally, coming in at around 5:20hours while I crawled round in 5:43. Certainly not quick but with both of us suffering knee problems, hers a longstanding cartilage issue, we were both rather proud of ourselves and after a month off the booze, we did what any sane person would and got hammered.

The biggest disappointment associated with the Marathon was that it happened on the same weekend that the big meeting was taking place which proved a significant day. By now we had set a deadline for everyone to have blogs, and more importantly, fundraising pages set up. Originally Charlie Campbell had been against using Just Giving because of the percentage they take of the money donated, but the rest of us were very much of the belief that in order to maximise our fundraising potential we needed to make it as easy as possible for people to donate, and that meant using Just Giving.

We then found out that Sport and Comic Relief do not accept donations from Just Giving for the same reasons Charlie Campbell had given so everyone had to go through an incredibly convoluted process to set up pages through the Sport Relief website itself in order to start raising money. We had taken the decision that the two sets of players would raise for Sport Relief while everyone else would raise for the Himalayan Trust (who thankfully do accept from Just Giving), and actually several people were already well on their way to reaching their £1,500 target – which was no small feat given the size of the target and the economic climate at the time.

The captains were also named that day, while the warm-up match between the two teams took place straight after.

I was slightly surprised when, in early September, I received a call from Kirt asking me if I would accept the Hillary captaincy were I offered it. Naturally I said yes, but wasn't I an umpire? He told me he was worried about the health of one of the members of Team Hillary who was a front runner for the job, and given how much I had put in so far it was only fair I should be considered. The phone call was brief, and has never been discussed since, so I do not really know how close I came, but it was an interesting twist.

Instead I sat in a meeting room with Kirt and Charlie Campbell and spent nearly three hours deliberating over the captaincy for Team Hillary, and had some input from Wes via speaker phone. We were honest about who we were choosing between and had actually sent out an email to our four leading candidates about six weeks before to let them know they were in the running and see how they would react.

The captaincy of each team was always going to be a bit honour, for Kirt and Wes were the front men of the trip and had agreed early on that they would not be considered for the roles. The idea was that people who had excelled since coming on board in April would be rewarded; we wanted leaders to emerge as there were plenty of people on the trip who were total strangers. Obviously being in London helped the causes of a few and damaged the hopes of others, but there is not much that could be done about that. Eventually we decided that Glen Lowis would make a great captain and we always liked the idea of having a Kiwi captaining a team named after perhaps the most famous New Zealander of all time. Jules Staveley would be his vice, a very close call between him and Jamo Peterson. Wes told us that Haydn Main was his choice for Tenzing and that it was a simple one, but he was struggling to decide over a vice. He asked my opinion on two guys, Gareth Lewis and James Carrington. I was surprised that Gareth was in the running, he lives in Oxford after all which made it harder to be involved but he was obviously doing something right. I gave my views on both guys, as I am sure Kirt and Charlie Campbell did as well, and it was Gareth who got the nod, mainly as it turned out for the work he had done in preparing fitness schedules for everyone and his rallying emails.

The vices had their own jobs to do, but for the captains this was a very big deal, and one that neither of them took lightly. They also represent two very different characters: Glen is a bit of a joker, very comfortable in his own skin and went out of his way to get to know everyone and befriend them all. Haydn is more reserved and perhaps a bit more intense but also very proud to have been not only selected as captain, but to come on the trip at all. Haydn was a complete outsider, who found out about the trip through Facebook, and had quickly emerged as the stand-out choice for the top job in his team. Contrasting styles certainly, but perhaps mirroring those of the guys they were chosen by.

I came to know Glen fairly well over the 12 months of organising, but Haydn was somebody I did not spend that much time with. I met up with him around ten weeks after we returned to the UK to ask him about the trip and specifically the job of captain and he spoke very openly about the experience.

Haydn found out about what we were doing through a friend who had actually climbed Everest who thought it might be something he liked the sound of. He then called up another friend of his, New Zealander Mike Preston who he felt might also be keen, and they met for dinner to talk it over before quickly deciding to get involved. Like most of the guys on the trip, Haydn was looking for something to break the monotony of life in the city and with a love of both sport and travel this seemed like a perfect fit. He had also done a lot of charity work and was a particular admirer of the Himalayan Trust so that was another reason to get involved, and perhaps why he threw himself so forcefully into the Events Committee as the events predominantly raised money for them.

Being a man who spent a large amount of time in front of his computer Haydn found it very easy to reply to emails very quickly and was always sending Wes ideas of things that they could do, and while he had no aspirations of captaincy, it became clear quite quickly that he was in the running and that only served to drive him on even more. I asked Haydn afterwards how he felt about the job at that time and his answer was a revealing one:

"*By September 2008, five months into the expedition planning, there were whispers that I was the front runner for the captaincy, which I took as a huge compliment, but I would admit that at this stage I started to have doubts as to whether I should accept it. My main concern was whether I would have the support of the guys in Tenzing, or more particularly their respect. In my predominantly rugby-oriented background, my comfort in captaining different teams derived largely from the respect I had from other players for my ability on the pitch, and yet I was far from the best or most complete cricketer in Tenzing. I thus spent considerable time thinking about whether I would garner the loyalty of the squad at the crucial moments. By late September I had not resolved this question in my mind, and frankly I have not since. This was a group of ambitious, strong-willed alpha males, and none of this would be easy, but I felt I had sufficient qualities to offer the team that I could make a decent stab at the job, in particular a truly fierce loyalty to boys in Tenzing and what I believed was an unequalled determination to win the game on Everest."*

So while Haydn loved the game of cricket, much like me, he was not a natural at it and this was a concern for him. He also did not have an easy ride of things in the months immediately following being made captain. Personal problems were one thing, but as the recession hit his job in an investment bank became increasingly insecure and he was made redundant shortly before Christmas. At that time he went home to Dorset and spent time with his family and later admitted to me that this was the first, and only, time that he was not putting Everest first. He decided as 2009 began that he would not do that anymore and had to throw himself back in fully to make the most of the experience.

I always felt that the weight never sat particularly easy on his shoulders. He knew that being the man in charge brought both responsibility and stature, but also difficult decisions, especially selection. He wanted people to behave normally around him and certainly did not want anyone sucking up in the hope of getting selected, but the knowledge that he was going to have to cut people at the 11th hour was hard for him and he felt it put a distance between him and the rest of the guys. Another thing he found tough was the division of power: with Wes being a vocal guy and quite a commanding presence, Haydn often felt a bit dwarfed in team meetings since Wes knew considerably more and would often jump in and take the impetus away from him. As a leader this was difficult to deal with and while Haydn is quick to say that Wes was one of the best friends he made from the trip, it did strain their relationship, particularly on the mountain itself.

Glen had no such problems with his team, and was certainly lucky in that respect. Kirt spent so much time organising the project that when there were Team Hillary get-togethers he was all too happy to let someone else take the lead and just spend a bit of time being one of the group. If there were question marks at times as to who was actually in charge of Team Tenzing, there were no such issues in Hillary - it was Glen's team and he was proud of it.

Like Haydn, he took the whole thing very seriously, but this seriousness manifested itself in different ways. While Haydn was seen at the Trim Trail just once for example, Glen was there every time. He loved the whole ethos of the trip, the opportunity to meet new people and be involved in something totally different to what he had done before was what got him out of bed in the morning. Haydn had won Wes over with ideas and creativity, Glen did his impressing with actions.

One of the big differences between the two teams is how they bonded. The first big get-together Team Hillary had was a rather monstrous pub crawl, all decked out in cricket whites, pads and gloves that very few of us can remember: it proved a great way to break the ice for a whole load of people who did not know each other that well. A couple of drinks in and it soon became clear that we all found the same rude jokes amusing and were quite happy to do stupid things in the name of comedy value. Hillary used this as something of a model and the first few meetings we had were not for training but for a curry at the Kathmandu Valley restaurant in Wandsworth and more than a few drinks afterwards, usually of Khukuri Rum. It was harder for Tenzing with a larger number of their team being outside of London, so when they did have a chance to all meet up it was important for them to turn it into a training exercise.

I felt that in making Glen captain we would get more out of him. He was clearly somebody who wanted to play a part but so far had perhaps held back because he did not want to appear to be making a run at the job or being overly ambitious and offending anyone (he could almost be

British). However, once given the job he certainly cut loose and made a point of letting everyone know exactly what was happening and when, and trying to coax as much out of the team as possible. It was not an easy ride for him either as, his sister in New Zealand was pregnant and due while we were away, meaning he had no chance of making it over there for the birth, and work was becoming an issue for him as well.

Driving back from one training session he told me that he had recently been offered a job abroad by his company, and a blog post in mid-December tells the full story:

"Sometimes, challenges are sent our way to test our resolve and hopefully, allow us to act and grow from the experience. Sometimes, it is opportunities that offer the greatest challenge, as we try to work out how to have our cake - and eat someone else's too.

Early last week I was offered a great job opportunity to work on something I've never done before and provide a real boost to my career and experience. Unfortunately, while it would not stop me being a part of The Everest Test, it would mean that I could not do the job of skipper justice. I wrestled for some time with the idea of how I could make the two work together, but ultimately realised I could not do so, and so have to resign the captaincy.

I've put a lot into this challenge, and the decision to take the captaincy had not been made lightly. We've got less than four months to go, and while there are guys in Team Hillary who could step up to the plate, I'm not ready to hand over the reins. If the last few weeks are anything to go by, it's only going to get busier and more intense, and to be anywhere but the centre of it all isn't something that I'd be able to live with. This is the single greatest thing I've ever had a chance to do, and I'm not going to compromise that when we're getting this close."

What Glen does not mention here, but told me in the car that night, was that his company was also offering to fly him back for important meetings and basically make it as easy as possible to fulfil both roles. But as he said, he wanted to be at the centre, and being present is the key to that. To turn down what would have been a terrific career move, and also something that he had been working towards for some time, in order to be part of this expedition, only served to boost my respect for him and be even more pleased that we had made him captain.

There was a feeling among a few of Team Hillary that while they were slightly behind Tenzing in certain aspects – who had, among other things, the Three Peaks Challenge penned in for October – they would be the ones who came good on match day because of a more relaxed attitude. This train of thought became somewhat derailed in the afternoon immediately following the announcement of the captains.

With the weather still respectable, a practice match was scheduled, but while the Tenzing guys were all present and correct, Team Hillary were able to boast just seven players, meaning more than half of the playing squad were missing. Although all had legitimate reasons, the meeting had been scheduled fairly early on. Still, four ringers were found but unsurprisingly Tenzing hammered Hillary.

Both captains' take on the event are as follows:

Haydn:

"The energy and belief in the Tenzing camp was incredible and when I won the toss the decision to field was an easy one. The plan: to get up close and on top of the Hillary batsmen and use the noise and spirit in the field to create panic in the top order. The result: with Gareth, Blinky and Tooves steaming in from each end, we ended the fifth over with five wickets for 10 runs. To their credit, Hillary put up some resistance in the middle, with a good knock in particular by Jamo, and they finished on 95 all out. But this was damage limitation; the calm before the storm that was Tenzing's demolition job with the bat. Led by the impressive Joe Williams and the experimental Peter Spence, the 95 total was chased down in 12 overs without loss."

Glen:

"I anticipated an evenly fought contest, with a Hillary victory well deserved at the end. What ensued, after being sent in, was nothing less than a shambles.

Team Tenzing, with the experience of a mid-week net behind them, had us reduced to about 5 for hardly any as the top order folded meekly. In stepped Jamo, the 7ft Hillary Man of the Match. Despite his heroic innings of 40 odd not out, we were undone for 95, an over and a half short of our 20. Still, we had hopes that while it may not be easily defendable, we could (and would) put up a good fight.

We couldn't (and didn't). Rotating the bowlers provided only fodder for the

Tenzing batsmen, who cruised to a 10 wicket victory in pretty quick time. Lesson learnt.

While I could spout off excuses, and there are many valid ones (we were 4 players short and relied on ringers, we'd never seen each other hold bat or balls... the list goes on), we were done. As far as motivation goes, losing like this serves only as a positive that we need to work on our training (fitness and cricket) and form a tighter unit."

There's no denying that this match was in the mind of both teams the day of the practice at Gorak Shep. It was a total mauling and while the Hillary excuses were valid, they were also problems of their own making. It did mean, however, that we had two very confident and very competitive teams ready to play and both desperate to win. We always knew this would be the case, but thanks to the practice match, and the response of both teams to it, the balance would be evenly poised come match day.

Brecon Beacons: Early 2009

CHAPTER FOUR

O ctober was a hell of a month. It started well and ended badly and represented some of our first serious setbacks.

The month began with our launch party on Wednesday October 8th at The Collection on Brompton Road. The venue was pretty flash and upon arriving and walking down the corridor to the main bar the place was covered with huge pictures taken of several people who were coming on the expedition which immediately set up the event. There were live acts and welcome drinks as part of the £30 entry fee and for once everyone had the chance to actually smarten up. We had become so used to seeing each other in training gear that to see people in suits or dresses made for a change.

Most of the thanks for what became known as the Trektator Launch Party, must to go to Lucy Brooks and Vicks Nicholson. Lucy was someone who had known the Drovers contingent for several years after being at University with Gareth and Jules. She came along to the meeting in Clapham and was soon using the word "Trektators" which she has since decided she wants to get into the Oxford Dictionary. She spent a bit of time persuading the guys that it would be beneficial to have some girls on the trip who were neither wives nor girlfriends, and we were all glad she put that effort in. For Lucy the trip was all about the charities and she took her fundraising duties very seriously and this party alone raised around £3,000. She also helped cajole others into raising more and was quick to come up with ideas of how this could be done.

Like many on the trip, she was struggling at work and was in desperate need of something to look forward to, the expedition becoming even more important to her when she was made redundant at the end of February. Rather than sit and mope she threw herself into all things Everest with even more gusto, swapping heels for trainers and pounding the pavements while also organising various scenic walks for the Trektators, although apparently her map reading leaves something to be desired. Unfortunately for Lucy the training had something of a negative impact as it left her with a dodgy knee and after she completed the Bath Half Marathon she looked like she could barely walk, which was not ideal with less than a month before departure and it would cause her considerable discomfort on the mountain.

Vicks had no such problems, being one of these people who enjoy throwing on the running gear, and even does so on holiday. Vicks found out about the trip via two different friends. She was about to take a huge career change, giving up life in the city for jobs working in some pretty obscure places cooking for people. Originally Alexandra Fudakowska had taken on the role of dealing with all the extra admin that Kirt and Wes struggled to get to grips with, things like collecting passport information and addresses, all the really exciting stuff like that. Unfortunately for Alex the pressures of her job got to a stage where she was struggling to do everything that she needed so she had asked Vicks to take over, which she happily did. It is probably fair to say that Vicks and Lucy perhaps tip-toed around each other for a while as the Trektators was very much Lucy's thing but Vicks tended to know more about the trip as a whole because she had more regular contact with Kirt and Wes. Despite this they are both completely non-conflict people so fortunately it did not develop into some kind of power struggle and they were able to each do their own thing to the best of their ability. Vicks also had a holiday to Australia booked from October to January so was away for a large part of the organisation, and even when she was back she was not based in London, so she essentially spent her life on her emails and mobile helping to find sponsors and file away information that would be needed at later dates.

The pair are exactly the kind of people you need on a trip like this: they are not looking for credit or glory, but just want to be involved in something unique and special. This is what the Trektators as a whole stood for, and in Lucy they had someone who was every bit as proud of their identity as the players were of their own teams and that rubbed off on all the others around her. I think once a few more of the girls started to come to the Trim Trail, it helped many of the guys who did not know them before and made everyone very comfortable with each other.

Shortly after the party however, things began to go awry. As with any expedition, people who sign up at the start later drop out and during October we lost seven people. Laura Hewitt is a friend of Lucy's and was going to be a Trektator. She was also instrumental in the organising of the launch party, but stepped aside early with a bad back. Charlie Meek and Charlie Brewer, both of whom were in Tenzing, also pulled out for differing reasons and both sent fairly heartfelt emails to the group. Charlie Meek said:

'Ultimately guys this trip for all of you will be one of the biggest, if not the biggest thing you will do in your lives, and I just didn't feel that I could do enough, or commit enough time, to justify my place on the plane, let alone the team. I would honestly say that withdrawing from the trip is the single hardest thing I have ever had to do. I was so proud to be a part of it, and to come to the decision in my head that it wasn't at all feasible was utterly heartbreaking. Most of you have already put in the most amazing effort to the trip and that is quite remarkable.'

Charlie Brewer echoed his sentiments: *'I felt fantastically privileged to be part of this awesome challenge and to get to know so many great guys who are putting so much effort towards both the trip and the fundraising. I'm absolutely gutted to be missing out but I really felt that after a long period of ill health I wasn't going to be able to contribute my best for the challenge in April. I wish all of those guys the very best of luck; I know you have earned it. Come on Team Tenzing!'*

Paul Stadden was another on the original list as one of our cameramen but we lost him as he simply could not persuade his fiancée to move their wedding day, while Ed Faber, another of the Reading University contingent who was coming as a Trektator, also fell by the wayside.

We did get one timely boost though as Graham Napier, one of the professionals who had gone to Base Camp in 2007, gave us his official backing, and Surrey County Cricket Club were made our official cricket partner. Kirt and Wes were still actively hunting for a title sponsor and I knew that talks were afoot with two different mobile phone companies, both of whom had offered around £15k to be our major sponsor. Right now however, we were still looking for a figure closer to £85k, which had originally seemed perfectly reasonable but was to prove somewhat optimistic.

Elsewhere the fitness regimes were gathering pace as people started to sign up for increasingly horrible events, the first being 'The Grim Challenge', whose name says it all. Undeterred by cold weather, 11 people gathered on a Sunday morning to stare at a small lake they would have to run through that was currently frozen, and watch as 4x4s broke the ice. The course was eight miles across, mostly frozen or thawing ground, which would involve several deep puddles/small lakes and crawling under some camouflage nets that were above one such icy hole. While everyone completed the course, the freezing feet were perhaps a good indication of how things might get higher on Everest. Miles Nathan in particular, had never run as great a distance in normal conditions, let alone on such a course. Everyone was elated to have finished, though.

When Team Tenzing decided to attempt the Three Peaks Challenge – scaling the highest mountain peaks in Scotland, England, and Wales within 24 hours – they were confident it would be a huge success. In total, it is 42km of ascent and descent interspersed with 475km of road travel, tough but achievable. The idea belonged to Gareth who, as vice captain, was in charge of fitness for his team and saw this as a great team bonding opportunity as well as gaining some valuable experience on some big hills. However, things did not go according to plan as Chris Beale (Blinky) explained:

"'South-westerly 50-70mph, gusts 80 to perhaps 100mph locally. Very difficult conditions even at low level, with any mobility widely difficult on higher areas. Significant wind chill. Torrential rain. Snow, soon turning to prolonged heavy rain. Will finish late afternoon as snow above 800m.'

Well, that was the forecast heading into Friday afternoon and it set me in to a bit of a panic. I decided that the raincoat I had wasn't going to cut it so I made my third visit to Cotswolds in 10 days and dropped another £90 on a half-decent jacket. I headed home to do my final packing before dashing to Heathrow for the challenge that lay ahead.

A few of the lads had been waiting at the airport a while and I met up with them and headed to the plane. After a bit of a bumpy ride that had a couple of the boys saying their Hail Marys we arrived in Glasgow. Haydn, having caught an earlier flight, was waiting with the video camera and took what turned out to be the only footage of the entire trip...

As we waited for the van to arrive we did last minute kit-checks and started to change into our base layers. I was pumped and really wanted to get stuck in to the challenge. After about 45 minutes, the van arrived and we all squeezed into its tight confines. A space we would get to know very well over the next 24 hours...

The drive to Fort William, where we were to start our ascent of Ben Nevis, was due to take around 2.5 hours. However after about 90 minutes on the road we were stalled by a nasty accident. We sat for a further 90 minutes while the wreckage was cleared, watching 'Cool Runnings' and generally reflecting on an entirely bizarre Friday night.

We finally got back on the road and were hoping to stop somewhere to fill up on some food and water before we started the climb. Unfortunately, very little is open at 3am in Fort William. We only had a few litres of water between us, but headed for the local Fire Station where we were able to fill whatever bottles we had.

We pulled in to the Ben Nevis Visitor Centre car park in a howling gale and steady rain. Tooves and Waters hadn't changed into their kit and did so in the van while the rest of us readied ourselves to make a start.

At a bit after 4am stopwatches were started and The General (Peter Spence) led off blazing the way with a head-torch brighter than a thousand suns. The going was immediately quite tough, especially for some of the lads who were in trainers. We eventually found the path up the Ben and started trudging up the stone steps.

There were frequent stops to adjust kit and remove layers as we made our way up the steady slope. The wind was gusting quite strongly now and we were being buffeted around as we tried to stay close to whatever shelter the sides of the hill offered.

After about an hour we left the stone steps and rounded a corner on to a saddle. We were immediately hit with huge winds directly behind us and started powering along. At this stage, the rain had picked up and the wind was driving this directly into my back. My 'waterproof' trousers were now completely soaked through and water was pouring into my boots. The brutal conditions and darkness *meant we missed the ridge that would lead us to the summit and we continued to walk with the wind behind us for some time.*

Eventually Gareth pulled the boys together for a serious chat. The conditions were getting worse. We had been walking for about 90 minutes and were still only halfway up the hill. The ridge that led to the summit was very exposed and the winds up higher were likely to be dangerous, if not deadly. We took a vote and a few of the boys were keen to go on. I didn't want to give up, but my opinion was that it was irresponsible for us to carry on as we would be putting our lives at risk, and potentially the lives of Mountain Rescue who would more than likely have to come and get us. G made a tough, but correct decision in the end and we turned around.

This is when it got hard.

The wind that had been at our backs was now directly in our face. Mike Preston and I estimated it was 120 kph gusting upwards of 150kph and the weather reports confirmed this later in the day. The wind was driving the torrential rain horizontally, right in our faces. It was impossible to look where we were going. Any time I lifted my head to look any further than my feet the rain stabbed at my eyes and face like a thousand pins. After a few minutes battling this wind I was tired and shaken. As we rounded a bend the wind picked up even further and I was blown a metre backwards. To steady myself I grabbed the closest large object which happened to be Joe Williams. Joe and I battled together for a few minutes, arms linked for physical and moral support and before long the whole group was walking arm in arm to make sure nobody got blown away. I was still unable to see any further than my feet despite Hillsy barking on and on:

'It's just wind. It can't hurt you. Look at it! Don't let it beat you. Look it in the face and swear at it!!'

The only thing that was going through my head at this stage was the drainage ditches that crossed the path every 50m or so. I was petrified of not seeing one and slipping in and breaking my leg. We clung together as a group and slowly made our way out of the worst of the weather.

Once out of the wind we were able to take a breather and recompose ourselves for the way down. We weren't out of danger yet and had to concentrate all the way down. People were getting tired and Tooves had a couple of good falls, one of which left him pretty close to the edge of a sharp drop.

As we made our way down the steps, with the lights of Fort William coming into view there was a sense of relief that we had all made it down. We hadn't made it to the top, but I don't think that would have been possible given the conditions.

More important to me than the challenge was the bonding of the team. We had faced some perilous conditions up there and had all stuck together, physically and mentally providing support for each other. If I ever get stuck in those sort of conditions again, I know who I would want beside me, grabbing my arm, yelling encouragement and leading the path through the rain."

That weekend was a real marker for Tenzing and helped bond them as a team. While they tackled the challenge with a large amount of naivety, they were incredibly unlucky as the north of England was hit with the worst weather in 40 years. They had also shelled out a significant amount of money in order to do this, and the fact that they essentially spent around £300 to be beaten to a pulp on Ben Nevis and then drive back to London still did not get them down. Speaking to all 11 who took part it was clear they each took the same thing away - the knowledge that they were with the right people who could deal with any situation.

All this activity was good for getting fit and healthy: living in London it was hard to get out and do some decent walking. Tenzing had tried to rectify this with the Three Peaks, and Hillary were talking about attempting it themselves, but it was a pain getting out to places like the South Downs or even as far as the Cotswolds just to find a decent hill. With this in mind the team weekends started to be planned, and for around six weeks in January and February they totally took over our lives.

While Tenzing were getting well and truly thrashed on Ben Nevis, Glen, David and Kirt were running the Cardiff Half Marathon, again fully padded up, thus claiming the biggest distance anyone had so far run in pads. After that was the Merrill Mudman in November: Glen (again), Tom, Jules and Charlie C took it on, with Glen and Charlie doing the full duathalon which consisted of a 7.5km run, followed by a 15km cycle and finished with another 7.5km run, again up and down hideous terrain that would break lesser men. Tom and Jules and opted for the safer option

of just doing the run and once again all four completed the course, with
Tom coming in a very impressive 6th in the run while after nearly two
and a half hours of pain Glen and Charlie both finished respectably inside
the top 100.

Then it was the turn of the girls to show that they were doing their
training too. Vicks and Paola Fudakowska had decided they wanted to get
some proper walking practice in and so rather than heading to the South
Downs or the Lake District they jumped on a plane and flew to Tanzania.
There they scaled the highest peak in Africa, Mount Kilimanjaro, and
while they both said they suffered shortness of breath on their way to
the top at 5,892 metres (19,330 ft)they both made it and had very few
problems. Their simple piece of advice was to go slowly and although
they admitted to being the butt of a few jokes from other teams on their
way up because of the slow pace they were going at, in a classic tale of
Tortoise and Hare, they overtook those who mocked on the summit push
as many were struck down with symptoms of Acute Mountain Sickness
and some did not even achieve their goal.

Both these girls were part of the Trektator team and while the original
idea was that these people would be the support crew who would provide
assistance up the mountain, in fact they did the vast amount of their
work preceding the trip. Vicks, for example, was organiser extraordinaire
and was someone Kirt and Wes could go to for advice and take on
time-consuming jobs. Paola and Lucy were heavily involved with all the
events that took place at various places across London, while Paola's sister
Alex also took on various administrative duties. Jen Gladstone was our
resident lawyer and Helen got herself qualified as an umpire while also
monitoring all the money that came in from that group. They created
an identity of their own and had several team get-togethers and training
weekends, just as Teams Hillary and Tenzing did.

By November both sides were doing semi-regular net sessions and
starting to find out who the better cricketers were. Team Hillary would
often do a Bleep Test or some other variety of horrible fitness session in
order to ensure everyone was exhausted when they went into bat, the
theory being that everyone would be knackered up at Gorak Shep so

we may as well replicate it as best we could. Two of Hillary's best players were also now getting among things with Kiwi Palmer returning from a year working in New York, and David Kirtley having finished the cricket season at Cardiff. Kiwi helped out with some coaching while David assisted in negotiating for MediRite to provide us with an enormous amount of medical equipment for the trip.

Many people were now training before or after work, and on the weekend. It was not necessarily organised events either, they would just grab a bike or put on their hiking boots and head off to somewhere remote that they had never been to before, equipped with nothing but a map. Some were naturally adventurous, but many were forcing themselves outdoors simply because the thought of Everest was beginning to cause some panic.

Some people overdid it and some people did not do enough, but people were making significant sacrifices in their personal and professional lives, and I was about to make one myself.

Alan Curr

Freeze mob: Trafalger Square

CHAPTER FIVE

I come from a large family where Christmases tend to be a pretty big deal. That year we were having a belated celebration as my parents and Helen would be in Australia until Boxing Day. I had planned to travel down on the 28th for our delayed Christmas but then things began to get complicated.

On my suggestion Kirt and Wes decided to draw up a disclaimer saying that anyone who pulled out of the trip after December 4th – the last day for flight issues - would not be entitled to any refund. We had already lost a nurse and a first-aider from the original list and with spaces to fill Wes decided to do something about our medics and went hunting. Word of mouth brought Ian Ditchburn to us, then notices went up in hospitals and ads were taken out. Before long we had four medics who were all great personalities. They were also willing to pay the £1,500, which was a real bonus since they all initially thought it was a trip that would pay them, but decided to come along anyway.

The four of them were all outsiders, only Ian had any connection to the group at all in that he knew Jamo Peterson. Ian, an amiable Geordie, had jumped at the offer to join the trip and had the added benefit of having been up to around 5,000 metres before as part of an altitude research expedition to Bolivia. He was easy to talk to throughout the trip, and expressed a willingness to stay behind if needed.

Teamed with Ian was Isla Cox, a GP based in Brighton; closet cricket fan, and someone with a wealth of expedition medicine experience. She made the effort to get to know the Trektators pretty well by going on several of their training walks.

Nick Walker and Breck Lord were the other two and these guys certainly held their own in the banter department. Nick was able to fit in immediately and with a background in the military was also full of the kind of jokes that are more associated with a locker room than a dinner party. He was also due to get married shortly after we returned home, and with another trip due he conveniently skipped all planning and organising. Nick and Breck had several things in common, but the main thing was their general decibel levels. Breck, an Australian, can be incredibly loud and had a laugh that could probably be heard in Tibet as we trekked up the mountain.

The four medics had met up several times before we left the UK and had a great dynamic between them as a group. They seemed to know each others' respective skill sets and complemented each other nicely. In the build-up to departure Isla sorted out all the supplies; contacted the airline and the Home Office letting them know about all the medication we were taking, and organised all the proper paperwork, while at the same time having a large amount of stuff delivered to her surgery. Responsibility for looking after all the kit and the one bag they labelled 'Really Useful' was split among the four of them and they were always working as a team. By the time we returned to Kathmandu people were quick to recognise the contribution these four had made as very few of us managed to escape totally free of illness. When it came to deciding who would stay behind at the necessary times it was left to the four of them to choose, but more often than not it was just the first person to treat the fallen trekker.

In dishing out advice and treatments whenever required, they proved their worth to everyone and nobody would be shy in speaking to any of the four if they were suffering. They also did an incredible amount of planning behind the scenes; Ian explains a little of what went on in those early stages:

"We took detailed medical histories from every member of the expedition, spoke to specialists if necessary and prepared for any potential problems. It was surprising how many medical issues a group of 45 young people could have. We meticulously organised two medical kits: a general medical supplies bag and an emergency bag. I remember as a medical student being asked 'If you were a GP what 10 drugs would you have in your bag?' It was a little like that but on a larger scale.

There was a lot to consider including: antibiotics, a defibrillator, resuscitation meds, protective equipment, airway kit, dressings, sedatives, oxygen, fluids, IV access, anti-emetics, rehydration sachets and even the emergency contraceptive pill."

So the spaces were filled, but it was becoming increasingly obvious that a reconnaissance trip would need to be made to Nepal before the trip took place. We decided from the start that we wanted to go about the whole thing in the right way by securing permissions and being open with the Nepali authorities on what we were doing. In truth, it was taken out of our control pretty early on when somehow the *Himalayan Times* picked up on our trip and ran a story on the front page, something that happened three times before we even got out there.

While we all thought this publicity was great, it actually posed a few problems. In the early planning stages Nepal was still a monarchy, but as of May 2008 it became a Republic and the political situation became embroiled in turmoil. Gaining permission from Parliament when the King was still in charge, despite his minimal powers at that stage of his reign, was relatively straightforward, but now various parts of government were being divided up and people wanted a piece of us. It was a saga that was to run and run, but since at this point not a single one of us had ever even met with Nir Lama and his people at Peace Nepal Treks who were organising all our logistics on the ground, Kirt had decided he would fly out for a week over Christmas. Needless to say, I wanted to go too and spent weeks agonising over whether or not I should be apart from the family and miss a friend's wedding taking place at the time as well.

Before a decision was made however, there were a number of other things to address. The relationship between Kirt and Wes was starting to show a few cracks, with the increased strain of still not having a title sponsor and issues over our charity choices dragging on. They began to disagree on the occasional path the trip should take: one such example was the use of a PR company.

When the expectations of the trip were first laid out we had no idea how much money we would be able to raise. Once we knew we would have at least 30 people in a playing capacity and that everyone would have to raise £1,500 the first target was just £50k. After that it grew to £100k but eventually we settled on the figure that got bandied around in the media as £250k - this was always a stretch target and was based on the fact that we expected to sell the product to a title sponsor at a cost of

£85k and have other, small scale sponsors as well. If we did this then the vast majority of those funds would go directly to the charities while what was needed would be used to pay off any expenses we would have, and as it turned out there were quite a few.

We thought a PR company might be important but at first had no idea what they cost. A company called Captive Minds impressed both the organisers with the way that they did things and their expertise in Expedition PR. They had worked quite extensively with Edward 'Bear' Grylls and helped build the brand that he has become, as well as David Hempleman-Adams, the first person to achieve the "Adventurers' Grand Slam" of climbing the Seven Summits (the highest mountain on each continent) and reaching the Geographic North and South Poles. They claimed to have been part of at least one world-record-breaking expedition or adventure since their formation in 2003 and saw ours as their next project. Marcus Chidgey was Founder and CEO, and was also pretty keen to come along.

Towards the end of 2008 there was a lot of discussion with them, and it became clear that if we were going with a PR company it would be these guys. Alex Rayner, the Co-Founder of the company, is Mr PR and has an incredibly infectious personality. He would often give the boys a lift when they were struggling for inspiration or motivation and is incredible when it comes to thinking outside the box. The issues we had surrounded costs, and the first agreement was that they had until Christmas to deliver a title sponsor worth £85k, and if they did so we would hire them full time and pay the fees they were asking, which at the time were around £20k. If they did not we would part company without any hard feelings. Things were not that simple, because if they were to come on board then part of the deal was that Marcus would come to Gorak Shep with us himself to help get media content off the mountain, and since we needed to give the names of all passengers to Qatar Airways by the middle of December, we simply counted him in. He was now coming regardless, which Kirt was fine with as he knew by now that they were here to stay whatever happened, and remained convinced that they would produce a sponsor.

Another big meeting took place in early December, this time at Lord's, one of several that would occur throughout the planning period. We decided that morning to conduct a 'Freeze Mob' at some of London's landmarks. This involved donning our cricket gear, not to mention rucksack, woolly hat, ski goggles and gloves and then enacting a cricket delivery. As the imaginary ball was bowled an appeal would go up and everyone had to freeze in their position for three minutes. Standing still for this time is surprisingly difficult, not helped by everyone else struggling to contain their giggles. As the umpire all eyes were on me when we did our first one at Parliament Square with Big Ben striking 11 immediately behind us, many passing tourists halted what they were doing to take a few photos and then ask a few questions.

That, however, was nothing compared to our sequel at Buckingham Palace. Where Parliament Square had people watching us from a distance, the Palace had a full crowd of people milling around when we arrived, most likely because of the imminent Changing of the Guard. We did not know of this, however, and as Hillsy and I headed towards the gates a convenient gap in the crowd opened up and the players took their positions immediately. Once the freeze began there was a big crowd surrounding us, who at first looked bemused but were soon posing to have their pictures taken with the crazy Englishmen in white clothing. One visitor even gave a high five to one of our frozen participants while saying, 'This is why I love London.' We later discovered he was from Texas and had absolutely no idea what was going on, but he and everyone else clearly found us more entertaining than the Changing of the Guard taking place behind us. A policeman did ask what we were doing but a quick-thinking Wes muttered it was for charity, while still trying to appear frozen. When asked which charity, Wes stammered: 'Er, the Prince's Trust?' and the Bobby walked calmly on.

The final freeze took place in Trafalgar Square and again a large crowd of confused people had pictures taken with us, prompting headlines such as 'Cricket brings Trafalgar Square to a halt,' in a couple of publications and a few websites.

Once we got to Lord's for the meeting I met Marcus for the first

time and as Kirt and Wes gave everyone an update on where things were
he was clearly impressed with how professionally this amateur project
was being run. Marcus was a similar age, but having created his own
business, travelled and got married, meant he was perhaps a little more
mature than many of our group. He was also clearly impressed as I ran
him through some of the coverage we had already received.

The fact that we had many contacts, and were already doing a
reasonable job of publicising ourselves, was what gave Wes reservations
about hiring a PR company, although he had originally thought it a
good idea. He felt that though it would be tough, we had the people and
dedication to run the PR ourselves, and save a whole lot of fees. He sent
me an email asking if I felt I could handle the PR side of things myself
and my answer was that I'd give it a go, but it seemed like a lot of work
for someone with zero experience. It was one thing trying to keep track
of what newspapers and radio shows we were appearing on, but quite
another to actually manage PR for an expedition. He had also asked
me not to mention it to Kirt as he knew that if we broke away from
Captive Minds then Kirt would not take it well. Wes was pleased with the
expedition blog that had been running since April and the website which
went live in September, and although these were both good means of
letting people know who we were and what we were doing, the hits we
were getting to both suggested it was really just friends and family who
were visiting. Marcus and Alex were about to sell themselves in the best
way possible by carrying out a highly successful Press Launch.

The major piece of news that came out at the meeting was the
decision to switch charity. While I was never involved with Sport Relief,
it was clear for a long time that the fit was not quite right. Nothing they
promised in the first meeting - from marketing to legal assistance - ever
came to pass. There was also always confusion about whether we were
raising money for Sport Relief or Comic Relief, and when it became
clear it was a Comic Relief year that was not a good fit. They also wanted
us to guarantee them a set amount of money and were unhappy that
we were splitting the proceeds we raised with another charity. When in
November they told Kirt that they would not be helping us with any

publicity – worried by 'Commercial Fatigue' they prefer to run their publicity intensively over two weeks rather than six months – with our aim of giving value to a title sponsor, this news was hardly ideal.

Wes described the quest for a suitable charity as his lowest point of the whole trip; here was a project people deeply believed in and were hugely passionate about yet nobody seemed to want to take the money offered since it was not enough - even though we could guarantee a minimum of £45k.

At around the same time Captive Minds told us that they had spoken to a businessman called John Ayling who, along with running several businesses of his own, is also Commercial Chairman of The Lord's Taverners charity. The Taverners had been discussed but not much was known about them. John said he loved the idea and that 'If they support the Taverners I will get them an £80k sponsor tomorrow.' Kirt and Wes practically ran to meet him.

The Lord's Taverners were founded in 1950 by a group of actors who spent much of their time in the Tavern at the famous cricket ground, and decided they wanted to give something back to the game they loved. The idea has always been to encourage people to get involved in the game, but with a special focus on those who might not otherwise have had the opportunity, hence their slogan 'Giving children a sporting chance.'

Half of the funds they raise go to cricket projects, so providing equipment and creating competitions for those at grass roots level, while the other half goes to special needs schools or organisations which help children to play disabled sports. In March a few of us were able to visit a regional event held at The Oval where schools were competing at 'Table Cricket' – based around cricket and table tennis - for a place in the final at Lord's and for those of us who were there for the whole morning it was a great opportunity to see the kind of project that we would be helping fund. Children with various disabilities were all having a thoroughly good time and also getting very competitive with each other.

At the meeting Kirt and Wes explained the situation with Sport Relief and said that the Lord's Taverners were very keen to get involved and would support us properly regardless of what we raised. It was put to a show of hands who thought we should switch and who did not, bearing in mind we were just four months away from our departure and had done eight months of work telling everyone of our alliance with Sport/Comic Relief and had already raised funds for them.

The decision was unanimous and we quickly moved on. The details of our relationship with the Taverners were still to be decided, but they were incredibly well connected in the world of cricket and were an excellent fit. A meeting was arranged for January 7th where we would discuss how they could help us and how much money we thought we could raise. They were clear from the start that they were not hugely bothered by the amount and that the £40k minimum would be fine providing they could piggyback some of our publicity to help raise their own profile. This was music to our ears. After the meeting we went downstairs to the indoor school and had a lengthy net session and another Bleep Test and a large group of us went out for dinner and drinks.

By now I was thinking very hard about what I would do about Christmas. I did not want Kirt to go out alone and felt that this was a unique opportunity for me to go on a recce trip, meet some local suppliers and government officials that would perhaps change the direction in which my life was heading. Yes I felt bad about missing Christmas and the wedding, but at the same time I felt it was time to put myself and the trip first. I was pretty pumped up and excited after the meeting, so come Monday morning I walked into the office and booked myself on the same flight as Kirt. We would fly on Christmas Eve, via Bahrain, and return on New Year's Day.

CHAPTER SIX

——

B y now the expedition was really taking over my life, I was giving everything to it and since Kirt decided he had to go out to
Nepal, and the holiday period was the only time he would be
able to go, it seemed inevitable to me that I would end up going too. I
didn't have to, but felt compelled. It was difficult for Kirt to skip Christmas, but people understood how important this was not just to us, but to
another 50 people, not to mention the guys in Nepal. My family were
largely supportive, if disappointed, as were my friends who were getting
married - so by the time we made our way to the airport I had managed
to assuage most of my guilt, although I still felt bad the whole time I was
away.

The flight over was fairly uneventful, a few drinks on the first leg
followed by four hours in an airport bar in Bahrain where we welcomed
Christmas Day by exchanging a couple of comedy gifts and had several
whiskies to help clear the colds we were developing. We arrived in
Kathmandu at around 6pm and as we came out of the airport I was
surprised at how many people were bustling around looking for business,
like taxi drivers and porters.

We knew Nir Lama would be there to meet us but as neither of us
knew what he looked like we thought this might have been a challenge
but fortunately we stuck out and he clocked us right away. Once we
packed into a taxi with his friend Bil and headed into town I was
immediately taken by how busy and noisy the roads were: I even saw
a truck with a sign on the back saying, 'Don't honk, just wait' which
made me laugh. As we approached Thamel, the tourist hub of the city,
the taxi driver told us that we would have to walk the last stretch to the
Guest House as there were road blocks due to so many people being
out celebrating Christmas. I was surprised by this given that Nepal is
predominantly Hindu and Buddhist, but sure enough the streets were
absolutely jam-packed, like being on the underground in rush hour.

The four of us braved the crowds, Kirt and I donning our backpacks,

Nir Lama (left) and Bil Tamang: Christmas Day in Kathmandu, 2008

and what is normally a five-minute walk took about 20, with me losing the others at one stage and becoming very concerned. I had never seen anything like it, but everyone was so happy and jumping around that it was hard not to laugh along with them, Kirt said it was like 2006 after the King agreed to relinquish his powers back to Parliament and impromptu street parties sprang up all over town. While I confess to an initial feeling of concern due to being in unfamiliar surroundings, once I got to grips with the fact that everyone was just having a great time I was able to relax and keep walking until I found the others. Dinner and a couple of drinks that night were fantastic as we slowly got to know Nir and Bil.

The original plan was to pack in as many meetings as we could during the first two or three days which would allow us to have some downtime afterwards and perhaps do some rafting or visit Pokhara, a beautiful town a few hours from Kathmandu in the shadow of the mountains and based around a huge lake. This never came to pass however, as we soon found ourselves neck deep in meetings. The first was Boxing Day morning with the Himalayan Rescue Association (HRA), which was our first of three visits, followed by a trip to Cricket Association of Nepal to meet Mr Binaya Pandey. These meetings were pretty different as the HRA wanted to see what they could do for us while the CAN wanted to see what we could do for them. Both went well however, we just had some negotiating to do with HRA who wanted to send eight medics with us and charge us handsomely. We politely declined as we already had our four medics and really just needed one altitude expert and some oxygen, but we arranged to meet them again on the 28th. Mr Pandey simply gave us permission to play the match on the spot; was delighted that we were helping to raise the profile of cricket in Nepal and offered to send letters to the Minister for Sport if required.

Each morning at 10am, Nir would arrive at the Kathmandu Guest House with a different person, all of whom would be involved in one way or another with our trip. This helped us realise how many people were part of our expedition in Nepal. The 27th was a Saturday so it was almost impossible to meet anyone, but Nir had managed to persuade his contact at the Ministry of Tourism to come and see us at 11am at the Guest House. This man, who I will refer to throughout simply as Smiley, arrived and was very friendly, but we soon discovered just how many departments we would need to get permission from. He told us that it would not be a problem as everyone agreed our expedition had great potential to benefit the country so it should all be a formality - this turned out to be a long way from the truth. Alarm bells started ringing and we agreed to go to his office the following day with the intention of meeting his boss. As Kirt would later write, 'The process of gaining us permission to do this had gone from being straightforward and certain, to convoluted and unsure.'

That afternoon I met Dharma for the first time and Kirt was delighted to see him. Dharma was the guide who took Kirt to Base Camp in 2006 where this whole idea began and Kirt was keen for him to come with us again – although he did not work with Peace Nepal Treks. They then decided it was time to introduce me to Tongba, a local beer that is served warm and drunk through a straw.

That night we hung out at a few of the bars in Thamel and as the night wore on it became apparent that Nir did not have a final sum of what we would owe him at the end of the trip, something that worried me considerably. I said to Kirt that we needed to get a number from him, if the cost was going to go up then people would understand if we told them now - as the trip was still some way away - but if we told them closer to departure it might not be so easy. Kirt became a little defensive, but later agreed and also told me that he had discussed the matter with Dharma earlier in the evening. Dharma was to turn out to be a very useful man to have around over the coming days as he had no personal agenda other than to look after the best interests of his friend: as he did not work for Nir he could also question him if he did not think something was quite right.

On Sunday morning, seven of us headed into the Government offices to put our case to the Tourist Board. Thinking back on it I am not entirely sure what we expected to happen, but in truth nothing much did. We were met by Smiley and we sat in his office for quite some time. There was lots of talking in Nepali so we had no idea what was being discussed, and after around an hour we were taken into another office and presented to the boss. We had a very brief chat with him, saying that we would like permission to play the match; that we had an environmental policy in place so would be careful not to damage the mountain by littering and would treat the area with the respect it deserves. Again, there was very little response, a smile and a nod followed by a short 'Thanks for coming' and we were back into the outer office again. We sat there some more while some quite heated conversations took place, which would often include long periods of silence, and then a little while later we left. All in all it was quite an odd morning and we really had no idea if we had made any progress at all, or even gone backwards.

During this time it became evident that Nir was an incredibly stressed man. Just a year older than us, he has built Peace Nepal Treks from nothing and runs it with family and friends. With the momentum of our trip gathering, and press coverage growing in both the UK and Nepal, he felt that if this was to go wrong, and permission not be granted then it would be the end of him, he would have to close his business in shame. Needless to say we tried to calm him down as best we could when he got into these moods, but such talk would become increasingly frequent as time wore on. The funny thing was that Kirt felt much the same way himself about everyone back in the UK. I was still trying to maintain the philosophy of 'Everything will be OK in the end, if it's not OK then it's not the end,' but concern was definitely growing.

That afternoon we paid a visit to Durbar Square, a small area in the middle of town that is full of Temples. In any other part of the world I would expect this place to be a bit of a haven of peace, but in Kathmandu it appears to be about the busiest thoroughfare in the whole city as motorbikes screech through it all hours of the day. As Charlie BN happened to be passing through Kathmandu on a family holiday for a couple of days, we decided to wander down to the Yak and Yeti Hotel and have a couple of drinks with him - the following day would bring more meetings and we needed to unwind.

We had also tried to arrange a meeting with the British Ambassador for that afternoon, but discovered that ironically he was back in London for the holiday, as was virtually the entire Embassy, so that option went out the window. Instead we headed down to the HRA again and their two head guys, Bikram and Prakash, told us they were happy to accept our proposed donation of £5,000 and would just send the one medic with us. We were hoping they would be able to supply us with some oxygen and a Gamow Bag, a large inflatable pressure bag used to treat Altitude Sickness. But we discovered we would have to pay extra for this, so we decided to keep negotiating. That conversation was just drawing to a close when Bikram suddenly announced that we had an appointment with the CEO of the Tourist Board. Kirt and I wondered if it would be with the same quiet man we had met with Smiley the previous day, but when we ended up at a totally different office we quickly realised that was not the case. After a short wait we were led into a significantly nicer office than the previous chap had, leaving me convinced this guy was more important, and had a very similar chat with him. He was more receptive to what we were saying and seemed happy to do what he could to help us. He said that it would need several people to sign off on the permission but that it should not be a problem, he could see the benefit for the tourist industry and welcomed our endeavour, even mentioning that in 2011 they are organising 'Visit Nepal Year' where they host an event each month and perhaps we could work with them on that. We left the office with our moods significantly improved.

It took some time to work out who the two people we had met were, but eventually we got to the bottom of it. The first man we met was head of the Ministry of Tourism, which is under the government. The second man was the head of the Nepal Tourist Board (NTB), which is an independent body.

That afternoon we ran through our itinerary with Nir and decided exactly where we would be each night. While this was largely straightforward, we made the call to have an extra rest day on the way up, meaning it would be a quick sprint back down. We were aware it would be difficult but felt it was worth doing in the interests of safety on match day. That meant our trek to Gorak Shep would be nine days, including two acclimatisation days. We would have two full days at Gorak Shep itself, with the match being held on the second of those, and then come back down in four days – meaning a total of 15 days on the mountain.

Nir met us the following morning and he was able to give us a price this time, around £36k in total for the group. This took us aback. When Kirt and Wes agreed on a price of £1,500 for the trip this was made up of £700 for the flights, £450 for the trek and £100 for insurance. This would then leave £250 per person as contingency for costs they had not thought of. Now we were looking at £720 per person for the trek. Kirt and I agreed we would need some more money from somewhere and so it was decided that we would collect a local payment in Kathmandu to cover the cost of everyone's food on the mountain. This would give us enough capital to have a breather again.

We had budgeted only £450 each for the trek, based on Kirt's own trek in 2006 where he had paid around £350. But where he had one guide, we would have around 20 guides and porters. Also, the cost of the internal flights from Kathmandu to Lukla had increased significantly since 2006, and we needed to pay for these, as well as food and accommodation. Still, given that we had now managed to get all our flights for free and only had to pay about £200 each for taxes, we felt we had enough to cover the costs.

New Year's Eve arrived with a nasty hangover and we made our way to HRA for a final meeting, when we quickly settled with what we had agreed in the previous meeting and if we needed to come back to them for oxygen or a Gamow bag then we would. We said goodbye and after an early dinner with Nir and Bil tried to get into the party spirit that was starting to stir up in Thamel. But we were both struck down with stomach cramps and fever, which did not abate on the plane. In fact, we were ill for quite a while after our return, but at least at our next meeting plenty of people told me how much weight I had lost!

Most importantly, we felt the trip had been a success and we had met enough people to at least make it plain sailing for Nir to get the permissions we required. The Sports Minister would not be a problem thanks to the CAN; the Home Office was pretty simple anyway, and thanks to our Environmental Policy - painstakingly drawn up by Kirt and Tom Sharland – the Forestry Commission were OK as well. The problems that remained were finally getting everything from the Ministry of Tourism, which we had received verbally but it would be some time before we had anything in writing, and then being granted entry to the National Park itself, which involved getting the permission of a man we will call Mr X.

In the next few weeks we had to make several financial decisions, the most significant one being whether or not we were going to employ Captive Minds. By now they were fully committed to the Press Launch, but Kirt was understandably worried that if we went through with this and then were denied permission by the Nepali Government it would be a disaster for all concerned – it would also leave him carrying the debt. A lot of very frank emails passed between Nir, Kirt and me updating on the situation, but we would often go a few days without hearing anything. We discovered later that one of the reasons for this was that Nir was going to the National Parks Office and simply sitting there all day until someone would speak to him, when he came home the electricity would be down due to Kathmandu being constantly subjected to power cuts, so he was unable to email. I can only imagine what was going through his mind all those hours he was sitting in these offices, basically being given the run around.

CHAPTER SEVEN

Feeling unwell seemed to be a rather inauspicious way to welcome in 2009, this seismic year in the lives of both Kirt and myself. It took us both close to two weeks to really get ourselves right again, and I was left pretty concerned at how I'd cope come April if spending just a week in Kathmandu had left me feeling that rotten.

Once recovered it was back to the planning, and there was still plenty going on. We had a meeting arranged for January 7th when myself and Kirt, plus Alex and Marcus from Captive Minds, were going to meet the top guys at the Lord's Taverners, along with people from Surrey Country Cricket Club who had also agreed to help us. That morning I had a call at 9am at Surrey saying they would have to cancel as all sorts of things were happening in the office – when I switched on the news and found that the England captain and coach had both been removed from their posts, this cancellation quickly made sense. So we met with the Taverners and one of the things they mentioned was the possibility of involving some of their celebrity members and perhaps current England players. They felt that opening batsman Alastair Cook was certainly an option as he is President of the Young Lord's Taverners, while Andrew Strauss was also likely to lend his name to the project. We had another group meeting planned for January 17th at Lord's and they had already looked into the possibility of Strauss coming down to do a bit of coaching or at least pose for a few photos. Unfortunately as we were sat in the room discussing this, over at Lord's he was being unveiled as the next England captain, so his time quickly vanished. Still, it did not take long to speak to the agents of the two players as well as arrange a meeting with Cook at a Taverners function and they were soon named honorary captains of the two sides. Since it was Kirt, Wes and I who met with Cook he was given first choice of which team to go for and chose Team Hillary. When this was announced at the meeting by Alex Rayner the whole room erupted and it was clear now that the project was starting to snowball, and what was more important was that the Lord's Taverners had already delivered

London press launch: January 2009

far more in the space of a couple of weeks that Sport Relief had managed in eight months.

Another reason that this was especially significant for us was the previous day we had made a decision of our own about whom we would go with for our kit suppliers. We were keen on Adidas – who were sponsoring then-England captain Kevin Pietersen – but decided on Gray-Nicolls who were already providing bats, pads, gloves and bags. This turned out to be the perfect fit, particularly once Pietersen lost the England job and the Gray-Nicolls sponsored Strauss took his place. We were in regular contact with the guys at the Taverners and it was brilliant to see such enthusiasm coming from them; in fact one of their team was so excited by the project she started talking about coming with us. Shona Langridge is Head of Fundraising and has a huge passion for the Himalayas, whenever we saw or spoke with her she was always incredibly excited about what we were doing, which made a huge difference to us, but when she kept saying she was going to come with us I actually thought she was joking until I found her that Just Giving Page was all set up for the Taverners, she was booked and she was coming! She was actually going to climb Island Peak, a nearby mountain that is 6,189 metres high that is popular among people wanting to get higher than Base Camp and be able to say they have climbed a Himalayan peak, but she made sure she would be there for the match itself and would end up presenting the Man of the Match award.

We had the meeting on the 17th and were able to run through the main points that had come out of our trip to Kathmandu as well as Alex Rayner announcing the two honorary captains. We also announced the involvement of Stick Cricket, an online computer game. Nick Toovey had contacted them asking if they wanted to get involved and they jumped all over it.

The week following the meeting I remember having six meetings in five weeknights, all related to our trip as the pace really began to gather, and one of those was with Paul Collins from Stick Cricket who offered us a trophy for the person who hit the most sixes in our match and also said he would like to support us by creating a computer game that would feature us, giving us a real moment from the film 'Jerry McGuire' when Bob Sugar says:

"I will not rest until I have you holding a Coke, wearing your own shoe, playing a computer game featuring you, while singing your own song in a new commercial, starring you, broadcast during the Super Bowl, in a game that you are winning, and I will not sleep until that happens."

The game itself was designed using Google imagery of the place where we would be playing and had the names of everyone involved. It launched just before we departed which made for a lot of very excited people and by the time we returned there were more than 9 million scores registered on it, driving a huge amount of traffic to our website. They were also kind enough to respond to a plea I made some months later for £500 to pay for the stumps (which we had branded up), bails and boundary markers.

Another who became involved in January was Jim White of *Cricket World* magazine and website. Jim is absurdly enthusiastic about all things cricket and seems to spend his days whizzing around the country doing interviews and watching cricket. Fortunately for us he absolutely loved The Everest Test and was keen do whatever he could to help us. He secured us 100 cricket balls from Tiflex as well as eight helmets and a selection of branded caps from Albion. On top of that the coverage we received from *Cricket World* in both their magazine and on their website was hugely welcome and has continued long after we returned.

We had news from one of the late joiners, David Christie, that North Face and Ellis-Brigham were willing to give us hefty discounts on certain products, we just needed to place our orders. Finally Joe Williams told us that Bulldog were on board to provide male grooming products.

We also now had our full allocation of people for the trip. There had been some unfortunate drop-outs, including two after the deadline for getting any kind of refund. The next issue to deal with was the Press Launch, which was scheduled for January 27th. By now I was speaking relatively regularly to Alex Rayner and he was working on another freeze in Trafalgar Square, on a Tuesday morning which is normally a quiet time for the press. We were all encouraged to send out the official press release that was drafted by Captive Minds to everyone we could possibly think of and when we arrived at Trafalgar Square we were not disappointed – and neither were they as nearly half of the group managed to take the morning off work.

By 8:30am we had a large group beginning to assemble. Since it was late January we had been worried that we might have rain on the day and be forced to abandon the whole thing, and just do a two or three-man interview in a nearby hotel. I later discovered that Alex was flying by the seat of his pants a little as the hotel room was not booked as a backup, so it was just as well the sun came out.

Before too long, two big green Lord's Taverners mini-buses showed up and parked on the square. There was also an enormous scoreboard with details of what we were doing standing at a 45-degree angle to Nelson's Column and as photographers and news crews started to arrive all of us began to feel like this was definitely a once-in-a-lifetime experience. All we needed now was for the pitch to arrive, but nobody was quite sure who had organised for it to be delivered.

Just as I was starting to fret a little I saw a white van pull onto the square and the wicket was unloaded. It was enormous, and looked like a Swiss Roll big enough to feed an entire school for a week. My first thought was to chuckle when I saw the efforts taken to manoeuvre the wicket around, but that laughter soon turned to apprehension when I remembered we were going to have to carry that thing for the best part of two weeks up and down a mountain.

The pitch was rolled out and the stumps set up and before long half the group were messing around with a bat and ball, which slightly spoiled Alex's mood as we were giving something of a sneak preview. He called us in and ran through what was going to happen. A repeat of the freeze, but this time we would bowl a real rather than imaginary ball and go up in an appeal and hold it for two minutes.

Charlie Bathurst-Norman and James Markby would be the two men batting and Team Tenzing would be in the field with Kinsey Hern chosen as the bowler least likely to suffer a case of the yips and send the delivery miles off target. While we were pitching ourselves as 'Ordinary people doing something extraordinary' we also wanted it made known that the match itself would be of a decent standard and very competitive. We had plenty of people on the trip who captain their various cricket clubs and play at a decent level, but we also had a few who fell very firmly into the 'village cricketer' category, and while Charlie BN would be placed in the former category, James was very much one of the latter! Fortunately he took up his place at the non-striker's end and we did not really worry about it.

The freeze was done and a few photos were taken, but in truth it did not have nearly the same feel about it without being surrounded by crowds three rows deep staring at us. The area was cordoned off for the press so the general public were not going to get in at street level, although a bunch of excitable children did come running down the stairs from the National Gallery whooping and hollering and then ran off again, which caused amusement. Once it was done we walked off and congratulated Kinsey for just about managing to hit the cut strip, and Charlie for actually stretching to get to the ball to make it look like he might be out in some way, and also for maintaining balance while mid-lunge. Alex soon came over and said the general consensus from the press was that they wanted to see us play a bit, so out we went once more and Kinsey was given the task of actually bowling a spell. Nerves still jangling he managed to do so, and Charlie decided to enjoy himself with the bat as well, coming down the pitch and sending the ball into one of the nearby fountains, giving everyone a good laugh. They would not have laughed so much however, if the previous ball he struck had ended up hitting a small child, rather than lodging in the wheel of its pram - a lucky escape. Next thing I knew Kinsey was retaliating to being hit for six by bowling a bouncer at Charlie's head which very nearly took him out and Alex was quick to signal a 'Not cool' look and I decided to call an end to proceedings. We even managed to get James Markby on strike for a few deliveries and make him look like a genuine cricketer.

After that was done it was time to mingle with the press. Former England players Mark Butcher, Chris Adams and James Kirtley were all there and joined in for the last part of the cricket before posing with us for plenty of photos. Suddenly it felt like graduation again as everywhere you turned another camera was stuck in your face and any expression other that wide-eyed enthusiasm was simply unacceptable. Then came the interviews, wave after wave of them, with people able to speak to whomever they wanted. In total the whole thing lasted little more than two hours, but by the time we had packed up and made our way to a nearby pub we were already hearing reports that we were on the lunchtime news on both BBC and ITV.

I spent the afternoon with Kirt and Will Simmons, who had missed most of the morning as driving up from Cheltenham had taken longer than he had expected, and our phones were going virtually non-stop as people called through to tell us they had seen the coverage or read about it in the *Evening Standard*. It felt good to be finally making waves and when I returned to the office the following day I had around 30 emails from various people on the trip sending attached news cuttings or links to online stories. During the next couple of days the story was picked up all round the world. Where previously a simple search on Google for 'Everest cricket' would come up mostly with miscellaneous Everest stories and the details for Everest Cricket Club...in Ohio, now our website and blog had shot to the top and every other story for pages was about us. Captive Minds had shown to any doubters that they had the ability to put our story out there and all we could do now was hope somebody would come to us with sponsorship.

Alex in particular had been gutted about missing out on being involved in the freeze mobs in December and felt we could have done more with them, so he was particularly pleased with how that morning went and emailed us all regularly with links to the news footage that appeared. ITV ran the story for more than 48 hours, something which was not missed by the team at Captive Minds. Everyone was delighted and excitement levels were at a real high thanks to Alex and his team.

The launch was also a good opportunity to see the difference of our two charities and how they each worked. They differed enormously, but both believed in what we were doing and were willing to help in any way they could. The Himalayan Trust made it clear early on that they had very few people who actually work for them in the UK, and those that do are volunteers, so they could not devote any manpower to helping us out but did send a couple of people down on the day. An old fashioned charity, they rely heavily on the goodwill towards the Himalayas, the Nepali people and of course Sir Edmund Hillary. What they were able to do, however, was let us use their name whenever we wanted and they were incredibly helpful when it came to supplying letters and giving us access to their contacts in Nepal when we were trying to secure all the permissions we required.

The Taverners meanwhile were more than happy to throw everything at the Press Launch, splashing their name where they could and dishing out Lord's Taverners branded caps as well as putting two of their distinctive mini-buses in the middle of Trafalgar Square by way of raising their profile.

This period in early January also coincided with Kirt being made redundant as the company he worked for folded. He was not the first person on the trip to suffer this fate as Charlie Campbell and Haydn were both also out of work, but Captive Minds presented Kirt with a solution. They offered to employ him, on a fairly basic salary, to work on his own project while also helping out occasionally on other things that needed doing. For him this was perfect as it meant that he could now dedicate himself full-time to sourcing corporate sponsorship, just at a time when we needed it most and were at our hottest. The next few weeks would be vital to the financial side of the expedition. Of course, by doing this it was now impossible for us to not take the full services of Captive Minds as our leader was heavily invested in them, and to a lesser extent, them in him.

At first, Kirt thought this would actually free up some of his evenings to relax a little, but since January that simply was not happening for anyone. We had reached a stage where virtually every night there was something Everest related going on: if it wasn't training it was a meeting about events; if it wasn't events it was finances; if not that it was how the filming was going to be done; or where we were with final permissions from the Nepali government, or how people were getting on with their individual sponsorships and where our Partners Program was at. This took up every waking hour of many of our lives, and while we tore our hair out at times, we all loved it really.

As time wore on it became increasingly clear that raising £250k was going to be beyond us, and an earlier target of £100k was more feasible. After the launch many newspapers and websites said that we had in fact raised that amount, which was being a little overzealous, and ultimately we were to raise around the £100k mark. However, both these charities were happy with what we could give them, and as we sat in a room with John Ayling he commented that it was a shame we had not carried out the project a year or so earlier as we would have got closer to £300k for a title sponsor. While I was impressed with his conviction I could not help but be a little sceptical.

Knowing that we would be raising at least £75k from the 50 participants, we decided we would split this with two thirds going to the Taverners and the rest to the Himalayan Trust. We also had plenty of fundraising events happening which would be weighted more in the favour of the Trust to even things out and of course worked on the assumption that several people would raise more than just the £1,500, David Kirtley and John Richards for example both set their targets at £5k. We had always said that unless you raised the £1,500 you could not come on the trip, but with names having to be given to the airline so early this simply was never practical. We stated afterwards that the deadline for fundraising would be September 1st 2009, and by a month after we returned most people were at their targets, but there were a couple who had not raised a penny. We had said that whatever you did not raise you would have to make up yourselves, but of course, that never happened.

By this point we had agreed that we would pay Captive Minds for doing the launch and then they were not obliged to do any work for us until we actually departed for the expedition, at which stage they would kick into action again, unless the elusive sponsor was found and fronted up plenty of cash. They were still confident that the attention and coverage we would get from the launch would be enough to convince a major company of the value they would be getting from putting their name to our trip, and so they could keep working with us full-time.

Apart from new charities, computer games and celebrity names that came our way in early January, the training schedules also went up a notch. Trim Trails became harder as people like Glen and Blinky in particular wanted to push themselves more and more. Meanwhile the weekend team-building trips were now approaching. Most of these had long been in the diary and each one proved memorable in its own way.

First up was a trip to Kinsey's farm in Hereford. Nearly half the people on the trip made the long journey from London to take part in the 'Fantasy Fitness Challenge' which was loosely based on a Fantasy Football format. As one person said afterwards, it was the taking of a simple concept and making it so complicated that most people had no idea what was going on for the first half of the day that made the experience so unique. Kinsey put in a lot of work coming up with various challenges that people would have to do on the Saturday, which would culminate in a five-mile run up and down the hills. All of this would take place after a night in the village hall, where several people put themselves forward for the Least Wanted Roommate In Nepal by farting and snoring for several hours.

The Saturday began with another Bleep Test, where this time Ben Jarman (BJ) registered a very impressive 14.3 in an empty chicken shed. After that was a rather old-fashioned game of throwing the boulder as far as you can, where newcomer Nick Mullineux impressed everyone with a throw of 6.7 metres and beat everyone else by almost a whole metre. Wes, meanwhile, managed to chip his own tooth and Hillsy nearly killed himself by throwing his last boulder straight up in the air and only getting out of the way at the last moment.

Next was a relay event where teams had to push a tractor tyre around a slalom course set up in the shed, a precursor to another event where the tyre was replaced by a giant hay bale. This particular event was interesting as Paola was about half the size of her bale and Blinky threw a small hissy fit about the crumbling state of his. The sense of humour failure by Blinky went virtually unnoticed however as the event before had produced an even more spectacular rant by Gareth, who in a game which involved shifting stones around (Kinsey using the opportunity to get some manual labour done) had a total meltdown after misunderstanding the rules. The competitive edge was starting to shine through and it was good that people were actually taking it all quite seriously. The tug-of-war and five-mile finisher, which most people agreed was more like eight miles, rounded off a brilliant day and another occasion when people got away from London and did something completely different to anything they had done before.

The very next weekend was a Team Hillary trip to Dartmoor. While not quite filled with the same absurdities that took place on Kinsey's farm, the country folk were treated to groups of men frying eggs in just their underwear at the top of a hill, and a man in a Gorilla outfit flying a kite, not to mention walking around 18km over the moor in deep fog. For Hillary this was a significant weekend as it was the first time the whole squad had got together and it established a dynamic and camaraderie that would remain for the next four months, much like the doomed effort on the Three Peaks had done for Tenzing the previous year.

The following weekend much of the banter that had set the tone for Dartmoor was repeated when we set off for the Brecon Beacons. In the end 14 people made it down for two nights sleeping in the pavilion of Cardiff Cricket Club, not an ideal place to hole up in mid-February but by now we were starting to get used to some unusual accommodation. The whole weekend was thrown into doubt at the 11th hour however as extreme weather threatened to make the journey from London a non-starter. Snow had caused chaos in London causing trains to be cancelled and all buses actually stopped running on one day as the roads were too dangerous. It had looked like it was easing up by the end of the week only for news reports to say that both Severn Bridges were closed due to 'falling shards of ice' that were smashing car windscreens. Needless to say this put off several people and throughout the Friday afternoon, emails were exchanged as to whether or not it was safe to travel. Eventually the majority decided to brave it, and promptly had the easiest journey down to Cardiff as the motorway was virtually empty.

The weekend was spent testing out our trekking gear and walking around in the snow. On the first day we climbed Pan Y-Fan in approximately a metre of snow. I am no skier, but several of the people there said it was some of the best 'powder' they had ever seen and wished they had brought their snowboards with them. This was particularly the case on our way down the hill as it became too difficult to walk down conventionally so, led by BJ, we slid and rolled our way down until the snow began to thin out. The following day we took on a more normal walk which would include taking in some magnificent waterfalls, and as it started snowing, Glen, Blinky and Kirt decided an impromptu Trim Trail session was needed - everyone else just left them to it. The walk took a little longer than planned as BJ and David managed to do a particularly bad job of map reading, much to the chagrin of James Butler and Tooves, but by the time we returned to the start point we all felt we had done a very good day's walking, many of the group carrying their expedition packs and we covered considerably more mileage than we would during any day of the trek.

The Bath Half Marathon was still looming large in March and for many people was a real source of fear, but it was becoming obvious just from looking at how the physical shapes of most people had changed that we were starting to become quite a fit and healthy bunch, despite the occasional slip-up along the way.

CHAPTER EIGHT

The weekends away and the seemingly constant announcements of new sponsors or contributors becoming involved really helped feed the enthusiasm of everyone involved. Kirt was still chasing corporate sponsorship and Wes and Vicks Nicholson were helping out with that too. Our two main photographers, George Powell and Will Wintercross, were also helping to get a few more stories and pictures in the press and things were going quite nicely. The real boost however, came around a month after the Press Launch in Trafalgar Square when Kirt sent around the following email:

"Right – this is a big bit of news. As you know the awesome team at Captive Minds have been wielding their media might and we have some big news to announce.

Departing with us on April 9th we will be accompanied by a television crew from ITN, the News Agency that produces London Today, London Tonight, ITV, NBC and many, many more news programmes. London Tonight is watched by 3,700,000 people every night.

I have a contract here that clearly states:

'ITN will broadcast on London Tonight, a daily update, every day of the expedition, right up to the World Record attempt and then a 20-minute special upon the return. ITN will also broadcast the team training in preparation and the return of the expedition to London.'

This means, in normal terms, we will be on the television every single day – at least covering the whole of London and likely to be nationwide as we reach the Match date. As I sat in the ITN offices, watching the news studio "Go live", I was left truly speechless as some of the biggest men in UK news thanked me (and duly all of you) for creating such a wonderful World Record, and leaving such a touchable legacy for London, UK and of course the Antipodean states we are delighted to team up with.

I was stunned further when our cameraman mentioned his last 'high-altitude'

Arrival day in Kathmandu: Mark Jordan shoots footage for ITN

filming was an emergency evacuation across the Hindu Kush in Afghanistan, while being shot at by the Taliban. ITN are definitely taking this seriously and you will all meet the cameraman Mark Jordan shortly as he becomes a fully fledged member of The Everest Test."

He was right, this was a big bit of news and a great boost for the guys before we set off - the last part however, did not quite come to pass. Most people only met Mark at Heathrow airport or once we arrived in Kathmandu, and while I have to say I got along OK with him, not everyone did. The first person he fell out with was Alex Rayner and this is not entirely surprising: PR people and journalists rarely see eye-to-eye. This became apparent on a day in February when a few of us went to the previously mentioned Table Cricket, a Lord's Taverners event hosted at The Oval, but Mark was there to film a piece for ITN. Alex was trying to coordinate it and the two were at each others' throats from the first minute until eventually they decided to simply leave each other alone.

Following the announcement of ITN's involvement came our entry-level umpiring course. Held on Valentine's Day, the course tutor said with a wink that this day was the highest attendance they had ever had.

While myself, Hillsy and Helen had agreed to take part early on, we also persuaded Paola, Charlie BN, Mark Waters and Hillsy's dad, Andrew (who happened to be over from Australia and otherwise wouldn't have been able to catch up with his son).

All the guys had often umpired in club matches and thus were confident of being able to pass easily. We were wrong. As Mark wrote:

"We studied everything. Everything. How to enjoy umpiring, how to be an umpire, how to stand like an umpire, what a ball is, what hat should I wear? Bails; wood-whittling genius, or cricketing necessity? What's an over? What's an under? How wide should my popping crease be? What's a popping crease? The lot.

We were given a practical demonstration of what an umpire should be prepared for and what they should carry in a little, belt-holstered, "Man-Bag". Bails; 3 of. Heavy Bails; 3 of. 6 coins, plus 1 extra. 1 pencil; pointed. 1 piece of card; white. 1 Towel; John Smiths variety. Ball Gauge - What? 1 copy of the MCC rules; thumbed. One semi-automatic Heckler & Koch sub-machine gun, 1 small dachshund, 1 penknife, 1 Complete Works of William Shakespeare, fruitcake and bog-roll. That should just about cover all eventualities."

By the time we came to sit the exam, none of us were overly confident, and were even less so after the event. Most of us scraped through, except Hillsy and Paola, who was not overly disappointed, as her only prior knowledge of cricket having been that it was played by people in white on a rather large field.

This left us with a dilemma. Mark and Charlie most definitely did not want to umpire, they wanted to play. Helen would step up but had never actually stood in a match situation, so she started going to the Tuesday night net sessions for umpiring practice. Hillsy managed to arrange a re-take, just five days before departure. All we could do was wait and hope he got through it.

CHAPTER NINE

B y the end of February everything seemed on track: we were receiving regular updates from Nir and while we had permission from some of the smaller Ministries, the Department of National Parks and Wildlife Conservation (DNPWC) were causing real headaches. Mr X is their man based inside the park itself at Namche Bazaar, and while he regularly visited Kathmandu he kept avoiding Nir, especially after Nir told him he would not pay him any money in order to get permission. Nir offered to pay for him to come with us, but nothing else, and so our problems began. The existence of this man came to our attention in February, when Nir sent us an email referring to him as 'a virus'. Kirt did some research and discovered that other event organisers had been forced into offering bribes in order for their events to take place. Other avenues had been tried to avoid this fee, but people generally decided it was simpler to pay up.

We contacted several people, including members of the Himalayan Trust and the people at the Nepal Tourist Board, who all tried to persuade him to change his stance, but we had no joy. He wrote a negative letter about our trip, claiming that we would damage the flora and fauna in the area. For those who have never been to Gorak Shep, the place is barren. Grey as gravel on a military marching ground. He was simply not going to allow us to play there, and was suggesting we play at Namche Bazaar instead, which is almost a vertical mile lower than where we intended thus diluting the achievement enormously.

Kirt decided enough was enough and we would just have to bribe him. It was not something anyone wanted to do, especially as we were still very short on capital, but if there was no other option then so be it. We knew Nir would be unhappy about this and Kirt was willing to fly out himself if necessary. As we were looking at flights to get him out there we received an email from Nir saying things were looking good and on Wednesday March 4th we heard that Nir had gone over the head of Mr X and reached the Director General of the National Park and

Above: Nokia sponsorship
Right: Bath half marathon

Wildlife Preservation, a man called Dr. Shyam Bajimaya, who would write a letter and confirm our permission. Finally everything looked to be OK, but that did not last long and exactly two weeks later everything was up in the air again, and with our departure just 22 days away, the whole expedition was in doubt.

On Wednesday 18th March Kirt and I received an email from Nir that threw us both completely. The first thing he said was that we did not have permission from the Ministry of Communication and Information, and that they were kicking up a fuss over the filming equipment we would be taking and the fact that we would be sending footage back to the UK without any official personnel having a chance to check it. For them the priority is to make sure Nepal is shown in a positive light, why we would do anything other than that is beyond me, but that was the situation and they wanted to charge a thousand US Dollars per cameraman, and since we technically had three, and three photographers, this was a considerable problem. This was the first setback, the next was when Nir went to collect our permission letter from the Ministry of Tourism he discovered they had decided that they wanted to collect a 'Royalty' from us. This had never been mentioned before, and this is where our relationship with Smiley began to break down.

They wanted to charge $4,000 because of how many of us there were, money we simply did not have. Nir knew we were short on funds and immediately said that he did not want to make any profit from us whatsoever, despite the fact that he had worked solely on our project for six months, he was now willing to do it for free as the pride in making it happen was all he wanted. It got worse; the Home Office had now decided to wade in too, following the attack on the Sri Lanka team in Lahore on March 3rd, they wanted to send three security staff with us at our own expense. The argument was that if anything happened to us it would be a huge embarrassment to the government.

The email went from bad to worse as Nir continued. The next problem was that every Ministry we had received permission from wanted to send somebody along as a liaison officer, again at our expense. Nir had already rejected one from the Forestry Commission and four from the Sports Council and Ministry, but others were refusing to let go. He emailed again the following day and it became apparent that people for some reason thought we were a bunch of wealthy, and possibly even famous sportspeople, and suddenly everyone in Nepal wanted to get a piece of what we were doing. The fact that we were paying for the trip out of our own pockets had perhaps been misconstrued, and the fact that everything was going to charity, in part to help the people of Nepal, had somehow got lost along the way. The second email opened like this:

"Some agencies are going to attack our expedition to stop it this time; they would like to start for the next time themselves. Because our expedition is a world record attempt the sports tourism are jealous and they would like to make the record themselves. I heard all this news behind my back. People and some agencies are really - really jealous with our expedition. Some people told me Peace Nepal Treks is going to earn Millions dollars with this project. I think this is not good situation in this moment for me."

It was obvious how upset Nir was, and he was quite clearly starting to panic. Up until now he was always adamant that everything was under control, but now he felt the expedition, and thus his livelihood, was on the line. If his reputation was damaged then everything he had worked for with Peace Nepal Treks would be destroyed and so for the first time he asked us to come back out to Nepal and help him. Much as I wanted to go, I couldn't as I was having a dreadful time at work and had no holiday at all. Since Kirt was now employed by Captive Minds he had that extra flexibility and was on a plane on Saturday 21st March. Both Wes and Vicks did what they could to see if they could go too, but eventually he left alone.

His time out there was as stressful as it was worthwhile, and if he had not gone I am pretty certain that things would have turned out very differently. One thing I discovered at this time was that Kirt had essentially kept all this information from Wes, and that only I knew all the details, while Vicks had a vague idea of what was going on as well. This was a perfect example of Kirt trying to deal with everything himself and not sharing the burden. Wes only found out when he did because we were having a meeting about accounts the day the first email arrived on the 18th, and the fact that he was about to jump on a plane was quite difficult not to mention. Kirt later cited the fact that Wes does suffer more from anxiety and that the last thing he wanted was for him to get sick again; while also telling Wes that there was an element of embarrassment if things were to fall apart at this late stage. Whether he was right or wrong to keep it from Wes, the bottom line is that Kirt got it done, but it was definitely detrimental to the trust between them.

Wes was having a difficult time of things anyway. The anxiety that Kirt mentioned is really more about the future and the bigger picture, rather than day-to-day stuff which he thrives on, and the overall feeling that he was being pushed to the side of the project was a lot more damaging than if he had just been told. The other issue was his passion to make a film about the expedition; he wanted it done properly so went looking for a Director of Photography (DOP) and we signed up a chap called Konrad Frost. Wes has always enjoyed working with a camera and as Kirt had been taking more and more on in terms of logistics, often keeping Wes in the dark, he now felt that the film was the biggest thing he was going to take out of all this on a personal level. He felt early on that in order to do this we needed a strong cameraman with a lot of experience who could capture footage that a less experienced person might miss. We already had Miles Nathan, a friend of Kirt's from Roehampton, coming along as a cameraman and production expert, but Wes wanted someone from outside who would be at a higher level. He thought at first he had found this with Konrad, a friend of Vicks Nicholson who has documented several trips of a similar nature to ours and had his work shown on some major television channels. Unfortunately, these two had quite a personality clash and Wes felt the whole thing was being taken away from him and moving in a direction he did not want it to go. This really got under his skin for a number of weeks and came to a head when we had a meeting with around ten of the major people involved in the expedition shortly before departure.

Konrad felt he was not there to film a cricket match; he was there to get in people's faces and capture the emotion the trip had, while also taking in the beauty of the scenery. Wes felt this was missing the point and that while the cricket was never going to be the major part of any documentary, it was the primary concern of the other 49 people on the trip and that needed to be taken into account. It was obvious Konrad was a bit of a one-man-show and would not be taking any direction, which was not what the original idea was at all. The following week Wes was fighting a bit of a battle with himself as he was very unhappy with the direction things were taking, when the answer conveniently fell into his lap. Konrad thought he would not have to pay the £1,500 that everyone else, bar none, had shelled out, since he was effectively coming in a professional capacity. This was something Wes had stated early on when his search for a DOP had begun, but this was only if he found someone who fitted the bill. Konrad was our age and while undoubtedly very good at what he did, he did not fall into the category Wes wanted, so simply told him if he paid the money he could come, but otherwise there was no chance. Konrad would not pay and that was that. I was disappointed at the time; I had only met Konrad once and liked the guy. I found him to be witty and sharp and thought he might be the kind of character to lift spirits on difficult days, but it was Wes' call and as joint Expedition Leader he had the right to make that choice. Speaking to Wes the following day on the phone he was a changed man, and the enthusiasm that had been lacking in the previous month or so was well and truly back, my overriding feeling at the time was that this could only be a good thing in the long run. A happy Wes in Nepal was vital for everyone, and he admitted that without the documentary he was questioning his whole purpose of coming, especially with Kirt taking on an ever-increasing workload.

Meanwhile Kirt was having some pretty hostile meetings out in Kathmandu, but he did manage to get the costs down to a level we thought we could cope with, as well as getting the number of people coming with us down to two security staff and one Government Liaison Officer, at an additional cost to us. A lot of this was thanks to Aamir Akhtar, the owner of the Shangri-La Academy and a former player for the Nepali National team who had been emailing us from Kathmandu the moment he heard about what we were doing in the press. He put

Kirt in touch with a large TV station called Avenues who then put out some advertising on their network about our trip and thus placed an embarrassment factor at the door of the government should they turn us down. He was due to fly back on the following Friday 27th March, and left without the paperwork he needed, but thankfully we received an email on the Sunday with the letter of permission attached and finally we were in the clear.

The weekend he departed was the same one that many of us had decided to go down to Cornwall for a final training weekend, and while down there I received a lot of questioning. Everyone knew Kirt was back in Nepal but nobody quite knew why, bar three of us. By about 3am I finally cracked under the strain of questioning from Joe Williams and briefly outlined the situation, his response was exactly what I expected when he admitted to having absolutely no idea that this stuff was going on, and why should he? He said the following day that for him The Everest Test was a fantastic trip away, an opportunity to do something totally unique and while he knew lots of work was going on behind the scenes he never fully appreciated what that work was. For him, it was just a question of doing what he was asked when he was asked and everything would work out, a sentiment which I think could be applied to a large number of people on the trip. This is fine as you need people to take a back seat and just enjoy the ride; if anything we sometimes had too many people trying to do too much.

There was however, one bit of good news waiting for Kirt when he returned. The efforts that had gone into finding a title sponsor cannot be overstated. Presentations were made, letters written and meetings had with more companies than I can think to name. I have already discussed the issues we had, alongside the fact that while so many people were happy to give us their products, nobody was able to actually give us some cash. Early on in the search we were in touch with Nokia, through Charlie Campbell, and although they offered us £15k we did not see that as enough at the time. When we were put in touch with them again, this time through a combination of George Powell and Vicks, it was agreed that we would snap their hand off if they offered the same amount and that is what duly happened. They came back in the form of Nokia Maps and it was good to be able to have another big name associated with the trip, along with Qatar Airlines, even if the money they came up with was not enough to cover our rapidly rising costs. If I am honest, the PR team they sent to look after us did more harm than good – insisting that certain items of kit be branded but then refusing to pay up when some items needed to be couriered up and down the country at a time we were struggling to meet a delivery deadline as it was. On top of that, they also wanted to gut the entire website that initially Wes and latterly Blinky had spent nine months working on, and replace it with something of their own. This turned out to be an unmitigated disaster as they essentially took down the entire site for two days while we were up on the mountain so nobody could find out any information and all the efforts we were to go through in order to post blogs and send back footage seemed to ultimately be in vain. It was a setback for followers back home, but thankfully we had gone to a lot of trouble to build up a mailing list so by the time we were on the mountain we were able to send back daily newsletters to everyone who had signed up to them, but for the random followers simply checking on the website after hearing about us on TV, radio or in the papers there was very little info. We were never compensated for this, or really given an explanation as to why it happened when it did.

However, being able to announce Nokia's involvement was a reason to celebrate and the guys who organised all our events did a cracking job and were able to really enjoy the fruits of their labour come March when we had two huge occasions. The first was a night at the Comedy Store in Piccadilly Circus which came about largely thanks to Chris Martin. Chris is a stand-up comedian himself and so managed to persuade a few friends of his in the industry to come along and do a show for us for free so all we had to pay for was the lease on the venue, which was kindly donated by the relative of someone on the trip, so all ticket sales went to charity. Fortunately for me, the event also fell on my birthday which saved me having to actually organise anything myself, which was just as well. As well as Chris himself, we had some relatively big names in

Russell Howard (Headline Act), Jack Whitehall and Jarred Christmas and it was a hugely successful evening. After that was the send off party at 24: London in Soho which sold out of the 400 tickets three days before the event on March 19th. Between the two of them these events raised around £10,000 which was a great effort and the latter was a chance for people to really let their hair down for a final time before the trip, and that's exactly what we did. We were grateful that Neil Laughton, a man who has set foot atop of Everest himself, and the Patron for our trip, was able to come along and say a few words to the slightly inebriated crowd. More on Neil later.

After these parties we were into the final throes of preparation and we just had two significant events left, the Bath Half Marathon and our final meeting on March 28th before our departure on April 9th.

After all the runs mentioned previously a huge number were inspired to sign up for this run as a way to test where they were fitness-wise before we departed and once again a whole bunch ran the race in pads. This took place on March 15th and 17 people directly involved in the expedition ran, while six friends of the trip also did and three others supported from the sidelines, proving it to be another excellent day out for us as a whole. Hillsy, Glen and Russell all padded up, but most of the credit was reserved for Kirt who once again donned the pads and gloves and tackled the course, making it 57 kilometres in total that he had run in full cricket gear during the last nine months. These runs are hard, and after doing my marathon I developed a new found respect for those who put themselves through such things. Those of us on The Everest Test always made the point that we were just normal people getting off the sofa and doing something. One person who really personified that was Mark Waters. The ginger Rocky was one of the oldest on the trip and left behind a wife and two young daughters to come to Nepal. He, like me, hated all the training and seeing as he lives up in Hertfordshire he never had the benefits of going to Trim Trail and training with mates, but while he was disciplined enough to keep going running on his own, he was also nervous as hell about running around Bath. His penultimate blog entry before the race tells of a state of mind I think many people who have run such races can appreciate:

"*I haven't been able to think about much else, I'll be honest. This is the one thing that looms over my Everest trip, like a vampire bat that's about to drop onto my head (what?…?!, sorry). This is the final hurdle that I need to get over before I can savour the excitement leading up to our departure in just over a month. The Everest Test has a great turn-out for the Bath Half which is amazing considering that most of us would rather cut our arms off with a cricket bat than run 13 miles. I understand that the field will be over 8,000. I've never come last place in a field of 8000 before but y'know, there's always a first time…*

Great Pulteney Street. The last remaining loaming of daylight.

The road sweepers finishing up for the day and leaning up against their brooms and having a pull on their rolled up fags. Another fantastic race; over for another year, they say to themselves. The pubs lining the route are full of cheerful runners and supporters, all pretty well greased now and enjoying the camaraderie of race day. Singing boisterous songs with celebratory arms round each other, raising their glasses to the Gods of Half Marathons and singing predictable songs like Sweet Chariot. Then the sound of very heavy; heaving breathing; more like a rumble. Like that bit in Jurassic Park when the big lizard hasn't turned up and the cup of water goes all rippley. Then the sound of water bottle tables being up-turned and the flocks of Starling taking flight from their evening roost.

A violent, wheezing sound now; a broken, unholy sound that reminds one of a Boeing 747 backfiring whilst taxiing in Wookey Hole. There. The silhouette of single, final and very lonely "runner", clutching at anything he can to make it up the final straight to the unmanned finishing line. Literally dragging himself by the lips along the final straight. The timer was turned off ages ago; Timex don't make a watch that goes up that high. All of a sudden the pubs spill out onto Great Pulteney Street and picking up any old rubbish they can find, everyone hurls it – plastic bottles, banana skins, shoes, small animals, kitchen appliances; everything – at my head; the old, ginger, fat-head for being too crap, too slow and basically far too pale for any form of competitive sport.

I then wake up, bolt upright, dripping in sweat; guts wrenching as if on a herring trawler."

Mark made it round in 2:18, and admitted afterwards that the aches and pains were all worth it, and glad the anxiety dreams would now stop.

While there was a happy ending for Mark, there sadly was not one for one of our other players, and come the final meeting it was down to me to make the announcement that we were to have one final drop out before we left the British shores.

When I answered the phone to Charlie Bathurst-Norman while sitting at my desk I thought - and hoped - he was calling to tell me that the recent discomfort he had been in from a long-standing illness had gone away and that he was fit and ready to go, but that was not the case. As mentioned previously, Charlie was out in Nepal with Kirt and I at Christmas, and had signed up to the trip without a moment's thought. He was a constant help with things like events and team building and was a vital member of Team Hillary, not least because he is a very class batsman. BN, as we all know him, had become a particular ally to myself and Kirt, somebody we could rely on for a sensible opinion and logical solution when we encountered problems and was never more than a phone call away. He was also instrumental in bringing on board some of our partners and he was very seriously considered for the captaincy. In the end, the main reason we decided not to make him captain was because we knew how much he had on his plate already at work and that he did not need to be in charge in order to give everything. Conversely we felt that Glen was someone with a lot to offer and making him captain would really draw the best out. It was fortunate that we were proved correct on both counts.

BN has suffered from stomach ulcers since 2002 and at one stage spent three weeks in hospital fearing that he was going to have his whole stomach removed. He was put on some pretty heavy medication which made his life distinctly unpleasant. He had mentioned about a week before the send-off party that he was having problems again and I became immediately concerned, but as someone who was involved in the organisational side of the party he dutifully turned up and played his part ticking names off at the door, but I knew something was up when he wasn't drinking and left very early. Five days later he called me and said he was a non-starter. I have honestly never felt so deflated in my life, he had sought several opinions from doctors and specialists and they felt with his stomach bleeding internally in the way that it was and with the basic facilities in Nepal, if things turned bad he would be in serious danger.

Not being one to ever miss a bit of history, BN titled his email to everyone stating the news as 'I am just going outside, I may be some time...' The email read as follows:

"A year ago I gathered on a snowy morning in The Duck in Battersea to start out on the incredible adventure that is now The Everest Test and with 14 days and 7 hours to go, it is with enormous regret that having lived and breathed the Everest Test every day since then, I will now be unable to join you on what will be simply a once in a lifetime experience.

Some of you are aware that I have been in and out of hospital over the last couple of weeks with a stomach condition and yesterday have been advised by both the Everest Medical Team and a specialist that it would put my health at considerable risk if I were to embark on such an expedition. To be given a tap on the shoulder and asked to stand down in the eleventh hour is a devastating blow for me and the thought of now not going back to Nepal where I spent Christmas and New Year is heart wrenching, let alone not to be able to walk up the hill to Gorak Shep and break the record for the...you know the rest, we've all said it enough times!!

Over the last year I have had some incredible experiences and also got to know some of you who were strangers to me at the start and it has certainly been an honour and a pleasure doing so every step of the way. Witnessing firsthand as well quite how much time, passion and personal sacrifices you have all thrown into this project to make it what it is today is simply astounding and it has been a pleasure to be involved in something as spectacular as this. None of us would have thought it even possible to ever be involved in something of such magnitude and to now be a couple of weeks away from commencing on an expedition that has both national and global coverage, backing from the both old and new greats of the mountaineering and sporting world and having the chance to personally hold a world record still makes the adrenaline run through my veins. It is a bitter pill to swallow that I will not be able to join you on that plane, miss all the panoramic views of Everest and all the experiences Rambling in the Himalayas, watching the game unfold, the world record be broken and of course be there for the celebratory meal in Thamel to watch Glen lift the trophy! It's possibly the hardest decision that I have had to make and if I had the choice, would crawl up there on my hands and bloodied knees. But having spoken to the doctors I have been advised that I could risk losing my stomach or worse and would be obviously a selfish act if I did choose to come. I think Al described it best with 'mate, this must be gutting for you'. Step aside Chris Martin...."

We had our final meeting a couple of days later and I stood up and said a few words for the benefit of those who had not heard and also announced that we were going to name the Man of the Match award in his honour, an idea that someone, although I forget who, came up with that morning. A few of us went round for dinner at BN's place a couple of days later and while he was on great form I could tell he was struggling with the whole thing, particularly with an enormous canvas depicting the hills of Nepal spread across his living room wall, something he picked up on his previous visit. As it turned out, it was a decision that was vindicated as he was to spend the day the match took place in a hospital bed; a lower point I am not sure I can imagine. He did not return to work until January 2011.

PART TWO

THE MOUNTAIN

Sagamartha: Goddess of the Sky more commonly known as Mount Everest

CHAPTER 10

W
e could not take part in The Everest Test without considering the stories of the mountain.

Western interest in the mountain began in the early
1800s when the Surveyor General of India completed a project to
map British territory in the region. In 1852 a young surveyor called
Radhanath Sikdar suggested that the highest mountain in the world was
not in fact Nanda Devi in India at 7,817 metres (25,643 ft), but another
on the border of Tibet and Nepal that was at the time simply known as
Peak XV, and a full kilometre higher.

Andrew Waugh, then Surveyor General, announced the news and
unaware of its Tibetan name Chomolungma, meaning Mother Goddess
of the World, suggested it be named after his predecessor George Everest
(pronounced Eve-Rest), a suggestion the Royal Geographical Society
agreed with and made official in 1865. Everest himself had always given
mountains names relevant to their location, but Waugh argued that as
both borders were closed by Heads of State who mistrusted westerners
it was not appropriate to give the mountain a local name. The Nepalese
have since given it their own title, Sagamartha, which means Goddess of
the Sky; this is also the name of the National Park in which it is situated.

George Mallory is one of the most famous names associated with
Everest as the first man to really have a serious go at the world's biggest
peak, the 1924 expedition being his third and final attempt, and it remains
unclear whether he and Sandy Irvine reached the top or not. before they
disappeared. Irvine's body has never been discovered although the search
continues, not least because his camera could prove the two made it to
the summit.

Mallory was drawn to the mountain after his first reconnaissance
in 1921 and continually left his young family for months at a time to
go back there. Mallory summed up the allure best. In response to the
question "Why climb it?" he replied: "Because it's there".

There was no reward in those days for accomplishing such feats, no real fame or money to take out of it, or a career in public speaking to return home to, as there may be today. Mallory knew this and in fact seemed to thrive on it: *"We shall not bring back a single bit of gold or silver, not a gem, nor any coal or iron. We shall not find a single foot of earth that can be planted with crops to raise food. It's no use. So, if you cannot understand that there is something in man which responds to the challenge of this mountain and goes out to meet it, that the struggle is the struggle of life itself upward and forever upward, then you won't see why we go."*

Thinking back to this early attempt, and the fact that it is still unknown if they succeeded, it really is one hell of an achievement that they even got as close as they did. Mallory's body was not discovered until 1999, a full 75 years after he went missing, and the man who found him, Conrad Anker, said that the kit he was wearing was not dissimilar to what you might see people wearing on the streets of Seattle in winter today – let alone six vertical miles up in the sky.

After Mallory and Irvine's ill-fated mission there were barely a handful of attempts for the next two decades, but after World War Two people once again began to look at mountaineering and exploration.

A Swiss Expedition, whose lead Sherpa (or Sirdar) was Tenzing Norgay, came close to summiting in 1952, but ultimately the accolade was to go to a British-led expedition the following year. The 1953 Expedition was led by John Hunt and was the ninth attempt by a British party, Tenzing was again the Sirdar for the attempt and the four strongest climbers were split into two pairs, with Tenzing in the second pair with New Zealander Edmund Hillary. The first pair, Tom Bourdillon and Charles Evans, came within 100 vertical metres of the top on May 26th, but turned around due to exhaustion. However, the trail they had broken and extra oxygen they had laid made life easier for the second pair up to the point now known as the Hillary Step, which is the final major obstacle to the summit on the south side of the mountain. Hillary and Tenzing were to reach the summit at 11:30am on May 29th 1953.

Since that day around 2,500 people have successfully returned from scaling Everest – and Apa Sherpa has climbed it 21 times (at time of writing) - more than 200 have perished to date, including some horrendous disasters. These days many people climb it on commercial expeditions and are guided up the peak. Such people are often labelled 'trophy hunters', but Everest is no normal mountain, and anyone who reaches the summit deserves immense credit.

Everest really hit the news in 1996 when nine lives were claimed in a storm that is generally agreed to be the worst ever seen on the mountain since climbing on it went commercial. As it happens, our Expedition Patron, Neil Laughton, was on the mountain that day and I discussed the events with him at length after we returned from our own trip.

That year commercial climbing was at its peak. On May 10th the mountain was seriously over-crowded when Rob Hall and Scott Fisher – two vastly experienced guides each with rival tour companies - opted to make their summit attempts. Despite a bad turn in the weather, their competitiveness drove them on to attempt the ascent. A further series of small, unfortunate coincidences would escalate into a catastrophe which ended up killing the guides and many of their clients.

Among Hall's clients was Doug Hansen, whom he had turned around the previous year just below the summit. He had offered Hansen a huge discount to return for another go and while one would not expect to be on the summit after 2pm, Hansen did not reach it until 4pm. As a storm came in he and Hall were trapped overnight, and by the following morning Hansen was dead and Hall on his own. He made it slightly further down the mountain, but rescue teams could not reach him because of the weather, and a second unprotected night on the mountain without supplementary oxygen proved too much. He did, however, manage speak to his pregnant wife Jan a final time on radio.

Fisher was also having trouble: his team had become split up and he too reached the summit late, at 3:45pm. Probably suffering ill health, he then encountered a badly struggling member of a Taiwanese team, Makalu Gau, high on the mountain whom he tried to help. The two of them survived the first night but by the time the rescue team reached them the following morning Fisher was too far gone to be helped down, although Gau did survive.

Several others were also stranded that first night, a mix of the two teams and their guides; 11 in total had got lost on the descent and huddled together for as long as they could in an attempt to keep warm and ride out the storm. They were barely 400 metres from their camp, but with poor visibility they had no idea how close they were.

Neil had arrived into the final camp on the day the teams were making their summit bids. He recalls:

"I remember trying to put up the tent at around 6pm and it was impossible to do on my own, it took five of us to erect it in deteriorating conditions. At that stage, it's difficult to describe, we didn't know and maybe we were being a bit too insular, but we assumed everyone was back down; normally they would be by then. Nobody told us there was a drama happening and that people were missing so we had no knowledge of the impending disaster.

"Clearly we were focussed on bringing people up and considering our own survival in the deteriorating conditions: we had certainly one climber missing from our group who had set off but hadn't arrived. Once the storm got going our communications started to fail and we could not make contact with any of the camps on the mountain so we were effectively on our own, fairly blind. We put a rescue team together to try and find our missing personnel but after that we had to hunker down and the storm raged on through the night. We were lying on our backs with our feet on the side to stop it flattening; there were six of us in a five-man tent."

Of the 11 that were stuck, six made a dash for camp in the early hours when they felt strong enough and promised they would send back help for the others. Guide Anatoli Boukreev had already made one unsuccessful attempt to find the missing clients but when half the group returned he went back to retrieve the rest, two were deemed beyond saving and were left behind. Several people went back to these two clients, Yasuko Namba and Beck Weathers, to see if there was any hope of getting them off the mountain, but at that height there are no emergency services you can call. Carrying an unconscious and barely breathing person down the mountain could endanger the lives of others, so the tough decision was made to leave them where they were. It was not until 16:30 on May 11th that Weathers stumbled back into camp, having been virtually unconscious for more than 16 hours.

Neil described it as a hideous situation, saying that he looked like a ghost wandering towards camp. He had lost his right glove, so his hand was so badly frostbitten it felt like porcelain, and he had severe disfigurement to his face, especially his nose. Weathers had no recollection of Boukreev rescuing the others, or anyone else checking on him. He recalls:

"Initially I thought I was in a dream. When I first came to I thought I was laying in bed, I didn't feel cold or uncomfortable. I sort of rolled onto my side, got my eyes open, and there was my right hand staring me in the face. Then I saw how badly frostbitten it was, and that helped bring me around to reality. Finally I woke enough to realise I was in deep shit and the cavalry wasn't coming so I better do something about it myself."

Somehow Weathers was to survive and return safely to his family. Neil did not reach the summit on that trip and it was another two years before he returned to Everest and successfully reached the top.

This catastrophe brought the commercialisation of the mountain into focus and the media gave the disaster serious coverage – even more so after one of the climbers, John Krakauer on Hall's team, wrote the critically acclaimed *Into Thin Air* about the events.

Durbar Square, Kathmandu

CHAPTER ELEVEN

The challenges of The Everest Test were of course not limited to the physical ones of scaling the mountain – we also had political problems to contend with. To be able to understand fully some of these issues, it is helpful to know something of Nepali history.

In 2006 political violence was rife throughout the country, mostly in opposition to the way King Gyanendra was running it and pursuing absolute power. Gyanendra took to the throne in 2001 in extreme circumstances when his brother, King Birendra, was killed in a Palace massacre along with several other royals. Birendra's son led the attack at a family dinner and was also wounded, later being announced as King while in a coma. He died three days after the attacks leaving Gyanendra as the next in line. The whole episode remains shrouded in mystery as many Nepali's believe Gyanendra to have been behind the attack, motivated perhaps by his brother's politics, and the fact that all of Birendra's family were killed while none of his own were, he was also out of town at the time while his wife and daughter were at the dinner but survived. There is however, no proof of this.

In 1991 King Birendra declared Nepal a Constitutional Monarchy, after an uprising the previous year, but this came to an end in 2005. Once Gyanendra was in power he had to deal with the Maoist rebels who had been fighting their cause since 1996 in a Civil War that would claim the lives of nearly 13,000 people. His reaction to the threat of the Maoists was to dismiss the elected government in 2002 and then declare a State of Emergency and send in troops when peace talks broke down. He appointed a series of Prime Ministers up until February 2005, when he decided to sack the government altogether and take total power himself. This did little to appease the Maoists who were continually growing in power, and even led to several of the minority Democratic parties joining together. In the long run it was the single most important event in ending the 240-year monarchy.

Between February 2005 and April 2006 there was continued

unrest, culminating in the 2006 riots in which Kirt was to become embroiled after his trek to Everest Base Camp. He was tear-gassed on a bus by the police who were going after some of the rebels, and saw rubber bullets fired into a crowd of protesters. Eventually the Maoists committed themselves to mainstream politics and by late April the previous parliament was reinstated and within weeks the majority of the King's powers were taken away from him, leaving him as little more than a figurehead. Kirt recalls the street parties that took place when the riots were over and the King agreed to give up some of his powers. He had never witnessed anything quite like it, people dancing and cheering, laughing and hugging each other. This went on for several days.

The Maoists began cleaning up their image, and stunned the world by winning the parliamentary elections in 2008. It was only a matter of time before the King was removed altogether and on May 28th, 2008 only four members of the 601-seat assembly opposed the decision to announce Nepal as the world's newest republic. Initially Maoist Leader Pushpa Kamal Dahal (known as Prachanda) was made Prime Minister only to resign a year later when his attempts to bring his foot soldiers into the army were denied. Since then another Prime Minister lasted barely a year and was forced to resign by the Maoist demonstrations against him in 2010, and it took another seven months, and 17 rounds of voting, for a new Prime Minister to be put in charge of another weak coalition government. As things stand the constitution, which was supposed to be written after the King left office, has still not been written. The deadline of May 2010 was not met, and as of May 2011 it is unlikely to be met once again.

It is thus clear to see how getting anything agreed in Nepal is challenging, as Kirt was finding out when trying to get our permissions. Deadlines are rarely met, or even taken seriously, and with the government in a constant state of flux it was almost impossible to tell who we should be speaking to – the Minister of Tourism, who we had met through Smiley and had suddenly started demanding royalties, or the Nepal Tourist Board, who we had met through the Himalayan Rescue Association and had so far been a great help.

PART THREE

THE TEST

At Heathrow on departure day

CHAPTER TWELVE

Despite spending more than a year preparing to go to Mount Everest, less than a week before departure I had no clue what I needed or where to obtain it. How can you spend that long planning for something and still be so utterly unprepared? We were due to depart on Thursday 9th April and here I was running around Covent Garden at the last minute trying to sort myself out.

I already owned the obvious bits of kit: boots, socks, gloves, but I had given no consideration to waterproofs, water bottles, bug repelling sheet covers, extra boot laces nor did I even really know what merino wool was. I enlisted Glen's help and he supervised my purchasing of baby wipes, Imodium, Dioralyte, vitamin supplements, ear plugs, and cough medicine during an outing in which we bumped into five other expedition goers.

We all headed to the pub and bet on the Grand National. Though I know nothing about betting, I just had to back a horse called Himalayan Trail. It fell at the first hurdle and I hoped this was not a bad omen.

The following day we distributed our official kit manufactured by MKK, including playing shirts and trousers, hooded tops and polo shirts. Irritatingly the fleeces were not given out as Nokia's PR Company wanted their logo to be added to them, which meant we would not receive them until we were actually in Kathmandu. Despite this little hiccup the guys involved focussed more on the positives than the negatives, what they did have rather than what they didn't, and everyone collecting kit that day was pretty happy with what they had. This was a trait that was as useful as it was needed during the coming weeks.

We also heard that day that Jonathan Hill (Hillsy) had passed the umpiring exam: this was a huge relief. As a competent cricketer who had given up the chance to play in order to umpire, when he heard in late February he had failed the course he was suddenly left without a role on the trip. He later admitted that had he failed again he would have seriously reconsidered coming at all. I did spare a thought for my sister

Helen however, who had spent the best part of a year learning about a sport she had always considered a bit dull, but Hillsy passing meant she was back to reserve umpire once more.

The following few days comprised last-minute preparations and very little sleep.

On the day of departure a group of us needed to be at Lord's by 8:30am for a press call. That morning we met Rebecca Stephens, the first British woman to climb Everest in 1993 and a trustee of the Himalayan Trust, and it was a real honour that she showed up to give us a send off. I also spoke to The Times' Patrick Kidd who promised to do a piece on his blog that day and keep people updated throughout, a terrific way for us to reach a wider audience.

The other big piece of news caught many of the group by surprise. Some months previously Vicks had realised our match day would be the Queen's 83rd birthday, so she wrote to Her Majesty to let her know that we would happily play the game in her honour. A few days before departure an envelope arrived from Buckingham Palace containing a letter from the Queen's Personal Aide saying that Her Majesty wished us all the best for our endeavour. It was further fitting that we were playing the match in the Queen's honour as news that the original Tenzing and Hillary had scaled Everest had reached the UK on the day of her coronation.

Buoyed by this excitement, our thoughts turned towards flying and everything was set to go smoothly as the logistics had been meticulously planned. Our entire equipment – including 450kg excess luggage generously allowed by Qatar Airlines – had been inventoried the previous evening by Nick Mullineux and his four-strong team; now would come the challenge of getting it to the airport, dealing with the transits, and then getting it on the planes from Kathmandu to Lukla.

The 50 of us were split into two groups of 25 for the flights out, so we also had to make sure we got there - with the first flight departing at 3.05pm, Addison Lee laid on a coach due to leave Lord's at 1pm.

But then the trouble started: Nick Toovey (Tooves), who was on the second flight leaving in the evening, had accidently taken our visa documents and permission papers into central London after coming to the press call at Lord's – luckily we managed to locate a place to print off copies and we hoped they would suffice.

Meanwhile, unbeknownst to us, David Kirtley had been embroiled in a precarious situation. He had planned to drive from Cardiff to London but just outside Bristol his car broke down, leaving him no choice but to embark on a nightmare train-taxi-train-tube epic. He made it onto the first train to Paddington but had quickly realised the bag containing his camera, outdoor trekking clothes and boots was missing. His new plan was to replace all these items at the airport shops but this would prove problematic.

At the airport we located our two desks and got a little over-excited by the TV monitors that said "The Everest Test" on them, making us all feel slightly more important that we were. Just as were finishing handing in our individual rucksacks and were about to move on to the central kit the complications really started.

Someone noticed that people at the far end of the Terminal were being moved outside and had heard the words 'Security threat'. In typical English fashion we chose to ignore the situation and hoped it would go away, also assuming that - provided we got our bags in and made it up the escalator - we would still be able to get on our flight and leave on time. That illusion was soon shattered as we were told to step outside, where we stayed for around 90 minutes, where we began an impromptu game of cricket outside Terminal Three. This meant David Kirtley had little time for shopping. However, around 30 minutes after our flight should have departed he learned his bag had turned up at Paddington. Luckily Mike Preston, on the second flight, was able to get to Paddington and pick up the lost bag and once David got hold of it in Kathmandu the only thing missing was the camera.

While this was unfolding we were also faced with the fact that our central kit was 25kg over the weight limit and, with Qatar having been known to charge £23 per kilo for excess, we were facing a bill of around £600. Fortunately with all the chaos, they simply stuck 'rapid transfer' stickers all over the boxes, opened up some double doors and pushed the trolleys through. What a relief!

We were then allowed to board the plane first - Kirt pausing to have some cheesy pictures in the cockpit with the pilot – and at 17:00, two hours late, we were airborne.

Many people I know see a flight as an excuse to drink as much alcohol as they can, and most Australian cricket fans will tell you with some pride how David Boon once consumed 52 cans of lager on a flight to the UK in preparation for the 1989 Ashes series, a story which the moustachioed man himself has always refuted. We were no different and several people decided to get stuck in, it was after all one of the last chances we would get to drink so why not make the most of it? That question was answered emphatically in Doha. We landed shortly after our connecting flight was due to take off and were immediately worried about getting both us and our kit through.

As we left the plane we were told our connecting flight was being held for us, so we raced through the airport with crowds of people looking at us curiously. A short bus ride to the terminal was followed by a mad dash through the terminal building before another short bus ride back to another plane. As we got on the second bus, we were desperate to ensure nobody was being left behind. Then word went around that Jules and his wife Victoria were missing.

It soon emerged that Victoria thought she had left her passport on the first plane and was having difficulty getting back on to retrieve it. I knew there was a lot more chance of the two of them getting on a later flight than 24 of us making one, so Glen texted Jules to say we were leaving and good luck.

Moments before take-off they walked onto the plane and we cheered. Turned out the passport was in the bag all along, and Jules had not seen the funny side....

More good news followed - all of our kit had made it to Kathmandu: it is huge credit to Qatar Airways to organise such a fast transit and successful transfer without losing a single item.

Now it really felt like our adventure was beginning.

Kirt meets the Qatar Airways pilot

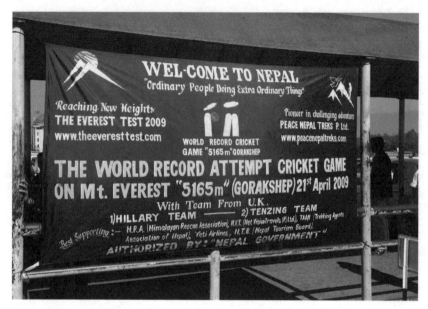

Our welcome to Kathmandu

CHAPTER THIRTEEN

Kathmandu is a funny sort of place. My first impression was that it was crowded and hectic, as people walked were they liked, motorcycles often drove along pavements and every vehicle would beep its horn at least every 30 seconds. But it's nothing compared to India – which will be another tale.

The city is built in a valley and surrounded by the Himalayas, but still sits at around 1,400 metres above sea level and is home to around 700,000 people. The city centre is relatively small and easy to wander around on foot, the old town being where you can find the temples and palaces, while in the tourist hub of Thamel you are surrounded by guest houses, bars, restaurants and shops selling everything from books and artwork to knock-off DVDs and trekking gear.

In the 1970s the city became a popular hang-out for hippies travelling through Asia, many of whom were coming either from or to India. They came from the USA, particularly California, and from Europe. Kathmandu was the final stop on the 'hippie trail' the popular low-cost way of travelling in that decade. It did not last long: the Government were not happy with the direction their country was headed. Trekkers were encouraged to visit, laws on drugs - which still exist today – were tightened and although there remains a hint of hippie culture it is certainly not the hotspot it was becoming then.

Now just Jochen Tole remains, a street on the outskirts of Thamel nicknamed 'Freak Street' which still attracts members of the hippie brigade. While so many westerners came to Asia in search of different ways of life, somewhat ironically it is the western flavour that lingers; a Pizza Hut and KFC can be found on Durbar Marg, one of the main shopping streets. Though there is no McDonald's as yet, there is a Yak Donald's on the Annapurna trekking circuit!

We were due to stay in the Kathmandu Guest House in the centre of Thamel, where we would be able to easily go into town and collect any final things we might need, as we were due to be up at 4am the following morning to catch our flight into the mountains. Unfortunately our long day of ups and downs was not over yet.

We had landed at around 10am local time and were met by Peace Nepal Treks, led by Nir Lama. Nir and Bil were the first two people I saw as I stepped out of the airport wheeling a trolley stacked to just below my chin with bags and equipment. Their grins stood out a mile.

Just behind them I noticed a huge banner they had made up for us saying 'Welcome to Nepal' and then giving the details of who we are and boasting that we were there to play the 'World Record Cricket Game.' I can happily say that it felt good and the guides were making an instant impression on the rest of the group too. The next thing I noticed was how surprisingly hot it was, the sun was blazing down and I was in serious danger of overheating! We hauled all the stuff over to our buses and gradually loaded them up and headed into town, the journey being every bit as fun as I expected as we swerved to avoid various objects such as other cars, animals and even the odd person.

On arriving at the Guest House we quickly moved into the garden out the back which was bathed in sunshine and helped everyone relax and start to feel at home. Being somewhere I already knew my way around had helped me relax too and we quickly ordered some drinks. Then came the sucker punch, Kirt beckoned me over to one side where a group of around five Nepalis were locked in discussion and all looking rather concerned, and just out of ear-shot told me there was a problem with our booking. 'What kind of problem?' I asked. 'The kind where they don't have enough rooms,' came the reply. This was not ideal but not necessarily insurmountable, so I told Kirt I thought we should stand our ground. About five minutes later nothing had changed and Kirt was looking particularly irritated: he had mentioned before that the alternative to fighting for our rooms was to move to another hotel that was admittedly nicer and had a pool, but was also some way out of town. Since we had made our reservation more than four months previously I felt we had a right to stay firm, so I wandered over to see what was going on. I asked the manager how many rooms short they were and his reply was simply 'Many.' So I rephrased the question to how many rooms they actually had, and the answer was eight. Since we needed 25 we were clearly some way short.

It was obvious that we had no choice so we picked up our bags and got back on the bus - again the group all took it well. Once we arrived at The Park Village Hotel, a good 25-minute drive from Thamel and in the wrong direction from the airport, it was at least a spectacular property with a huge swimming pool and inviting bar.

The other flight would arrive later but the first flight still had a busy day ahead. A quick shower and change and six of us headed off to the offices of the Himalayan Rescue Association for a pre-arranged press conference that was due to start at 12:30, and following that we had an appointment with a local cricket academy at 14:30.

We felt if we could help raise the profile of the sport in Nepal, even just a little, it might be of some use and was something that could leave a legacy. Aamir Akhtar ran the first and only cricket academy in Nepal which we had agreed to visit; do some coaching, and donate some equipment. After the press conference we left the HRA offices and headed across town to the Shangri-La Cricket Academy where we were met by Raman, Aamir's partner in running the organisation.

Apart from providing a place where people can have a net practice and do a little fitness, Shangri-La also opens its doors to young people who don't necessarily play cricket. On weekends they have a group of orphans, many of whom live on the streets, come in and play around for a few hours. They had invited these children in to meet us and when we arrived they were playing a game that involved throwing a rugby ball at a tree stump. Kirt, Glen and I joined in and it was considerably harder than it sounds. Spending time with these boys and girls was a great experience and the six of us from the conference were later joined by a whole load of our team who wanted to be involved.

Aamir arrived a little later. In 2006 he became the first Nepali to play at a serious level outside of his country, after playing some Surrey second XI matches; at the same time he was playing an important role for the Nepal national side as well. Unfortunately a dispute with those at CAN meant he is no longer being selected, so instead he has turned his attention to help grow the game in Nepal his own way, this has included recently securing Reebok as the first major sponsor of Nepali cricket.

We moved on to some interesting cricket sessions where 20 people squeezed into a single net while someone batted. The kids loved it, and many of them were particularly excited by some of the cameras on show. Victoria Staveley spending most of her afternoon surrounded by about five girls staring at her digital camera while George Powell showed the children the shots he was taking with his fancy Nikon camera, fitted with a huge lens.

After a while we decided it was time to donate some equipment. The Lord's Taverners had kindly given us three enormous kit bags to distribute where we saw fit, and this was definitely somewhere that deserved it. Helping sport at the grassroots is the only way to really develop it and increase the numbers: with some decent kit now available to them, hopefully more people will come to play at Shangri-La and it can become a place that develops talent, and maybe they will unearth the next gem that could help the Nepali team achieve their ultimate goal of qualifying for a World Cup.

After that we were kindly presented with a small plaque thanking us for coming to visit and wishing us all the best for our match at Gorak Shep. When we saw Aamir again before we flew home at the end of our trip, he also brought us a whole load of Shangri-La t-shirts which several of us wore on the flight home.

One of the criticisms I read about our trip from people who knew nothing about it was why were we donating cricket gear when we could just be giving money or medical supplies. Playing sport for a living is not really an option to Nepalis right now, but plans are afoot to change that and with the amount of money coming into cricket right now, including to the Associate and Affiliate nations of the ICC, things could change for them very quickly.

That very year Afghanistan went from playing at the same level as Nepal, and beating them in the World Cricket League Division Five to seal promotion, to qualifying for the World Cup and being granted full One Day International status. Because of that Afghanistan has received a

lot of attention in the world media and if they can build on that success
in the coming years then it might indeed be possible for those players to
make a living from the game, why can't the same be done for Nepal?

The ongoing problem for any smaller country is that they do not
have kit, it is not like football where balls are quite easily accessible or
a substitute can be found - bats, balls and stumps have to come from
somewhere, not to mention pads, gloves and helmets. By donating three
of these bags given to us by The Lord's Taverners we have helped with
this problem, even if only in a small way. Aamir and Shangri-La had
already shown us how cricket was helping bring kids off the streets in
Kathmandu and keeping them out of trouble: had we just donated a lump
sum of cash you never know quite where that might go. Furthermore, we
were donating all our left over medical supplies to the Himalayan Rescue
Association, and particularly the team at the Himalayan Trust School in
Kunde which some of our group were able to visit.

Given that I had not managed much sleep on either flight before
heading straight out to Kathmandu I was slightly reluctant to go and meet
the second flight that was coming in that afternoon at around 16:30, so I
passed the baton to Jamo and went back to the hotel with the intention
of a quick sleep. This never actually happened as the traffic in Kathmandu
was so hectic that we just decided to jump out in the centre of town as
our minibus wasn't really getting us anywhere and needed to head on to
the airport. We went back to the Kathmandu Guest House for a quick
drink and while we were there had a rather interesting encounter.

I had heard that a man had arrived at Nir's office looking for Kirt
while we were at Shangri-La and Nir and Vicks were trying to sort out
satellite phones. Well, he then arrived at the Kathmandu Guest House,
thinking we were staying there - since we had been moved it was actually
a stroke of good luck that he bumped into us as we were only there
for around 45 minutes and we later found out it was his third visit to
the hotel that day in his attempts to track us down. Since we were all
wearing our branded polo shirts it was easy to spot us and over he came,
an older man carrying a small book. After exchanging pleasantries in the
way one usually does with a man who does not speak the same language

as you, we ascertained that his name was J R Joshi and he was an author who had written a phrase book and wanted to give it to Kirt as a present. While with us he wrote a small message inside that wished us luck and that our journey was important for all of Nepal. It turned out he lived some way outside the city and had made the journey in especially to find this chap he had read about in the newspapers. It was a small incident but incredibly touching as it showed how our trip had reached people that we never expected it would.

On closer inspection of his phrase book we discovered it was also quite an amusing read, and when I was out in Nepal for three months the following year I met him again and his book became something of a Bible, with proverbs such as: "Moustache does not stop eating" and "He who does not know how to dance says floor is not smooth."

After that we jumped in a taxi back to the hotel and actually arrived after the people on the second flight. In this second group were Wes and Haydn and I needed to let them know Kirt wanted to get everyone out for dinner that night at a bar called Rum Doodle, well known in the area and one of the few places able to accommodate a large group.

Now Wes was here people were looking to him for direction, so when I told him Kirt had booked a restaurant for us all in town and he said he was too tired after a long flight to go into town and would rather stay back and sort his kit out, many people decided to do the same.

However the decision was made on behalf of everyone and several Tenzing players later admitted to being annoyed at not being invited out to dinner and were surprised to hear that the invitation had simply never reached them as neither Wes nor Haydn wanted to go. Truth be told, Kirt had originally only booked the restaurant for Team Hillary and the Trektators, but decided he needed everyone there to speak about what was to happen over the coming days. He was furious when I met him later and said that the others were not coming. I should point out that he had not slept properly in almost 24 hours and had eaten only aeroplane food so understandably he was starting to fray a little around the edges, and this was about to get worse.

There was a big group of us assembled at Rum Doodle, and like Kirt

I was also suffering from a serious lack of sleep and an appetite befitting a large bear at the end of hibernation, so was very much looking forward to a massive steak, as this was also the last time I would eat meat and drink beer before the match. Remembering how sick I was after my last visit at Christmas I was determined to be careful this time around, with the exception of tonight. We were upstairs on the veranda and the sun had now set when I spotted Kirt once more pacing around on the far side of the room while Nir sat at a table for two with several of his entourage close by. I immediately got the impression that something was wrong, which was not difficult to figure out.

Minutes later he beckoned me over and told me the issue was financial. One of the jobs to be done was collect R120,000 (around £100) from each member of the expedition before we left for Lukla the following morning. We had put the vice captains in charge of this, Jules for Hillary and Gareth for Tenzing. This wasn't a problem and although a few people were having difficulties withdrawing money we knew we had enough to cover it.

However, it now looked like Nir was still unsure of what the whole trip was going to cost us. Up to this point we had paid £30,250 from the UK, plus $10,800 on arrival and still had a further £5,000 to come. We felt sure this would be enough but from looking at the calculations it appeared that might not be the case. As we sat in the corner of the bar, staring at numbers scribbled on the back of an envelope with tired eyes and empty stomachs both our heads began to spin. Kirt finally lost his temper, he snapped at Nir saying that this simply could not be right, we must have enough cash to cover everything, he then marched over to the table where the majority of people were oblivious to what was going on, and demanded to know who had not yet paid their money to Jules.

As always in these situations there were blank faces as nobody likes being put on the spot, but before anyone had a chance to respond he shouted: "I don't care what the issue is or what the excuse is. Everyone knew this money had to be paid so just pay it," and with that he came back to the table and told Nir this whole thing was doing his head in and he was going for a walk. I should make clear that this was the first and only time Kirt lost his temper and failed to keep outside issues from the rest of the group. He had not actually said anything was wrong, but it was clear that everything was not going to plan. Meanwhile I was left with Nir trying to explain that Kirt was not angry with him, just the situation.

After about five or ten minutes Kirt came back in and sat down with Nir and I. At this moment Smiley, from the Ministry of Tourism, turned up and tried to make conversation. Given that he had originally told us we would not have to pay for any liaison officers or security officials, and had then gone back on that, and that our current issue was a financial one, his timing could not have been worse. Smiley was clearly disliked by some of Nir's team, one of whom happily gave him the finger behind his back as he shook Kirt's hand on the way out. I don't think this whole episode helped anyone.

Kirt said he would go and change some more money up into Nepali Rupees as this was the currency that would be easiest to use on the mountain and off the two of us went. Once out of the restaurant Kirt really began to vent his fury. It is fair to say that during the final few months leading up to departure he had felt a huge burden on his shoulders because if we had failed to get permission from the government to play the match, then he would be left footing the cost of 50 very disappointed people, made worse by the fact that each of these were now his friends. He had often joked with me that in a worst case scenario he would have to pack his bags and live the rest of his life in Guam.

He also felt he was not getting the backup he needed from his fellow Expedition Leader. So angry was he that the people on the second flight had not come to dinner that he spat the words: 'Tenzing are dead to me, and I refuse to speak to Wes on this entire trip.' As we stood in the tiny Travelex on a pitch black alleyway, changing US Dollars into stacks of rupees I did not have a great deal to say, other than 'You'll be fine after some food and some sleep' – I think perhaps a female might have been better suited to the situation.

We handed over another $3,300 and said we would sort the rest out later on. I was also given an enormous wad of rupees to look after which was to make me nervous for the next four days. We ate dinner, had a couple of beers and by the time I got back to the hotel and had met up with some of the guys from the second flight I was feeling a little better, but still had a sense of trepidation about the coming days.

The following day was the last real hurdle we had – or at least so I thought at the time. If we could all get on the flights and make it to Lukla in one day to start the trek then surely we would be all right from there, but getting there would be a challenge since the flights only go if the weather is OK, and as good as it had been today, there was always the possibility it may change tomorrow and the tight schedule we were on could have been thrown up in the air.

I slept fitfully that night, and while Kirt calmed down a little after dinner the events of that evening seemed to set the tone for the relationship he would have with Wes and the other team as a unit for the rest of the trip.

One of the many bridges along the trek

CHAPTER FOURTEEN

A s it turned out I need not have worried about the flights, even if they were a bit hairy. A 03:45 start is never ideal and that was a feeling I could tell was shared by many of the group as people made their way bleary-eyed to the front of the hotel. A few hellos were exchanged with people I had yet to see and then we were off on another cover-your-eyes drive through Kathmandu, even at that time in the morning you could not escape the beeping horns and people walking aimlessly into the middle of the road. Spirits, though, were good and once we arrived at the domestic terminal and started loading up our bags the usual banter began.

Amusement levels rose when we noticed that the Nepalis did not believe in weighing each bag separately and adding them all together to see if they were too heavy to go on a plane, but just piled one on top of the other on the set of scales until the right weight was reached, and then all were taken to a plane and bundled aboard. Time saving and effective if you ask me.

As we stood on the tarmac gazing at the Yeti Airlines plane that was supposed to be taking us to one of the most dangerous airports in the world with a runway just 20 metres wide and a 700-metre drop at one end, I decided not to mention to the guys around me that just six months earlier another Yeti Airlines plane had crashed killing 18 people and leaving the pilot as the lone survivor. It would probably not have made a difference mind you, since Hillsy was white as a sheet before he even boarded the plane, and looked gradually sicker throughout the 40-minute journey.

In truth, it was fine and our resident comedian Chris Martin kept our flight amused for most of the journey. I actually dozed off for a while mid-flight, I think largely due to the fact that things were now out of our hands, the trip was finally underway for real, and the organisers had done everything possible. There was a spontaneous eruption when we landed safely on the 12° incline at Tenzing-Hillary airport.

After that we went to collect our bags and spent the next few hours milling around Lukla waiting for the luggage to arrive. We were lucky in that we had left much of the central kit - including the Flicx wicket that was both heavy and awkward to move - at the airport on arrival so we could load it straight onto the planes that morning rather than having to deal with it at the hotel. We had a quick brunch at a local hotel and many of the guides picked up bags and took them across there, unfortunately they moved too quickly for some members of the trip, including Joe and Vicks who both assumed their bags had not arrived yet and were stood waiting at the airstrip for quite some time. Still, it gave everyone a chance to get used to the altitude of 2,800 metres as well as have a laugh at the 'Starbucks' on the street, unsure if it was a cheap imitation or if the real thing had indeed reached this far flung corner of the world.

Waiting for us at Lukla was Dharma who had been fantastic during our December recce trip and since he was not an employee of Peace Nepal Treks Kirt had assigned him to George Powell for the duration of the trip to help George find the best spots for photographs and carry some of his heavy gear.

We were now complete in terms of our trekking group as well as porters and guides and when we eventually set off from Lukla in the early afternoon it was the first time that the 50 of us had actually all been together at the same time. It was an extraordinary situation when you think of the amount of meetings and socials. Everyone had made it, but there were several people who had never even met. For those of us involved in the organisation it had been one of the plus points getting to know everyone during the course of a year, and now the chance had finally arrived for everyone.

We were all there now, about to begin walking. The first day begins nicely, actually taking you down from 2,800 to 2,600 metres, thus abiding to the principle of 'Trek high, sleep low' which I must have heard 100 times from various people in the days before we left, although our route was fully mapped out. I honestly think some people thought I was just packing a tent and cricket bat and wandering off into the Himalayas!

Of course this was the point when I would discover just how

underprepared I was, and it did not get off to a good start when one of the guides, an excitable fellow called Prem, decided to tell me I looked pregnant. I guess the twelve months of training had not paid off as much as I'd hoped and needless to say I did not wear that rather tight shirt again. Another problem I had was my rucksack: despite the fact that everyone told me it was supposed to sit on my hips I took all the weight on my shoulders, since everyone on the trek was carrying full packs, some weighing up to 25kgs. It was no real surprise that when we arrived at Phakding I was unable to move my shoulders and neck for about five minutes after dropping my pack. What I could do nothing about however, was the fact that my pack also had no outside pockets, which meant that my jacket and fleece were tied to the thing so that I could keep such things as chocolate bars, water purification tablets and sun cream in those pockets instead. All in all, I looked like a bit of a novice.

Upon arrival I decided to meander around this small village and see what it had to offer. I was with Kirt, Hillsy, Wes and Miles and the five of us ended up at a cafe just around the corner from the teahouse where we were staying and having a cup of tea. It made for interesting viewing as Wes clearly had no idea that Kirt had got so angry with him the night before and although he had chilled out considerably since then, he was still holding a grudge. It was a pleasant way to pass 45 minutes or so and the owner told us he was about to leave to live in the USA and train as a pilot.

After a dinner of the staple mountain diet of Dhal Bhat - rice and vegetables with meat as an option - the decks of cards came out, another trekkers staple. I had my last scheduled drink until after the match, and it was more of the local brew, Tongba, which I had been introduced to during my previous trip. Tongba is to the Nepalese what vodka is to the Russians and Guinness is to the Irish, and I developed quite a taste for it, despite its appearance. It is essentially warm beer, based on millet and made by cooking and fermenting whole grain millet, and then leaving it to ferment for around six months. You drink it through a straw that is sealed at one end but with a small hole, pin-prick size, that allows you just to get the liquid. Hot water is poured into the container and after around five minutes you go to work on it. The container is then topped up until all the alcohol is sucked out. Apparently you can tell the Tongba is finished when you start to feel the heat through the clay container you are drinking out of.

Dharma has a close friend living in Phakding and he would be staying with her and her family that night, and so a few of us went to meet them. Hillsy, Vicks, George, Miles, Jonathan Woods (Woodsy), John Richards and Will Simmons all joined and tried out the local brew. It is safe to say everyone was slightly suspicious of what they were about to taste and needed Kirt and I to lead the way to be sure it was not some kind of elaborate wind-up. We were in a small room with no windows and a large container of hot water being boiled - it was a guest house but we were clearly not sitting in the part reserved for guests!

After the first one most of the guys headed back but Kirt, Will and I stayed for another and before long were actually a little drunk. It was great to finally see Kirt properly relaxed, he was in his element now and this for him was what the trip was about. We were chatting to some local people, exchanging stories with them. There was a young boy there, perhaps 15 years old, who loved cricket and promised he could not wait to hear about our success. By the time we sauntered back to the tea house we discovered we were locked out. Fortunately I could remember which room I was in so banged on the window until a less-than-amused Hillsy came to let us in.

It had been a good day and a great night and was probably the most relaxed many of us were to be for the rest of the trip, it was only going to get physically more demanding from here, and it was to start in just a few hours with a long and painful hike to a village called Namche Bazaar.

The following morning I awoke with a foggy head: this would not have been so bad if it were not for the fact that the others were all fine. Kirt especially was grinning away and telling anyone who would listen that Tongba does not give you a hangover. The previous time I had tried to stuff I was inclined to agree with this theory, this time however my feelings were slightly different. While everyone else forced down some breakfast I made do with a few cups of tea and decided to stock up on chocolate for later – not ideal preparation for a day that had bothered me since I first looked at what this trek would actually involve.

The name Namche Bazaar, immediately conjures up images of small bustling streets and plenty of active shops and cafes. The reality is not all that far from this. Once you reach Namche you are deep in the Khumbu Valley region, of which this is the largest village by far. It is the very heart of Sherpa country but has changed dramatically in the last 30 to 40 years as the impact of tourism has played a large part in defining it. Along with the many guesthouses that now take up the slopes on which it is based, there are hundreds of houses where people live and the population is thought to be around 1,500 (it is difficult to give an accurate figure as many people will work and live there during the trekking season but head back to Kathmandu in the quieter periods). There are also a couple of bars and restaurants along with internet cafes which are often a hang-out for the younger population, as Jon Krakauer wrote in *Into Thin Air*:

"Teens hanging out in Namche carom parlours are more likely to be wearing jeans and Chicago Bulls T-shirts than quaint traditional robes…most of the people who live in this rugged country seem to have no desire to be severed from the modern world or the untidy flow of human progress. The last thing Sherpas want is to be preserved as specimens in an anthropological museum."

Along with internet cafes and the popular music that is often heard as you walk around the town, tourism has brought significant amounts of money to the area. Most houses now have running water and there is also a dental clinic that is able to provide good quality work to the local people.

There are problems that have come with this change in lifestyle however. Our expedition is as good an example as any, and while I cannot speak for all the others, the time I have spent in Nepal is the first time I have really become friends with people who are significantly poorer than I am, and it is common and normal to then want to help those who have played a part in such an experience as trekking in the Himalayas. While it did not happen on our trip (as far as I am aware) it is not unusual for visitors to end up sponsoring the child of one of their guides to help that child get a good education, but while this may seem like a wonderful act of kindness on the surface, it can also bring about difficulties. In *Touching My Father's Soul*, Jamling Norgay's book about his own climb to the summit of Everest, following in the footsteps of his father Tenzing, he talks about this specific problem:

"For instance, when two brothers go trekking with different groups and one of them returns with a foreign sponsorship for his child and the other doesn't, the seed of family and clan division is planted. The have-nots have been turned into the haves overnight…Foreigners' charity is not always based on merit or performance and the often arbitrary and excessive nature of these changes can upset a social balance that has developed over centuries."

He goes on to say that the best way to really help the people of the region is to invest in community projects that will bring more schools and hospitals to the villages, in the way that the Himalayan Trust has done in Khumjung, a school widely regarded as comparable to many of the private schools in Kathmandu as well as having the advantage of being away from the temptations that city life can bring.

Once The Everest Test began moving along officially I went out of my way to find out as much about the area as I could, and I was not the only one. Many of us bought and exchanged books, along with any other information we could get our hands on. However, most books on Everest really breeze through the trek as far as Base Camp, often in as little as a page or two, so I had to look further afield for specific information. A brief web search told me that the walk to Namche Bazaar was one of the hardest days those on the trek endured, and despite being so early in the itinerary it was not uncommon for people to struggle badly on the steep climb that takes you into the village itself. Kirt had told me this already, but I was determined to find more evidence, and when I found some footage of professional sportsmen gasping for breath when reaching the village and stammering about how hard the walk was, I wished I had not gone looking.

The walk was fairly gentle to start with, similar to what we had encountered the previous day with a few ups and several downs before we reached Monjo where we would break for lunch. After lunch was when things would get tough, a long and arduous climb would take us to a height of 3,440 metres above sea level, so around 800 metres higher than we had slept the night before. This was where people were first likely to begin experiencing problems with altitude and it was especially important to keep hydrated throughout the day, as once we began the climb there would be few, if any, places to refill our water bottles. The effects of altitude were not all we had to worry about on this trip however: we knew most of us would endure stomach bugs and unpleasant toilet experiences at some stage, and for some this was a more frightening prospect than Acute Mountain Sickness.

It is well known that getting the runs is a common part of trekking life, but this knowledge makes it no easier to deal with. My own stomach is not my strongest asset. The long drops (a simple hole in the ground) are not the easiest of things to use and it was either the Tongba or the nerves that meant I had visited the bathroom three times before we set off that morning. I should point out that I was devastated to discover by the third that there was actually a perfectly normal porcelain toilet upstairs in the teahouse that I could have used all along.

Since running water was now something of a rarity we all had alcohol gel to spray on our hands, Nir had also brought his own cook as part of his team for us as he did not fully trust the chefs in the tea houses along the route and understood the importance of getting us all to Gorak Shep fit enough to play the match. I did not know at the time, but while I was worrying about the almost certain lack of facilities on the route ahead, another man was to have a far worse time than I.

The previous day, as there were so many of us, we walked in the same groups that we had flown in with. This made it easier to keep track of everyone and it was simply impossible to all walk together; this was to become something of a bone of contention later on but for now everyone just got on with it. That morning at Phakding we were told we would be in the same groups again and that everyone on the first flight would be heading off first. Everyone that is, except for me.

I was moving in slow motion that morning and had spent the best part of 20 minutes just trying to close my rucksack. This was to become a theme each day I as jumped on, sat on and punched the thing until I could get the zip to close. Unlike most normal rucksacks, mine closes at the side in more of a suitcase design, very handy when you are trying to keep your clothes in good order, but when you really do not care about that and just want easy access to everything, it is far from ideal. I was also slightly delayed as I had asked Russell De Beer, our formal Royal Marine fitness trainer, to adjust the straps so that I would not endure quite the same shoulder and neck issues as I had the day before.

I was actually quite happy with missing the group as this meant I would be walking with a totally different set of people, many of whom I had hardly said hello to on the trip so far. While I knew everyone in Team Hillary pretty well, there were several people in Tenzing who I had spent little or no time with.

As Secretary I was lucky in that everyone on the trip knew who I was because more often than not I would be emailing them asking for money or telling them what flight they were on, but it was harder for some of the guys who maybe lived outside of London or had joined the teams late.

All of us knew that Namche would be the last major village we would pass through so if we needed to buy any more gear, as several people did, this would be the place to do so, all we had to do now was get there. As we set off spirits were good and before long we were crossing more bridges and I spared a thought for Jules who the day before had admitted to an 'almost paralysing' fear of heights which was hardly ideal given the bridges we were crossing were both high and not all that safe looking, not to mention frequent, meanwhile below them the often rapid waters of the Dudh Kosi (Milk River) flowed noisily. This was also my first day using trekking poles, something I was not sure of when I brought them with me but became increasingly grateful for as time wore on.

Every so often the team would burst into song, or at least hum a tune, the Indiana Jones theme being particularly popular when crossing the bridges, and the guides would look at us as if we were quite peculiar. The mood was helped by the continuing good weather and several people were beginning to go that wonderful shade of pink that most British people seem to reach when exposed to the sun. Chris Martin had a particularly unfortunate experience when he forgot to put sun cream on his ears and they blistered quite badly, meaning he spent most of the remaining days trekking with some very odd headgear on to try to protect them. It is worth mentioning that with every 300 metres you gain in altitude, the UV radiation increases by approximately 3 per cent, and we were going up to 5,165 metres.

On our way up one of the slopes and shortly before our first drinks stop - where we would briefly catch up with the guys in front - something unusual happened. As we were all carrying our packs we were soon building up a good sweat and while most people dealt with this by stopping regularly and drinking plenty of water, one of our party decided to do what had crossed many of our minds. James Markby had been eyeing the river for some time and it was not long before he gave in to temptation, and on finding a spot where the water was not too rapid and he would be able to lower himself in without doing any damage, he quickly took off all his clothes and moved towards the water. Not usually one to be shy in front of the ladies he got in and the amused crowd was briefly jealous of how nice it looked in the water, but the urge to follow suit was quickly dispensed with when Markby squealed like a child and hopped out as fast as he could go, being sure to tell the ladies that it was the cold water that had had a certain effect on him.

When we caught up with the others for a quick stop I heard about Jamo who was having all sorts of trouble with his stomach and visiting the toilet frequently. By the time I spoke with him at lunch he had been seven times and when he eventually reached Namche he was well into double figures. Of course one of the worst problems with this was that he was losing so much fluid and so needed to constantly rehydrate, fortunately he tackled the afternoon climb without any disasters, but with most of us being aware that he had eaten plenty of the chicken the night before, many decided to avoid meat for the time being.

Our staple lunch of chapatti and vegetables was again consumed and the talk centred on the upcoming walk. Most people were by now aware that this was going to be tough and so we kept telling ourselves that this is what we had trained for, this is what the Trim Trails in Battersea Park in the cold, wet and mud were all in aid of. For most of us the trip was not just about the time we spent out of the UK in April 2009, but the time we spent off our sofas for the 12 months previously.

With all this under our belts we had every right to feel confident about a 1,000-metre near-vertical climb to Namche Bazaar. For the most part of the trek, when things began to get tough you could look around you and take in the stunning scenery which would always give you a lift, but on this climb we were surrounded by trees so when you were able to lift your eyes from the floor all you generally saw was trees and sharp drops to your left. We encountered plenty of people coming down, as well as plenty of yaks, and were constantly told that it was not much further to go. What I thought would take around two hours ended up taking nearly four. I can cope with someone telling me that a walk will be another hour for example, as I can mentally prepare myself for that, but being told it is just another 20 minutes three times really pushes my sanity to the limits, and that was what we dealt with virtually every day on the trek. It is generally referred to as 'Nepali time'.

As I was in the second group I knew I would be among the last in, but surprised myself in that I was actually feeling OK, the altitude was not affecting me really, but I am a slow walker and was happy with my place at the back of the group. As we became increasingly spread out I was left with Joe Williams, Neil Sharland and James Butler and before long we also caught up with Marcus Chidgey who appeared to be struggling. About two thirds of the way up there is a spot where the trail levels out slightly and local people sell fruit to trekkers, and as we arrived a large number of our guys were just starting to leave. Joe particularly was puffing at this stage and as I gave him one of my Snickers bars we said we would just keep going at our own pace - it was still only around 15:30 so there was a while yet before it got dark. Butler came over to join us and suggested that Neil, who used to run the Trim Trails with his brother Tom, wouldn't be hanging around with us slow guys at the back, but sure enough as the others moved on Neil remained, happy to go at our pace. I have already mentioned what a machine Neil is so was surprised to see him waiting back but pleased that he did as it was the first time, and turned out to be the only time, I actually walked with him. The five of us were also making a good team.

As we set off Joe immediately started to struggle, he had been complaining of feeling dehydrated and looked like he was suffering a little from heat-stroke. The dust off the trail was also making life difficult for Marcus who has always suffered from asthma and from here on was moving especially slowly. I have never walked at such a slow pace in my life. It was literally three steps and take a break, but this was also my first time really seeing how people helped each other out. Each time the three of us at the back thought Neil and Butler had moved ahead we would turn a corner and they would be there waiting. We discussed how epic this walk was becoming and how in years to come there would be films made about us to rank alongside *Gladiator* and *Titanic* as films that filled the big screen.

"There are no heroes on days like today, boys," Butler would keep saying as we inched slowly towards the top. Eventually Namche came into view, and as we came round a bend I saw the ginger face of Will Wintercross staring at me, camera in hand. Will was on the trip as part of the Press Association and would play a major part in helping tell our story to the world through his photos, and he had also come on that final training weekend to Cornwall which was the first time he would really get to hang out with people on the trip. He had come back down so we knew it was not far to go from there and on we went. Shortly after we caught up with Mark Jordan of ITN who was taking some footage from the side of the path, and Marcus said he was going to wait with him and they would tackle the final stretch together; reluctantly I left him behind. We also caught sight of Lucy and Miles who were helping each other up the hill, and I was soon joined at my side by Jamie Zubairi (Zooby), another of the Trektators and unofficial photographers, who was also finding it tough going.

We slowly filed into Namche, and it was practically dark by now, at 17:30 and the others quickly vanished as people who had saved a room for them came and showed them the way. Having felt pretty good all day I was now tired and having come round a corner and seen another big slope I was starting to get to the end of my tether. I also had no idea where I needed to go and was particularly peeved when I saw Wes sticking the video camera in my face and then disappear without letting me know where I needed to go in order to sleep that night; as Expedition Leader who had gone with the first group that day and thus been there for hours, I thought he would know and be a bit more helpful.

Eventually I found a cafe inside a tea house where a few people were and slumped into a chair and quickly drained some tea. A message was given to me that Hillsy had saved a bed for me, but the bad news was that it was in another tea house further up the hill, and it was also on the top floor at the end of a very long corridor. With my sense of humour drastically beginning to fail I dragged myself up to where I needed to go and eventually managed to get some directions. On arriving at the room I was then told by Hillsy that there were not enough beds, but that the good news was he had found me a room on the ground floor, so he picked up my bag and took it down to where I would share with Dave Christie, a particularly amiable Australian.

While a small group had gone out to try some yak steak at a local restaurant I took a very cold shower and found my way into the dining area to exchange stories of the day with those who were about. Most people had very similar experiences to me, walking in groups of four or five and encouraging each other upwards. It was great to know that you could pluck anyone out of the entire group of us, and they would all respond the same way and get along like a house on fire; most people agree that is the biggest achievement of the whole expedition.

After some dinner I moved off pretty early to scribble in my diary and get some much-needed rest, but before doing so I heard and saw a few things that worried me. First of all Neil was really struggling to eat his dinner, which made me immediately concerned. I tried to convince him to force it down but he really did not want anything. My reading in the build-up had told me that loss of appetite is one of the first effects of altitude and given that Neil had surprisingly been with us at the back all the way up I began to realise that maybe there was more to his walking slowly than just wanting to hang out with the rest of us back there. All in all most people were feeling pretty worn out, and Glen put it well when he later wrote:

"The day's trek had been incredibly intense, and as I spent the evening trying to suck in as much oxygen as possible, I began to feel more and more ill. On arrival at Namche, after one of the most physically demanding days of my life, bending over to untie my boots made me feel dizzy, and rolling over in my sleeping bag at night left me breathless. It was a really tough day for all of us, and one that we'd all look back on with little fondness."

I also heard that Mark Jordan was getting upset at the fact that we were making relatively light work of the trek so far as it gave him little to report back to ITN. His job was to document the drama that unfolded and so far there had not been a great deal: sadly his objectives differed to ours in that we wanted no dramas whatsoever. At the point where I had left Marcus behind with him earlier he was also heard to snap indirectly at Lucy and Miles for watching him film, when all they were doing was taking a break as Miles was exhausted. Mark certainly had a difficult job, his bosses back in London expected certain things from him and he was meant to deliver no matter what. Added to that, he also had nowhere to undertake the time-consuming editing - he was treated like everyone else on the trek and had to share a room just like we did, which on a tiring day such as the one we had just experienced left him stressed and impatient with what was going on.

Marcus, as the PR guy, sensed things were starting to get a little tense so tried to ease the situation and a meeting began to take place in the tea house where the second group (of Team Tenzing and some Trektators) were sleeping. Rumours were beginning to circulate that Mark was unhappy and that he might just walk off the expedition if he did not get his way, which were of course complete nonsense, and so Wes moved quickly to try to stop those among his group. He told everyone to cut the guy some slack as these were not exactly ideal working conditions for him and he was under a lot of pressure that we did not necessarily know about. Marcus backed Wes up and they began to search for ideas of how they could fix the problem. Someone suggested faking some kind of near-death experience which received nothing but laughter so was passed off as a joke (we never found out if it was meant to be), and the next idea was to have a porter race, one that Mark himself had mentioned earlier. This involved carrying something in the way the porters on the mountain do, strapped to your head, and racing up a slope outside the tea house.

At this stage Wes began to get worried as the paths outside were not exactly smooth terrain and felt that someone getting injured in this way would be pretty unforgivable. His stance was that his responsibility lay with the people on the trip and to getting maximum exposure for the sponsors, but felt that there was a line in danger of being crossed for the sake of PR that had no direct benefit to anyone on the trip. He also felt that it was tempting fate to suggest the trek had not been hard enough so far and that it was still early for the mountain to throw something at us. Twisting an ankle or taking a heavy fall simply would not be worth it and he was not willing to force anyone to do something like this. A few others isn the room got a bit hot under the collar about the whole thing, but eventually talk diverted to how good it would be to get one over on Team Hillary and as soon as the discussion wound down Mike Preston told Wes he wanted to do it for the team. Mike is a quiet guy, but absolutely enormous. He rowed at age group level for New Zealand and I would not want to line up against him in any sort of race; all in all Wes was pretty happy as he felt that if this thing was going to happen it would now be for the right reasons.

Meanwhile in the Hillary tea house, Kirt was getting stressed about the whole situation, not knowing that it had been overcome pretty easily in the other building. As had become a habit, he was at first trying to overcome the problem on his own without sharing the burden and as such was winding himself up, not knowing that Wes had found out from Marcus. In turn, this led to Wes getting frustrated and feeling that Kirt was deliberately keeping things from him, which he almost certainly was after the episode on the first night. It was settled that the race would take place the following morning, despite a few dissenting voices (one of which I admit was my own). Little did Mark Jordan know that he was about to have just the sort of situation that makes for good TV.

Ama Dablam

Mike Preston (left) and Dave Kirtley in the porter race at Namche Bazaar

CHAPTER FIFTEEN

That morning I awoke to the sound of Dave Christie swearing under his breath that a second camel pack (a very useful piece of kit that I of course did not have) had broken like the first, so he now had to find one in Namche. He returned muttering even more about how prices were definitely rising as we got higher, but once his annoyance subsided he returned to being the politest man I know. We knew the porter race was due to happen after breakfast. I was not overly interested as I thought it was fairly senseless anyway, and was also trying to be more neutral as the match approached. Zooby summed up the views of several:

"The whole thing is farcical anyway and I hope that it doesn't get shown. If Jordan wanted the thing to be less like 'The Sound of Music' then he should speak to the people at the rear of the train. There are enough of us there to get dramas out of."

Of course I spent a good 20 minutes wrestling with my rucksack once again, and it was actually this which caused me to miss the race.

Russell De Beer and Mike Preston were slated for the challenge, but Russell was feeling a little worse for wear. He had taken on the climb the previous day with the gusto you would expect from a former fitness trainer in the Royal Marines, and had even overtaken the guide by the end. Unsurprisingly he now felt absolutely awful and was even quieter than usual. David Kirtley manfully stepped up for Team Hillary and lined up against Mike, the enormous New Zealander, with his porter sack strapped to his head. They probably only raced about 10 metres, up a slight hill, and both were wearing their playing kit, so it actually made for a good spectacle and a decent bit of fun. By all accounts it also made for pretty reasonable TV and Mark was happy that it had passed off without a hitch, and even had a group of guys do a fake cheer and celebration after it was run. Nick Toovey sums the event up nicely:

"Like clichéd Westerners on tours, we'd marvelled at the amount of weight the Porters were able to take up the hill, many of them carrying huge loads of

circa 50kg stacked into baskets that were strapped around their foreheads. I asked Dharma how long they could expect to do this for, expecting a response of 5 or 10 years before their bodies give way. 'For life' was the matter-of-fact response. The result of the race is still one that's up for debate. Mike was the clear leader before a stray elbow from Dave knocked Mike's strap off. Mike crossed the line first but without his pack. Hillary claimed this made it ineligible. Counter-claim was made of misconduct, and I slipped off to buy a water bottle before the arguing bored me to death."

While Tooves was not the most competitive man, the majority were fiercely so and any opportunity to gain some extra bragging rights was generally taken. Admittedly, I had stirred this up myself early on when I started running the expedition blog and continually mentioned how many people from each team turned up to which event and such like, but really these guys needed no encouraging.

We knew that a few people were struggling; Jamo was not 100% after all his visits to the bathroom the previous day, while John Richards was having similar problems. Neil had lost his appetite and gone slower than many would have expected, but now Glen was showing signs of feeling bad as well. His appetite had also gone and he was getting stomach problems as well; combine that with Russell's suffering and Team Hillary were not in particularly good shape. The effects of the altitude were definitely starting to show and we knew that this was only going to get worse as we got higher. The following day we were only climbing around 300 metres and would be at our destination by lunchtime, and after that we would have a much needed acclimatisation day.

It was another early start and we were on the trail by 8am. I was in the first group this time and as soon as I started walking I felt exhausted. With Namche being in a valley, as soon as the porter race was done we had to begin our walk on an uphill slope. I found when I was training for the marathon the first 20 minutes of running was always the worst, but once I pushed through that I was generally OK. That is why it was better to be running in Richmond Park rather than on a treadmill because in the gym if I still felt bad after 20 minutes I would just stop, yet it is not that simple in the middle of a park when on completely the wrong side, it's either carry on or lie down and die: while the second option was often tempting I managed to get past it.

I felt the same that day in Namche, and I had also made a mistake with my clothing that I determined not to repeat. I had worn shorts each day of the trek so far, but as we got higher I knew it was likely to get colder. I had failed to get my hands on any trekking trousers and had intended to buy some in Kathmandu; that was before a conversation with Charlie Bathurst-Norman the night before offering to lend me a pair of his. When I looked at them for the first time that morning I sensed they may not be such a good fit, but as I had no alternative I squeezed into them and set off.

Within minutes they were falling down, and they were to infuriate me throughout the day. This is not because they were too big: I could barely get them over my hips so had to undo the Velcro on the sides, of course this meant my lovely green boxer shorts were now on display to all, but that was the least of my concerns. Carrying my 20kg pack meant that the bottom was continually rubbing the small of my back, and basically pushing the trousers down, so the entire day was spent trying to pull these things back up and maintaining my calm when all I really wanted to do was scream "why me?" and shake my fists at the sky.

I was soon towards the back of our group, as usual, but as I looked ahead I saw a climb that put what we went through the day before to shame. This was practically vertical, but thankfully I was assured it was only a brief climb. In fact, that morning we were told there were three different routes we could walk between Namche and Khumjung, and we had chosen the quickest, but most physically demanding, route. I say the quickest, I think by this point the guides were starting to realise that their idea of quick and our idea of quick were different. After regrouping at the bottom we started off up the steps and were making steady but slow progress. I had a few people in my group who I had not yet seen a lot of, my sister Helen being one and one of the medics, Nick Walker, being another.

As we walked the conversation was what I had come to expect, ranging from tedious days in the workplace to different techniques of going to the bathroom and every so often Nick's radio would crackle into action. The radios were essential on the trail with such a big group and only a few people had them: Kirt, Nir, the medics, and the more senior guides. They were mainly used for checking everyone was OK and finding out where people were, or in Nick's case the occasional story or rude joke. As soon as you heard a radio make a noise everyone listened, partly from nosiness, but more often because it was either good to know how others were getting on or to hear an amusing anecdote. This time however, it was neither of those.

Nick was the most experienced doctor on the trip and when he heard Isla on the other end say Neil Sharland was in trouble below us he became very serious. Even despite Neil's problems the previous evening I was surprised: at breakfast (three cardboard-like pancakes not improved by jam) he had said he felt much better. We called out to those ahead of us to wait and ended up staying where we were for around half an hour. Not all of us stayed: Mark Jordan raced back down to get shots, as did Neil's brother Tom.

Those in pairs - Helen and I; the Fudakowska sisters; Jules and Vicks Staveley and Kiwi Palmer and Rebecca 'Sugar' Demery - had all spoken beforehand and agreed if one of us became sick the other was to carry on regardless. Helen and I were adamant on this, we had put too much into the trek to give it up because of the other. If I had become ill and Helen had ended up not reaching Gorak Shep, I'm not sure how I would have dealt with that.

Kirt had also made the point at our final meeting that we really wanted to avoid feelings of guilt if someone had to be left behind: they would be left in good hands with at least a medic and a guide. Privately I think it was all of our worst nightmares. For Neil - one of the people who had helped train us all and get us physically fit - this was a setback and a shock, and perhaps even more so to his brother. Tom did not even think for a second about what he was going to do, and raced back down the hill to join him.

Helen admitted afterwards that while she understood Tom going down, she and Alex F did talk and say they were worried it might set a precedent should anyone else with siblings or spouses get sick. It was clear Tom and Neil were going to stay behind, but fortunately we were still early in the trip and were resting at Khumjung the following day so they would have a chance to catch up, but that might not be so simple when we got higher up the mountain. Ian was the medic who opted to stay with them.

We did all know what the deal was: if we got ill we got left behind, plain and simple. Safety was the first priority, the cricket match a close second, and personal relationships were not to impact on anything. Wes had brought this up in discussions over the Team Hillary captaincy. He did not feel Jules was a good candidate because once on the mountain his priority would be with his wife and if she got sick we could lose him as well. Jules was adamant that this would not be the case and that they had an agreement. He even said she would give him a kicking if he did stay with her, but had that situation arisen it would have been interesting to see what would have happened.

When we all began moving on, the usual people trying to keep spirits up, there was definitely concern among everyone, firstly for Neil, but also for ourselves. We were only at 3,440 metres and had more than a mile to go vertically before we would start running around a cricket field. If they were not before, the dangers we faced now were very clear.

It was bad enough for us having to lose one of the team, but for the families back home it must have been awful. Mark Jordan captured Neil being laid out flat on the dusty ground and then being attached to a drip. In the footage he looks as white as the snow and when these images were broadcast on the 10pm News that night, people were unsurprisingly worried. Fortunately, Tom was able to contact his parents, telling them not to worry if they saw the news, but all the other parents – without the benefit of assurance – were suddenly considerably more concerned. ITN were inundated with calls from various people during the coming days wanting to know if Neil was OK, while several parents, and one pregnant wife, rang our emergency contact Philippa Mullineux. She was supposed to be able to contact us regularly but satellite phone problems meant we were only able to reach her intermittently. So instead people began to call Captive Minds, who had enough on their plate already, but once again Alex Rayner did his best possible pitch to everyone who phoned in saying that he had personally spoken to their loved ones that morning and everyone was doing fine. While this may have been a slight stretch – Alex spoke to nobody but Marcus while we were away – it helped calm the nerves and that was what mattered.

While the phone calls to Philippa were in this case understandable, at other times she would have various parents calling her worrying about such things as bedbugs and the fact their son was not getting enough TV time and so affecting his fundraising. I'm not sure these were quite the emergencies she had imagined dealing with when she signed up for that most thankless of tasks!

It was quite a long walk up, passing the highest airport in Nepal at Syangboche, whose runway is just a cut strip in the middle of a hill which yaks can wander freely across. The airport and the nearby Everest View Hotel were built for the same purpose when in the late 1960s a Japanese company had the idea to welcome wealthy tourists. However, when the doors opened in 1973 the first group of visitors became sick from altitude within hours of their arrival: not good for business. Solutions such as including oxygen tanks in many of the guest rooms could not help; people continued to become sick and before long the airstrip was shut down. It reopened some years later, but only for transporting cargo to the mountains.

At the hotel, business declined rapidly, as the wealthy clients it was designed for were largely unwilling to trek for a few days in order to visit, which is the only way to adequately acclimatise. It has now reinvented itself as a property known for quality food, and of course it still has the magnificent views. In 1999 the Guinness Book of Records also recognised it as the highest hotel in the world. It is still a one-mile walk from the airstrip, and about a 300-metre climb to a height of around 3,900 metres, and that is a mile that I really felt.

Once again I was walking with Joe Williams and James Butler and this time we were also joined by BJ, Wes and Russell De Beer. Joe was typically unsympathetic to Russell's plight as he was clearly struggling

Above: Battle of Trafalgar, The Press Launch in January was an idea which came from the freeze mobs carried out a month earlier in Parliament Square, Buckingham Palace and Trafalgar Square (below).

©George Powell (above), ©Jamie Zubairi (below)

Above: Richard Kirtley leads the group up Pen-Y-Fan in the Brecon Beacons after some heavy snow. **Below:** From left to right: Gareth Wesley, Alastair Cook, Richard Kirtley and Alan Curr at a Young Lord's Taverners evening.

©Alan Curr (all)

Above left: The front page of the Independent on Tuesday 14th of April showing Ben Jarman in front of Everest. **Above right:** The whole group at the Hillary school in Khumjung.

Above: John Richards (left) and Will Simmons give out kit to excited kids at the Shangri-La Cricket Academy in Kathmandu.

©Will Wintercross (top left), ©George Powell (top right & bottom)

Above left: Richard Kirtley and Nir Lama discuss finances and politicians at Khumjung. **Above right:** One of the many porters carrying a ridiculous load we passed on the trail.

Above: The ladies of the trip who were the core of the Trektators.
Left to right: Alexandra Fudakowska, Rebecca Demery, Lucy Brooks (behind), Paola Fudakowska, Jen Gladstone, Isla Cox, Victoria Staveley, Helen Curr, Victoria Nicholson.

Team Hillary from left to right.
Back Row: Miles Nathan, David Kirtley, Chris Palmer, Ben Jarman,
Jamo Peterson, Jonathan Woods, Glen Lowis (C) Tom Sharland, Will Simmons
Front Row: Russell De Beer, John Richards, Chris Martin, Richard Kirtley,
Charlie Campbell, Jules Staveley.

Team Tenzing from left to right
Back Row: Nick Mullineux, James Markby, Neil Sharland, Mark Waters,
Haydn Main (C) Kinsey Hern, Gareth Wesley, Mike Preston
Front Row: Joe Williams, James Carrington, Gareth Lewis, Chris Beale,
Nick Toovey, Dave Christie, James Butler.

©George Powell (all)

Above: The teams lined up with the umpires central while central while James Markby read 'The Man in the Arena'.

Above: This shot by Jamie Zubairi (Zooby) with Joe Williams in the foreground would later appear in the New York Times.

©George Powell (top), ©Jamie Zubairi (bottom)

Action Shot: Chris Beale (Blinky) attempts a diving return catch during the match while an avalanche happens in the background.

©Will Wintercross

Party time: Richard Kirtley (Kirt, left) pops the champagne straight into Gareth Wesley's (Wes) face during the presentation ceremony before.

Above: Everyone lines up for a group photo in the aftermath.

©Will Wintercross (all)

still, and said to him: "Russell, how does it feel to know that right now, at this very moment, I, Joe Williams, am in better physical shape than you?" Fortunately Russell was to able to see the funny side and said that he would not make the mistake of racing up any hills again and that he accepted altitude sickness was not a myth. We crawled pretty slowly up to the hotel, and were met on the way by a bunch of Australian tourists who said that they had seen us on the news and did not think we would achieve our goal as it was so cold at Gorak Shep and had been snowing up there. This was hardly a boost to our confidence, and the kind of thing we would get used to hearing as the days wore on; they did at least wish us luck.

Once I arrived at the hotel for a much-needed cup of tea and chocolate bar, the clouds had almost totally engulfed the peak of Everest, but at least Ama Dablam was still visible and looked as spectacular as I had hoped. I have a huge amount of respect for that mountain, and find it difficult to take my eyes off, even though at 6,812 metres it is more than 2,000 metres (6,560 ft) lower than Everest. The guys who had reached the hotel earlier had some great views of Everest and the other mountains surrounding it, particularly Lhotse, which at 8,516 metres is the fourth highest in the world, and neighbour Nuptse, which is a series of seven peaks, the highest being 7,861 metres.

We had a brief pause but, behind schedule after the long stop for Neil and wanting lunch sooner rather than later, we pressed on. That afternoon we wound along slopes on the edge of the mountain for a while, and took a bit of a battering by the wind and the dust, before descending down to Khumjung. I was at the back again as we left and walking with Wes once more. An extract from my diary reads: *"I had a nice moment with Wes on this final 45-minute walk as he turned to me and said: 'Fucking good to be here with you man, after all the work and everything we've put in.'"*

Having been annoyed at him the day before, I have to say I felt a bit different towards him after this exchange. I had always spent more time with Kirt than Wes so when they had their differences it was always Kirt's side that I heard. But Wes had also invested more than most, and cared about it passionately. Not only that but he was clearly grateful to the people who had helped it come alive; so what if he was a bit irritating when behind the camera? OK he often asked people to repeat bits of conversation so he could get it on film, but it was his passion. Nobody complains when they are asked to pose for photos for someone else's camera and this really was not all that different. Not to mention the fact that he was going to have to spend a lot of time when the trip was over editing hours of footage to make it into something that every one of us would want to have and he was doing that just as much for the guys who came along as for himself.

His passion for getting the right shot did cause him a bit of bother at the end of the walk however. When we came to the top of our final flight of stairs and looked down on Khumjung village, and the school that we had looked at photos of so many times, he was keen to film those of us at the back walking down towards it. Off we went leaving him perched at the top of the stairs where he decided he did not have the right shot and would wait for the second group to come through so he could film them. Little did he know they had taken a totally different route and came into the village from another side. While we were sat drinking tea and having lunch, Wes was sitting alone on a rock for a good 45 minutes before giving up and coming down to find everyone.

Everybody was now relaxed as the next day we could take it easy and do what we pleased. There were options of acclimatisation walks and visiting the local hospital, while a small selection would be going to visit the school built by the Himalayan Trust and coaching cricket to some of the children. If none of that was up your street, one path led to a nice bakery serving apple pie and tea and there were more than a few who spent the afternoon with their feet up playing card games.

That first afternoon at Khumjung plenty of people took the opportunity to shower, wash their clothes or catch up on writing diaries, while a few joined in a game of cricket outside our tea house with the local children. It was difficult to escape the fact that we had left three people behind however, that after just three days' trekking we were already losing people. While Tom wanted to stay behind with his brother,

Ian had put his own trip on the line. Each team was now down a player and we were one medic light. We all hoped they would catch up, but there was no guarantee.

Not only that, but word also reached my ear that a certain Warden of Sagarmatha National Park, Mr X, was once again making noise about us and threatening to stop us progressing further up the mountain.

Gareth Lewis entertains the kids at Khumjung School

CHAPTER SIXTEEN

Now at Khumjung, Tooves was beginning to feel a little worse for wear and John Richards was showing no sign of improving. Glen was still a concern so the three medics left all had their work cut out already. It was agreed before departure that we would have a time set aside each morning and evening when anyone suffering could speak to the 'On call' medic and as the trek wore on these sessions became increasingly popular. That afternoon I suffered my first real headache of the trip and decided to catch up on a bit of sleep, which did me little good, but the pain I was experiencing that day was nothing compared to the headaches caused by the issue of getting permission to enter Sagamartha National Park.

There was still time for Mr X to make one last attempt at stopping us. This was something we did not discover until we were at Khumjung, but he tried to invoke a rule which requires permits for a foreigner to enter any national park in Nepal and he also cited public pressure to stop the team, without saying who or where this pressure was coming from. We did not know that while we were trekking the steep climb to Namche, Nir's mobile was ringing off the hook with journalists in Kathmandu wanting to find out more. Once again it was the Director General of the National Park and Wildlife Preservation, Dr. Shyam Bajimaya, who came to our rescue. I discovered afterwards that most reports actually stated we had been denied entry and were left stranded after people were sent to intercept us at Monjo, the place we had lunch before the climb to Namche, which was not even slightly true. One thing reported that was true was that Mr X had now got himself into some rather hot water with his bosses, as an article that appeared in *The Himalayan Times* stated:

"Chief Conservation Officer [Mr X,] said the team had not completed all the necessary formalities. Peace Nepal Treks had applied to the Minister for Forest and Land Conservation, Kiran Gurung, to provide permission for the teams. Department of National Park and Wildlife Conservation has sent written order to the minister of the protected area. However, the national park wrote to the ministry

that they couldn't allow the foreign team to enter the area as it would be against conservation laws.

An official at the Ministry for Forest and Land Conservation said, "Minister Gurung is out of station and so are other officials," adding, "We would decide whether or not to allow them in once the minister or officials return."

The issue has, however, become a bone of contention between the ministry and the national park. Gurung said, "We have allowed them so nobody should stop the teams."

Director General of Department of National Parks and Wildlife Conservation, Laxmi Prasad Manandhar, opined that the teams should be allowed to play cricket in the area as the minister himself has sent a written order.

They were eventually granted entry into the Sagamartha Conservation Area to play the cricket match scheduled for next week after the director general of National Park and Wildlife Preservation, Shyam Bajimaya, directed the staffers to let the cricket teams in. Meanwhile Gurung has also asked Mr X to report to the Ministry for defying his orders."

The Nepal Tourist Board were also angered by the actions of Mr X as they had previously made a public statement saying that we would help to boost tourism which had started to fall because of the 'frequent strikes and crippling 20-hour daily power outage.'

The upshot is that Mr X will no longer be able to cause problems for people wanting to access the national park. As I stood outside the tea house listening to Nir and Kirt tell me all this I could not help but firstly be amazed at the persistence of someone trying to stop us purely for his own selfish reasons, and secondly at quite how much of a stir we had caused. I was to find out the full extent of it later, but even at the time the fact that we had managed to get a corrupt government official removed from office (he now works at the Nepal National Society for Earthquake Technology) was quite an achievement. Not only that, but since the new democracy did not actually have any laws in place to deal with an expedition like ours they had actually had to write some, so we have contributed in our own little way to the new constitution of Nepal, should it ever get finished of course.

The last thing left to do that evening was to pay the final balance to Nir, or at least as close to it as we had with us. He showed us that the final balance, including 'Royalties' and fees for various licenses was around £42,000; still considerably higher than we had planned for and without any profit for Peace Nepal Treks. Still, by the time Kirt and I had gone over the numbers we felt sure that we had enough to cover it all and it was great to get that monkey off our backs. Much as we both wanted to crack open a beer we decided to refrain, perhaps the first time ever we have both agreed on such a decision, and went back upstairs to join the others for dinner.

I would like to say that was the end of the financial worries, we certainly felt it was at the time, but upon returning to the UK there were still plenty of bills left to pay. The airport taxes came to around £8,500, plus the £5,000 given to the Himalayan Rescue Association for their doctor to come with us and to keep a helicopter on standby, not to mention the fee to Captive Minds and the costs incurred for getting kit branded and delivered up and down the country; the £75,000 total that was paid by the 50 people on the trip was not even nearly enough. The £15,000 given by Nokia for sponsorship helped, but we still wanted to give some of that to our charities, and in the end we had to ask everyone on the trip to make a donation to help towards the outstanding bills. Even with this, it took Kirt around 18 months to actually pay off the remaining debt.

There were a few things to be discussed in the tea house, mainly about the visit to the school the following day. As it was not term time the school had sent out invites letting people know that we were planning to visit and were not entirely sure how many would be there, especially as many live so far away. Just that morning Tooves had talked to a lady who ran a shop in Namche who told him she walked to the school in Khumjung every day for ten years; at first it would take her two hours, but she eventually got it down to one and a half. It certainly put our lives into perspective when he told me that. Still, if there were only 30 or so children there, as the school expected, then there was no point in all of us turning up and crowding the session, so the tough task fell to Kirt and Wes to decide who was going to take part. I had discussed the situation with Kirt briefly beforehand and said I did not mind stepping aside for someone else as it was really important for me to do an acclimatisation walk, going above 4,000 metres. I came to regret this enormously, but such is life. A few people were pretty disappointed to miss out, but the priority did go to people on the second flight that had missed the session the others had at the Shangri-La Academy, which meant David Kirtley was left on the sidelines, something he told me later as we roomed together that he was seriously gutted about. It was a classic situation of not being able to please everybody, but mostly people took it fairly well. We were also told that each of the three teams - Hillary, Tenzing and Trektators - would be separating shortly for a practice session in order to prepare for 'The Everest Factor,' a totally absurd idea dreamt up by Jamo to entertain all of us as well as the guides. It would be essentially three groups singing three songs each and the medics would take up the role of judges. While several people filed off to practise, a little underwhelmed by the whole situation, I am not sure anyone quite knew how entertaining it would end up being.

Life in the Himalayas was always interesting to observe, the people were as friendly as the living conditions often were not. Many of our guides would tell us that they live a simple life, but a happy one. Perhaps it was with that in mind that Jamo came up with the idea of The Everest Factor, a chance to have simple fun in the form of a good old fashioned singsong. I have to admit to being slightly dubious when I first received the email about the event, but at least appreciated the line stating that judges were under strict instruction to award points on enthusiasm above talent. As we sat in the main room of our tea house discussing which songs we should go with, I could not help thinking that this could go either way, storming success or utter catastrophe. Fortunately Jonathan Woods (Woodsy) got everyone going by launching into a version of 'Afternoon Delight' which he had memorised since laughing uncontrollably at its use in the Will Ferrell film *Anchorman*, and our first song was in the bag. After that '500 miles' by the Proclaimers seemed a logical enough option with the idea of a bit of acting at the beginning involving Kirt, Miles Jamo and I while the final option would be 'Wonderful World (Don't know much)' by Sam Cooke.

As we practised it was priceless to see a Nepali family consisting of a mother and her two children watching us with wide-eyed amazement as we belted out some truly dreadful renditions of these classic songs, forever getting the words wrong or cracking up with laughter as someone let off a hideous fart. Such things are always a risk in a roomful of men who are eating plenty of eggs. Still, as the session wore on, we discovered that Team Hillary had a joker in the pack in the form of Jules Staveley who shocked us all by demonstrating an ability to actually sing in tune. After we finished I wandered back into the other building and found a few of the Tenzing guys wiping tears from their eyes after laughing so hard, and decided there and then that this event was clearly going to be a huge success. With that in mind I headed off to bed and spent the night trying to shut out the sound of David Kirtley snoring.

The following morning I was late getting up, around 8am, and after breakfast I heard that there was a decent walk taking place that should last about five hours and go up above 4,000 metres. I thought about it for a while and decided why not, so at 9am I set off with Kiwi, BJ, Blinky, Nick Mullineux, James Carrington and James Markby, along with a couple of guides. I had not met either of the guides before - with such a big group it was quite easy for that to happen - so I tried to speak with them early on but discovered that their English was not great and since we were starting with a steep climb out of the village it was best to leave speaking alone for a while. We were soon out of Khumjung, heading back the way we had come the day before, and it felt good to be walking without a heavy backpack for once and instead just carrying my camera and water bottle. After around an hour, as we were heading back towards the airstrip at Syangboche, we saw three familiar figures coming towards us. We were very pleased to see a much healthier-looking Neil Sharland, flanked by Tom and Ian. We chatted briefly to them and it was clear that Neil had made a full and very quick recovery. He admitted afterwards that watching the group leave was easily the low point of his trip as he began to worry about whether he would make it to Gorak Shep at all. After a year of preparation he really thought his trip might be over. Fortunately having his brother with him really made a difference and of course Ian was quick to make sure that he took on lots of water. The effects of altitude can be exaggerated by dehydration and that was exactly what had happened to Neil and he was certain not to make the same mistake again. The rest of the trip was relatively easy for him. He also received a terrific ovation when he reached Khumjung and greeted the others.

We continued walking but could not help but notice that we were consistently going down. Nick had a phone which told you what altitude you were at and we were consulting it fairly regularly. After a while the guides pointed out to us where we were going and said it was another four hours away, meaning we would most likely be doing a nine hour walk on what was supposed to be a rest day, and we were now down to 3,400 metres and staring across a valley. The idea had been to go high, spend a bit of time there and come back down again, but obviously there was a miscommunication somewhere and while the guides were taking us to the right place, they had chosen a route that was a long way from what any of us wanted to do. After a quick discussion we agreed to turn back and were back at Khumjung by midday.

Some of the guys were particularly annoyed by this episode, particularly Markby. This was made worse by everyone telling us how great it had been at the school; there were around 60 kids there throughout the morning and after a while everyone who was around ended up getting involved in one way or another. Seeing the photos made it clear what a brilliant time we had missed. On top of that we also found that there was another walk that afternoon that would definitely go above 4,000 metres, so in fact we would have been better off relaxing in the morning and then going on a proper walk in the afternoon. I was disappointed and it put me in a bit of a bad mood, but after an afternoon in the bakery with a few of the others who decided not to go on the walk I quickly got over it. The walk the seven of us did was not a complete waste of time as I had some good chats with the guys, particularly BJ and Nick, the latter of whom had climbed Kilimanjaro on his honeymoon and also spent almost a year doing the round-the-world clipper race. It was because of his experience at such things that he was given the role of quartermaster and spent every morning and evening monitoring where all the central kit was.

When we were back in the UK I asked everyone to fill out a questionnaire on the trip, with one of the questions being what their trip highlight was. Of course most put the match itself, but several said that the day at the school was for them the best part of it. Of course we tried to mix with the local people as much as we could, but having a full morning set aside to spend time with them and see where they go to school and how they amuse themselves was very special.

Khumjung School was built in 1961 and was the first project Sir Edmund Hillary took on as part of the newly founded Himalayan Trust and began life as a two-classroom building which could hold around 50 people. Nowadays it caters for pre-school, primary and secondary students and can take up to 350 pupils at a time. Because of the success of the project the Himalayan Trust became inundated with requests to build more schools in other areas and has ended up building more than 25 schools within the region to date. As I mentioned previously, people would walk for two hours a day just to get their education, because they wanted to.

The following day, day five on the mountain, we would arrive into Tengboche, to get our best look at Everest yet, and for some of us our first. We were well and truly in the trip now, halfway to reaching Gorak Shep in terms of trekking days. We had experienced a few setbacks and I think deep down we knew we would experience a few more before match day, but for now we could enjoy where we were without complicating things too much. By the time we reached Tengboche however, the minds of a few were starting to drift towards the biggest cloud over the whole expedition, the issue of selection.

The captains in front of Everest at Tengboche

CHAPTER SEVENTEEN

W hen we arrived I finally had that first proper look at the mountain which had claimed the lives of so many in such tragic circumstances, and still held the bodies of some of the greatest climbers of our generation. It was a strange feeling, a mix of awe and shame: knowing these stories I wondered 'Why do people continually want to climb this thing?' The answer however, was right in front of me as I came round the corner and saw almost our entire group having their picture taken with the mountain in the background, while Kirt stood quietly to one side simply staring for around 20 minutes before I decided to disturb him, and then a few of us all simply stood and stared. The mountain holds a draw, as discussed in Part Two, and it now had a hold of every one of us, and we were only going a little more than half way up!

Tengboche itself is a tiny place, home to a little more than 50 monks and a handful of families, yet it receives approximately 30,000 visitors a year. This creates a few problems for the area and the quest for sustainable tourism is ongoing, particularly as the periods of highest demand on the facilities are also the periods of lowest supply. For example, water is extremely scarce during the cold winter months, but as this is the time when the views are almost guaranteed to be clear the visitors pour in.

The monastery is what the town is really known for: established in 1916 it then suffered considerable damage during an earthquake in 1934 and had to be repaired. On January 19th, 1989 however, an electrical problem caused the entire facility to burn to the ground in a fire which destroyed precious old scriptures, statues, murals and woodcarvings. It was rebuilt with help from numerous places, not least the Himalayan Trust, and reopened in 1994. It now relies heavily on tourist donations.

Spirits were soaring - while the walk was quite tiring, it was finished by lunchtime and we had a free afternoon. Most of us spent a good 20 minutes or so sitting on the slope with the famous monastery to our left, but with our attention firmly focussed on the mountains in front of us.

At 8,516 metres (27,940 ft) Lhotse ranks fourth on the list of the world's highest peaks and stood proudly to the right of Everest as we looked, its sharp peak offering a contrast to the smoother peak of the highest point on earth. Several people chose to take a quiet moment alone to stare at the sight before them, but before too long groups were developing and the cameras were out. George Powell decided this was a good moment to take photos of virtually everyone in front of the mountains, which was just as well because shortly after lunch the clouds came in once more and they totally disappeared. The stand-out shots were of the two captains, in their team shirts with Team Hillary and Team Tenzing across the back, standing side by side; the shot of Kirt and Wes looking delighted at how things were going, and the team photo of the Drovers. Hillsy had carried with him the flag that he and I had taken to the Cricket World Cup in 2007 and the 13 guys who were part of the Drovers Cricket Club took the chance to gather round - one for the club website.

That afternoon, after several hours playing cards in the local bakery, I wandered up to the monastery with Vicks and James Markby, and as we walked in I saw Tom, Zooby and Haydn already there. It was a fascinating experience, leaving your shoes at the door and sitting cross-legged on the floor while the monks chanted non-stop. I noted in my diary shortly afterwards that the sound is one that if you heard it while sitting in your living room it would drive you utterly bonkers, but in the Monastery it was incredibly peaceful and relaxing. This was proved by the girl behind me who was sat with her eyes shut and when one of the monks came round handing out biscuits we realised she was actually fast asleep. Most people during the afternoon, and some the following morning, made the visit and I think it was totally worthwhile.

Zooby, ever the artist, took the opportunity to do some sketching and chat to some of the monks. His write-up of the experience says:

"We got ushered into the inner courtyard to wait for the monks to take their places inside the building. One of the monks is really old and has to be almost carried up the stairs. Inside, we take our shoes off, observe the 'No Flash' signs and we're greeted by loud music of various horns, cymbals and pipes. It's quite dark apart from the lights from the windows and the flicker of the electric lights which

sometimes go off and we're plunged back into darkness. I get stuck into sketching the scene but as the light is so low I'm not getting a clear image. The sound of the monastery at prayers is amazing. It's the low drones of 30 voices all reciting the same verse at different points of their breath. Transfixing. I'm sat opposite the monk that looked through my sketchbook earlier and I sketch away. He reminds me of a friend's dad. I look up during sketching once and I see that he's looking directly at me, his lips moving, the sound of his voice mixed in with the other voices. He's noticed that it's him that I've been sketching a lot of. Oh shit, I've done it now, I've ruined his concentration. He smiles and starts to giggle but still maintains the chanting. Thank god. Must be all that meditation that they do, either that or he's perfected the art of keeping his lips moving and it'll look like you're singing."

As I left the Monastery I walked down the steps to discover an impromptu game of cricket taking place. I really should not have been surprised, since I was on a cricket tour, but it still looked a little odd! James Butler was doing his best impression of a petulant child when he was not allowed to bat, and David Kirtley was having his ear bent with the old classic 'You're not even the best cricketer in your family' chat. Several of the guides were getting involved, Dharma in particular impressing everyone with a spectacular diving catch. The game went on for hours, which was an encouraging sign for later on, even though we still had more than a vertical kilometre to climb.

After the game wound up and everyone made their way back to the tea houses I had a quick chat with Kirt and discovered that he was coming under some pressure from the medics to hire some more porters for the final stretches as they were uncomfortable with all of us carrying our large rucksacks. It is true that we were still yet to pass any other group of westerners carrying loads anything like what we were, but I felt that generally people were coping very well. The girls especially were showing no signs of feeling ill or being overly tired which was impressive, although we should have suspected as much. The medics had been a little spooked by the difficulties suffered by Neil Sharland, as well as the sight of someone being carried down the mountain, nobody sure if the person on the stretcher was dead or alive. It did transpire that a Japanese tourist had died on the trail while we were there, it was never confirmed if it was indeed him we saw that day.

Since we would be breaking the 4,000-metre barrier the following day they felt we needed to start being more cautious. After dinner that night we had a talk from the four of them, where they told us the story of the Japanese trekker, and told us to make sure we went to them if we were feeling rough in any way and not to keep it to ourselves. The medics would do their best to get everyone up the mountain, and there was still time to stay behind and catch up later, but AMS can be deadly and we were not to take it lightly. That night the queue outside the 'surgery' was something to behold and I am confident that the medics spoke to more people that night than they had the rest of the previous days put together.

Still, Kirt was reluctant to hire extra porters, simply because we did not have the cash. The decision was taken to hold off for another day and see how people coped as we got higher. The answer, unfortunately, was not particularly well. Several of the group, Including Wes and Kinsey, had filled up their water bottles from a container that had previously contained kerosene and as a result quickly felt particularly sick. After it became apparent that they were not as sick as first feared the jokes began to fly, getting called petrol-heads by a few of us while Tooves sang the line from the Kings of Leon song 'Revelry' which goes: 'With a fire in my bones and the sweet taste of kerosene.' I am not entirely sure Wes saw the funny side at the time, but he did later on.

That night I roomed with Gareth and it was he who was beginning to fret a little about selection. Haydn had not quite been himself during the last couple of days and Gareth felt that, as vice captain, the issue of selection was really weighing on his shoulders. Unlike in Team Hillary, where Glen had made it clear that selection lay with him and only him, although he would seek advice, for Tenzing it was much more a question of Haydn and Gareth discussing things, while Wes had some input as well. Gareth told me that the two of them had very different ideas of who should get picked in the final XI and there were a couple of people Haydn was thinking about leaving out that made Gareth's mind boggle. I said that there was no point getting too worked up about it at this stage as the match was still several days away and a decision would not need to be made until the night before, or possibly even the morning of it. Still, it was an interesting insight into what the captains must have been going through and how their experience differed to that of everyone else. I had not seen much of Haydn and was unsure whether to go and give him my input, but eventually decided to stay out of it Gareth knew my thoughts and since they were the same as his there was really nothing I could do.

The following morning we had hoped to receive a blessing from the Head Rimpoche at the Monastery but unfortunately he was not there so while a few people went and sat again as I had the night before, we did not manage to get the blessing as hoped. Glen and James Butler meanwhile, were up early to do a shoot for ITN which involved hanging out some prayer flags. In late March they had done a presentation at Avon School in east London to a group of children aged between 4-11 years old with the aim of both inspiring and educating them. Their presentation went really well and both these guys proved to be total naturals in front of the kids, something that surely helped when they arrived at Khumjung and certainly surprised Butler who was absolutely terrified about the whole thing. The kids had spent a week learning about Mount Everest and Nepal and had prepared prayer flags with their own hopes and prayers for the guys to take and hang up for them. That morning they tied the flags to a bridge with Ama Dablam and Everest in view and the idea is that every time the wind blows the flag the prayer goes up to the heavens. Once the ink has faded that is when it is thought to have been answered. What was written on these flags really touched the guys who collected them, with things like 'I hope my Daddy is happy in Heaven' and 'I pray one day they find a cure for cancer' while one even wrote, 'I pray Amy Winehouse will stop doing drugs.' The footage went out on the news report by Mark Jordan that night and it was very well received.

It was an early start for those guys as we were on the trail by 8.30am to begin another long walk up to Dingboche. This would be the first time those who did not do the acclimatisation walk at Khumjung would go above 4,000 metres so it was always going to be a test, but once again we began with a downhill walk which frustrated a few of the guys, but by now many of us were getting used to it. Tooves was getting increasingly upset, primarily because he had been assigned the 'Dick of the Day' award. This came in the form of a cow bell which was tied on to the person's rucksack to make him stand out as a complete idiot. Thus far Markby had worn it after his skinny dipping episode; Kirt for leaving his trousers behind at a drinks stop; Butler for asking if the Jews played any role in World War 2, and now poor Tooves. His was almost certainly the dumbest as we were now a week into the trip and he had only just discovered you had to wait half an hour after putting your purification tablets in your water before drinking it: this probably explained his dodgy guts.

Again the views were spectacular as Everest was in front of us most of the way and as we began the climb we finally began to notice it becoming colder. We spoke to several people who were on their way back down and each of these were decked out in warmer clothing. These people said they had heard all about us and generally wished us luck, while there was still the odd doubter that we would achieve our goal which only served to spur us on. This was a spur that many of us needed as the walk in was pretty exhausting: Dingboche is another village that seems to go on forever and we walked past several plots of land growing crops and holding animals before finally reaching our destination. I roomed with my sister that night and after settling in, made my way into our front room. I was pretty gutted to hear that there were a few rooms with en suite bathrooms and several single rooms as well since I was feeling pretty rubbish and had not slept at all well the night before, mainly thanks to Gareth getting up five times in the night. Perhaps it was just as well that he grabbed one of the rooms with an en suite.

It was a while before the last few people came in, and in that group were Haydn and Glen, along with a couple of the medics. Breck and Glen were sharing an extra pack between them and Haydn was looking as green as the Incredible Hulk, only without the strength. Everyone was worried about him and he was quickly put into a room and tended to by the medical team. He did not emerge for dinner that night and I was not to see him the next day either. It was a worry to see somebody in that shape; we were now at 4,410 metres so if someone was struggling badly with altitude the only real solution was to descend, so everyone was hoping it was something else like dehydration or a stomach bug. One man worrying more than most was Gareth, who now had people coming up to him and saying that if Haydn's trip was over he would be the one taking on the captaincy. Gareth is not generally one to show his emotions when he is under a bit of pressure, but he admitted to being pretty concerned about Haydn and all that came with him getting sick.

"The only problem I personally had faced was coming into Dingboche, Haydn the Tenzing Capt had been suffering and went straight to bed when he got in and didn't get up for an acclimatisation walk the next day. He was suffering from dehydration and altitude sickness and was in danger of having to go down a day. Some people joked I might have to step up to the plate.... the joke suddenly hit home more than it had ever before, I would have to cut the four guys who couldn't bat or bowl, I would have to lead the team and I would have to start thinking about everything to do with getting Tenzing to win the match. Oh dear...."

This was the first time that we were genuinely worried about somebody having to drop out altogether. Wes had struggled and obviously we had left Neil behind at Namche Bazaar, but we were always confident that those guys would be OK and have sufficient time to recover. This was different and a few people knew it.

As we settled in for the night I soon heard a commotion and it turned out we were not the only group around who were having difficulties. As I had Ian in a room one side of me and Isla in a room the other side, it did not take a genius to figure out that something was wrong when they were both roused by Kirt knocking at their doors. As it transpired there was a French lady on another trip who was experiencing some symptoms of pretty advanced AMS, staggering around as if drunk and seriously confused about where she was. The medics treated her for both a cardiac problem and AMS with some of our medication, under the advice of Motti, our doctor from the HRA, but since they did not have the tools to do a thorough examination and the only real cure was to descend, the guides and porters helped her down to Pheriche where there was a medical centre. It was dark by now but still only around

10pm, and can by no means have been an easy journey being at least a couple of hours.

My cough had also returned, and with the walls as thin as they were I received several cross words the following morning, and with the weather also beginning to deteriorate I could not imagine it clearing up any time soon. The night before there was some heavy rain while tonight it began snowing, which led to an amusing incident with Mark Jordan. He was doing a live broadcast to the studio in London, talking about the day and people becoming sick while standing in the snow with Marcus to one side shining a torch on him since there was no other lighting. As the area was absolutely silent by now they were quite clearly audible to those nearby but while everyone in our group knew what was going on, the German tourists nearby just thought they were being noisy Englishman and one decided to give Mark a piece of his mind, having no idea what he was doing. It gave us all a bit of a laugh when we heard about it, and from seeing the footage it looks like the guys in the ITN studio were pretty amused as well.

The following day was another allocated rest day, but once more there was not a whole lot of rest involved. The day began with a birthday celebration as Kinsey was turning 28: the guides had organised a cake and everyone gathered around to sing Happy Birthday, but the fun and games was saved for later. For now we had another acclimatisation walk with the idea being to head up to 5,000 metres for the first time, spend an hour or so up there and then come back down. Once again we were not carrying our packs which made life slightly easier and as we hit the dusty track most people seemed to feel all right. Haydn was left in the tea house trying to consume a bit of food and more liquid, but other than that we were all present and surprisingly I was soon up at the front. Not quite as far forward as Mike Preston and one or two others of course, but still going along OK and actually feeling fine. The weather however, was anything but fine and for the first time it became noticeably colder and windier as we got higher, a real insight into what it would be like during the next few days. Nobody is quite sure of the exact height we reached as the weather set in and the group had become quite split, showing what would happen if we all tried to walk as one group, so we stopped somewhere around the 4,900 metre mark and sat for between 20-40 minutes before going down significantly faster than we had climbed.

The acclimatisation walk above Dingboche was highly worthwhile and I think eased a few worries that some people held about reaching 5,000 metres. We had heard about the dangers of altitude so many times now that it was almost impossible to not be constantly thinking about it, and that paranoia perhaps made people think they were struggling more than they were. The slightest headache, which I would shake off without thinking about it back home, suddenly became a serious concern and thoughts of my brain swelling and nose bleeding would happen instantly, when it was just because I was wearing normal sunglasses rather than prescription ones that day. Speaking to people afterwards it was evident that I was not the only one thinking like this and while several people were experiencing headaches on the walk, none were too serious.

We were back in time for a late lunch and then spent the afternoon us we normally did, playing cards and talking nonsense. What was in everyone's minds however, was what would be taking place that night. As it was Kinsey's birthday, and he had spent the entire day walking around with balloons tied to his head, Gareth had emailed round before departure suggesting we do a comedy night where everyone stands up and tells a joke or sings a song or whatever. Much like the singing bonanza at Khumjung, a few people were understandably nervous about this and felt that it would be made considerably better by several pints of beer, which sadly was not an option. Zooby typically put it best by saying:

"I was a little afraid that I didn't know Kinsey enough to write a poem especially for him despite my asking him over the course of the past few days a random set of questions, which I thought might help. He's one of those enigmas that follows their own logic but seems rather odd to the outside world. Something I completely identify with."

Still, people prepared pretty well and there was certainly an assortment of jokes, rhymes and even a rap.

Chris Martin took charge of the evening with Gareth lurking beside him and they opened the event with a typically ridiculous song about milky tea, which was the staple drink at every rest stop and tea house along the trek, and had become something of a running joke among the group. After that the scene was very much set for a whole host of absurdities, but before that really kicked off Hillsy read out a rather heartfelt poem that his mum had written for us simply congratulating us on what we were doing. It was a nice reminder that we were inspiring others back home by this world record attempt, even if at the time we were all crowded into a very dark room in celebration of a man sat in the corner with his face painted blue and yellow, just for the hell of it, while everyone took turns to tell generally bad jokes.

Again two of the medics, Breck and Ian, shone with their unique brand of humour; each I think aided significantly by the ability to do foreign accents (does Scottish count as foreign? I think it does when in Nepal), while some of the girls re-wrote 'Old MacDonald' to 'Old MacKimbo had a farm' which of course he does. Then Will Simmons did a phenomenal Billy Connolly impression followed by Woodsy doing a brilliant version of 'The Italian Man Who Went To Malta'. Although Woodsy did a great job, he was not to be the star. The Sharland brothers had called me into their room earlier that afternoon asking for some help in re-writing 'Bohemian Rhapsody' and while I had to admire their ambition I wondered quite how they were going to do it. After they explained they were just doing a couple of verses, generally taking the piss out of each other, I listened to what they had while giggling like an infant and afterwards informed them that they most certainly did not need my help. Even then however, the pick of the night was still to come. Joe Williams stood up, quickly wishing Kinsey a Happy Birthday before admitting that he had indeed stopped to poo in one of his fields during the training weekend on the farm; then donned a hat that was a Shark's head, and morphed into MC Shark. He was flanked either side by Jules and Miles who were now in their alter egos of Base Camp 1. The rap that followed is right up there with the most absurd thing I have ever witnessed and had the room in absolute hysterics. It might just seem plain odd to the casual observer, but that is the beauty of a group of people bonding over the course of a year, we had all learnt to appreciate each other's sense of humour, no matter how bizarre they may be. A search on You Tube of 'MC Shark and Base Camp 1' will reveal this rap: words simply cannot do it justice.

Once again the evening was a roaring success and asked afterwards which was preferred, this or the singing, the comedy just shaded it. What most people preferred was not having the competitive aspect and everyone just getting up and doing their thing. It was a great time to do it as well, it was purely coincidence that it was Kinsey's birthday on the day we had arranged to rest but people were tired and tense about the next few days so a chance to unwind and enjoy each other's company in a relaxed environment was exactly what everyone needed. Wes managed to film most of it and it was just a shame that Mark Jordan could not at least have been there to see it, since he was busy editing again, as it might have given him an idea of the kind of people he was with and shown us in a different light to how he had seen us so far.

While we were on the acclimatisation walk the day before we were able to see a large part of where we would be walking the following day, so for the first time we had some idea of what to expect as we set off. The day was also significant as Kirt had finally succumbed to the wishes of the medics and hired extra porters for the final two days' climbing. I think the final straw for Kirt was Haydn's woeful state and he felt that if people were going to get sick after Dingboche it would be tough for them to catch up and so he wanted to do all he could to prevent that. The system was that you would buddy up with whoever you were rooming with that night and then share one pack between the two of you for the walk to Lobuche and then the following day to Gorak Shep. This was convenient for me as I was in with Helen at the time and we proceeded to pack all heavy things into my pack and then hand that over to the porters. When I lifted Helen's pack I was amazed, it was so light and easy to carry I felt the next couple of days would be a breeze: how wrong I was.

Walking in front of Ama Dablam

CHAPTER EIGHTEEN

A s we set off it was good to see Haydn back on his feet. He admitted that he was having huge problems with the food and was not drinking enough. As a confessed fussy eater he was rarely having breakfast on the trek and had not brought anything in terms of snacks with him either. The good news was that he was not really suffering from AMS as such, it was more the effects of not eating and drinking enough that were causing all the problems and if that was rectified he should be OK for the next couple of days. He was not quite himself, but he was walking and that's what mattered.

We began over a flat expanse where we walked in large groups and spread out. I took the pack at first and it was relatively pleasant as we walked across the open space: for the first time in a while we were not confined to walking in single, or double, file. Spirits were high too, as those without packs were able to enjoy the walk a bit more. That did not last long however as we began to climb once again; we were walking across pretty rocky terrain now and for the first time it really looked like we were at a significant height as there was less and less natural vegetation. Of course, the mountains around us were now looming larger than ever so it was fairly difficult to forget where we were anyway. On top of that people were particularly quiet: that was not necessarily unusual, it soon became clear it was because a number of significant people were beginning to struggle.

By now I was towards the back and as we crossed a small wooden bridge over a gushing river I started chatting to Will Simmons. Will is not a big talker; in fact one of the guys admitted that his Billy Connolly impression the previous night was the first time he had heard him speak, but to those he knows he is as chatty as anyone. He is also a pretty healthy individual, one of these irritating people who are naturally fit and does not have to do a whole lot of work to stay that way. He is a mean cricketer, too, and had just taken up the role of captain for Cheltenham Cricket Club, which was a pretty big deal for him. As he lives in Cheltenham it was difficult for him to be involved as much as he would have liked in the team building but he was trying to fundraise as much as he could as well as raise awareness in Gloucestershire of what we were doing, and one of the ways he was doing it was recording a verbal diary on a small recorder he was given by the local radio station, so that they could take clips and play them on air later, since he and Hillsy had already been interviewed a couple of times.

Like most blokes on the trip he did not want to complain when he was feeling bad, but he told me that he was struggling and simply had not been able to shake off a headache for the last day or so and despite being given a bit of help by the medics he was still feeling dreadful. I was pretty worried by this, and became even more so when we reached our lunch stop. We were in a place called Dhukla at around 4,620 metres (15,155 ft) where there is a lodge and small shop. Everyone took the opportunity to stock up on chocolate since it was cheaper here than it was in Dingboche and we were convinced it was only going to get more expensive as we went higher. Who would have imagined that we would have thought £2 for a Snickers bar would be a bargain?! We had covered quite a lot of distance but still had more to go including quite a steep climb right in front of us so the stop turned into one of our longest yet, but that may have had as much to do with the condition of Will as anything else.

By now Will was unable to eat and was slumped in a corner away from everyone else, hidden behind bags and what looked like a giant satellite – it was in fact a dish that is used to heat water. (A black metal pot of water is placed on the dish which is then pointed towards the sun. A large pot can be boiled in no time at all, saving valuable fuel).

It was clear that Will was going to struggle to leave this spot, particularly with a steep climb following. I also discovered that Kirt was feeling pretty ropey as well, something that he was doing his best to hide but he admitted later that this is when he started on the drug Actazolamide (AKA Diamox) for an unshakeable headache.

I was also pretty uncomfortable now as my stomach was churning once again and I was told with some authority that the toilet in Dhukla would be the last half-decent one I was likely to see until our descent in four days' time. Given the state of this toilet, my hopes were not high for what would follow. Tooves was in the same situation and no doubt a few others were as well, the hand sanitiser was now being used at an alarming rate and I was increasingly grateful to David Kirtley for sorting it all out for us. We had also been advised to start doubling up on our purification tablets in our water as quality was only going to decline and this did not do a great deal to help my peace of mind.

Eventually the decision was taken to leave Will here for the night, Isla this time would stay with him, along with a guide and a porter, and they would hope to catch up the following day. This was a big blow, even though we knew it was coming. There was still the rest of today to go followed by a half day from Lobuche to Gorak Shep - if Will was still feeling rough the next day he was going to really struggle to be there in time for the match. There was tremendous doubt over Will, even though he had not needed to be hooked up to an IV drip, and everyone was concerned.

As we set off I do not think there was anyone in our group who was not feeling terribly guilty about leaving another man behind, but we tackled the climb ahead as we did all the others - slowly. Upon reaching the top however, we were suddenly standing in a quite breathtaking place. Known among the Sherpas as Chukpo Lare, this surreal, incredibly peaceful place, is in the middle of the mountains and has views of all the surrounding peaks. It is filled with shrines and graves, with the only people buried here being climbing Sherpas who have died either on Everest or the nearby mountains, while there are many memorials to others who have died in the Himalayas. The site was identified and sanctified by the Tengboche Lama in 1970 after six Sherpas were killed during a Japanese expedition involving a man who skied down Everest. It has an increasing number of people there, again as a reminder of the people who give up their lives in the name of mountaineering. Jamling Norgay writes about the place in his book:

"Those cremated at Chukpo Lare all died untimely, accidental deaths. Reincarnation becomes complicated when one's normal life span has been abruptly

foreshortened. Dead bodies do not immediately become empty vessels, and Sherpas believe that a vestige of the living person lingers within and around the corpse for some time. If a body is left on the mountain without proper death rituals, its consciousness can wander and possibly cause harm. For climbing Sherpas, Chukpo Lare is an arresting reminder of our mortality, and of the insignificance of man in the shadow of a giant mountain. We always stop there to recite a prayer."

There are many monuments and prayer flags at the top when you first come onto the plateau on the way up, but scanning the horizon there are many located on the surrounding ridge as well. Away from all of these however, just off to the right on its own, is perhaps the most famous one. As we stood reading some of the carvings about the achievements of those buried here, Kirt came over and told me that this was where the memorial to Scott Fischer is, whose body remains high on Everest after the 1996 disaster. It is large, but by no means the largest, and is decorated with a drawing of the man, in sunglasses and ponytail. We paid our respects and continued on. I discovered later that Zooby, walking in the other group to us that day, was particularly moved by this place when he discovered a memorial to Alex Lowe who had been killed in an avalanche on Shishpangma in 1999. Lowe was regarded as the world's best climber at the time, and his friend Conrad Anker – the man who had found George Mallory's body that same year – was a survivor that day.

"Walking around, I found a boulder tucked into a far corner where there is a simple carving to someone. It's stupid to cry over people you don't know but I guess it's like watching films where you invest in the truth of the film and something sad happen; I can't help but cry. I don't know who this person is but I've invested in the truth of this mountain that it can be unforgiving and that there are dangers on it. I can only imagine what went on. I suspect that our little trek is nothing to whatever Alex Lowe had gone through. If I get back down I will find out who this person is and what they did and why an anonymous friend carved their name in a rock. It's simple but beautiful, out of the way of the main route through this place. And sitting by the rock, looking around, it's like we're being watched by the Gods on all sides in their towering majesty. No wonder they chose this spot as the place to place the monuments to the fallen. They can rest protected."

Again the walk continued in the way of the morning, lots of climbing over big rocks and paths that were mainly gravel tracks. We were all moving pretty slowly and despite the fact that my mood lifted as the afternoon wore on, I was still right at the back. Now walking with Kirt, Marcus and George with Gareth and a few others just ahead, the buildings of Lobuche came into view. I had heard a lot about this place, and none of it was flattering. Essentially it is not a natural settlement, rather a place that was built specifically for trekkers to spend a night as the walk from Dingboche all the way to Gorak Shep, or indeed Base Camp, was too much for most westerners. So it is really a bottleneck, often full of people crowded into small tea houses that were in no way built for comfort. The other problem is that at a fraction below 5,000 metres most westerners are now suffering from some altitude related illness or other and thus are so lacking in energy that even the most basic of functions is a huge chore. In my mind this place was going to be simply dreadful, I could not get the description that Jon Krakauer had written out of my thoughts:

"Three or four stone toilets in the village were literally overflowing with excrement. The latrines were so abhorrent that most people, Nepalese and Westerners alike, evacuated their bowels outside on the open ground, wherever the urge struck. Huge stinking piles of human faeces lay everywhere; it was impossible not to walk in it."

As you can imagine, this was not my idea of heaven. Yet as I approached I felt pretty good, in fact, I felt better than good, I felt elated. I have no idea why. Perhaps it was because I knew we had just a day of trekking to go before we reached our destination, or perhaps it was because I was feeling good that made me feel even better. So out came my iPod and I blared out a few songs for the benefit principally of myself but those around soon joined in when some stuff by Flight of the Conchords came on. We came into the camp, the last people there and I dropped the rucksack and poles outside before going into the tea house where most people had congregated.

Stepping into the tea house seemed to instantly flick a switch in my head, the switch being marked very clearly as 'PAIN'. The headache that came on was like something I had never experienced, I was suddenly dizzy as hell and felt sick to my stomach. I was not wearing my glasses so my vision was not great anyway, but now it became even worse, blurring at the edges as if a dark mist was swirling in from the sides, and even the quiet chatter of people next to me made me want to scream at them to shut up, if only I'd had the energy. I spotted an empty table in the far corner of the room and stumbled over there, slumping into a chair and just looking at the table. I do not really remember a great deal about what happened next, apart from it not taking long for a few people to realise that all was not right. Kiwi Palmer was quickly on hand to force a whole load of Dioralyte-loaded water down my neck but after almost two litres of water I was feeling no better at all. Medic Ian was soon across to give me a dose of painkillers and I remember thinking he was crazy as he handed over about six different tablets to take, but I swallowed the lot and said a short prayer. I had not even looked into getting a room for the night and had no idea what the situation was around me but Hillsy soon arrived and said that he had a bed saved, originally for Will, but it was in the other tea house, so I struggled to my feet and watched as he picked up both our rucksacks before following him.

I quickly collapsed into bed and lay there feeling utterly sorry for myself. Hillsy and I looked at each other and I remember him muttering the immortal words: "it's not a holiday is it?" before giving me a quick lecture on the importance of drinking as much water as possible, and perching three litres by my bed. Up until that point Kirt was pretty strict on us not buying water because of polluting the region, hence why we all had so many purification tablets, but now he accepted that people may need clean water quickly so gave the nod for people to buy what they wanted. Before too long Hillsy brought up a bowl of garlic soup, something that is supposed to alleviate the symptoms of AMS - we had consumed plenty of over the previous week or so – and told me he would bring some dinner a little later.

I can only describe the next few hours as the darkest of my entire life. When I spoke to Haydn, Will and Neil later on they all confessed to feeling the same way in their moments, but when in that condition there simply are no logical thoughts in your head. After Ian came in and saw me again, this got even worse. He said the words I already knew but really did not want to hear, 'I can say with almost total certainty that you have Acute Mountain Sickness.' Given the amount of water I had drunk since arriving he felt it was unlikely to be dehydration-related and that simply my body was struggling to cope and that I should actually ease off the water a little. I made a colossal effort to eat the food he had brought me in an attempt to show that I still had my appetite so it could not possibly be that bad, and he simply told me to see how I felt in the morning. I too was on Diamox now and it was only a matter of time before the side effects kicked in, chiefly pins and needles and constantly going to the toilet, not ideal.

As I lay in the dark my thought process was unbelievably negative. I felt that if I awoke the next morning feeling like this then it was over for me, I would be made to descend and would miss the match. More than a year of planning and training, along with three years of dreaming, would be for nothing. How could I face my friends back in the UK? The people I had bugged incessantly for sponsorship and those that I had bored to death about this magnificent project that I was so heavily involved in? Not to mention the Christmas I had missed with my family. It seemed cruelly unfair and I felt my only option would be to resign from my job with immediate effect and flee back to my parents where I could curl up in a ball of shame for months on end. Like I say, there is no logical thought process when your brain is that fuddled, all I could focus was the worst case scenario. I never even considered the fact that I might wake up and feel fine the next day.

It did not take long for the Diamox to kick in and I soon needed to pee. Having been led blindly into the building I had no idea where any bathrooms were so I staggered down the corridor and then down the stairs. I could not see much and soon just made a beeline for the outside, once I figured out where that was. It was dark now and so I just went outside the tea house, leaning against the wall and not caring if anyone could see me. The realities of Lobuche were now very much coming into focus and I would go through the same routine three more times, much to the consternation of a few passers-by, before I eventually worked out where the bathroom was.

By around 9pm Hillsy convinced me it was a good idea to go downstairs. I was feeling slightly more with it and actually felt a fair bit better as I walked down to where everyone was. I encountered Zooby on the stairs and it was honestly like I was having a conversation with a Zombie. Zombie Zooby I called him, the two of us must have made quite a picture: he had no idea who I was and could hardly get a sentence out, I was not doing much better. I managed to deduce he was going back to his room and that certainly seemed the best place for him so I left him to it. I found a space and sat down, I cannot tell you who I was with, I know Hillsy was there, and Jules who was also struggling, and the Fudakowska sisters along with Jen Gladstone who was convinced I looked better than earlier, which lifted my spirits slightly. I then just looked around the room as everyone did what they had done every night so far on the trip: play cards, chat, write in their diaries, but everything seemed to be moving in slow motion. At first I thought it was just me, but I gradually realised it was everybody. While I felt too awful to write in my diary that night, I managed a few words the following day:

"Hillsy came and got me up at around 9pm, I think, and I sat downstairs for an hour or so with some very spaced-out people. Zooby could barely see straight, Alex F couldn't do her 2x Table; it was weird, and quite frightening. Jules wasn't looking well either, and neither was Haydn. It was an utterly dreadful night."

Kirt wandered in to see how people were and seemed relieved to see me up, but he looked like Hell as well. I heard Joe was also struggling, while Haydn came past, once more greening out like the Hulk, and told me that Joe and Zooby would most likely be staying behind in the morning and carrying on with Will in the afternoon to catch us up. That sounded like a pretty good idea to me so I asked to be kept informed on the situation before once more staggering back to my room. I have to say that at times like these you really do appreciate the support of those round you and all the team-building and work we had done to create this environment was totally worthwhile. Hillsy I would expect such things from, and Kiwi as well, but having a few of the girls, who I barely knew, as well as Haydn (who was struggling himself), Tooves and Jules all wanting to help was an amazing boost and said a lot about the special bunch of people we had cobbled together. And I know I was not the only person who felt that way.

It was a fairly restless night with several trips to the toilet and my cough still getting worse. Most of us had walked from Dhukla in down jackets for the first time and many had something across our mouths to try and stop our throats being too badly affected by the dust. Gareth particularly looked like some kind of bandit with his handkerchief across his face and cowboy hat he'd bought in Botswana. Still, by morning, I felt marginally better and was assured it was not too long a walk so was determined to crack on. Simply, there was no way I was staying behind. The headache had eased, but was still there, but I felt more like myself again and was suddenly aware of how spaced out I was the previous night when I was unable to find practically anything. My belongings were scattered between the two tea houses as I had left them in various places in my desperate state the previous afternoon. Trekking poles were in one spot, hat, glove and sunglasses in another while I had no idea what I had done with my sister! Once I found Helen she gave me a few bits and bobs to carry and insisted on carrying the pack first up. I did not kick up a fuss and let her get on with it, but made sure we swapped later on, if only to convey the impression that I was OK.

I was in the first group to depart this time, and once again had that now all-too-familiar feeling of despondency at leaving two others behind. I had heard that Joe was not all that bad, just in desperate need of a rest, while Zooby was a bit more of a concern. They both wanted to reach Gorak Shep for very different reasons, but the disappointment they would have felt if they did not make it would have been as crushing as for any one of us. With those two in mind, and Will behind them, we set off, most people seeming confident they would catch up with us either that day or the following day. It was now April 19th and we had just two days before match day, something of which everyone was keenly aware.

Day Nine was our final day of trekking upwards and by now nearly everyone in the team squads was beginning to become nervous about the match, or more specifically, whether they would be selected for it. The decision to have two squads of 15 had always seemed logical as we were convinced that some people would be left behind, but as we departed Lobuche we were only missing one player from either side and a Trektator, so even if those guys did not make it in time, the captains were still going to have tough decisions to make about who to select. I'll talk about the captain and selection matters later, but the mindset of the guys in the teams varied greatly. Some were convinced that they were in and had no concerns about it at all, but others were beginning to panic slightly.

I had a small insight into what it would be like to be one of the captains when the Stick Cricket game went live. I had told the people there that we had squads of 15 and they said that was fine, they would have a squad and the starting line-up can be changed manually at the start of the game, of course the only people who would ever bother to do that would be the four who were left out of the original XI. I did not want to cause any upsets by picking a team myself so just emailed the list of players across to Paul Collins saying who did what and left it to him to sort a batting order and final XI. When the game was released I received several emails from people left out of the starting line-ups who were less than impressed, while Woodsy and Will had somehow been left out of the game completely. Will, who I am not sure has ever made a phone call in his life, actually rang me to see if this was some kind of message that he was not going to be selected on the day, while Woodsy emailed me saying that he was so angry he had already killed two people in his office. I simply banged my head against the nearest wall and said a quiet thank you for not being a team captain.

Another thing I was thankful for was actually being an umpire and so not having to worry about being selected. Many were certainties on each side, the captains and vices obviously, along with Kirt and Wes, so in each team had eight places up for grabs. Of course Hillary was now down to 14 people with the late withdrawal of Charlie BN, but Tenzing would have to leave out four people. Tooves was one person beginning to fret enormously:

"I began to think about the different characters within the 15 of us in Tenzing and who were the likely starters. Obviously captain, vice-captain, and Wes were certainties. Blinky, due to his tireless work on the website, was going to be another definite. That left 11 of us to go into 7 spots. I began agonising over whether I had contributed enough in the lead-up to the trip. Kinsey and Mike had hosted days at their houses, Dave Christie had organised and managed huge discounts and orders for kit, JC had nailed down the flights from Qatar.

I had organised the Stick Cricket game, pulling in over 3 million hits before departure, but had worried whether this had been lost along the way or whether it would be considered as a nice extra, rather than an actual contribution. Adding into this mix is a torturous record as a youngster in just missing out on sports teams. It's funny how memories as old and as seemingly irrelevant as those come back when you're grappling with self-doubt, twisting your mind into thinking that there's a curse and getting you into a bad frame of mind."

Another who was struggling was James Markby. Always the joker and rarely one to show that he gives a damn about this kind of thing, Markby was beginning to realise that his chances of selection were pretty slim. As I lay in bed in Lobuche feeling like death, I heard Hillsy having a chat with him in the room opposite, which essentially went along the lines that Markby knew he was unlikely to make it as he had been unable to contribute a huge amount to the organisation of the trip for various reasons, and had no real cricketing ability to fall back on. He was now aware that he had put himself through a considerable amount of effort and expense to get here, and was not feeling overly well either, only to be told that he was not in the starting line-up. I was too spaced out to hear what Hillsy said to him, but it seemed to have an effect and Markby would go on to play an important role on match day. It was the same all round, and from discussing this with people after the event, made for two very different walking groups on the way to Gorak Shep.

That day we were split back into our flights, so the two teams were back together, minus the guys and medics left behind. The mood in the Hillary team was generally a very good one, we knew it was our last stretch and while the walking was pretty tough over the rocky ground, we knew we were on the cusp now of achieving what we had set out to do. Meanwhile in the Tenzing camp things seemed a bit more strained that day. This probably had something to do with both Haydn and Wes struggling a little, so the leadership was a bit down, plus Joe was always good for some comic relief but he was not there either. It sounded like morale was low as they set off, and I am sure leaving Joe and Zooby had something to do with this, but it became compounded as people argued about when to stop and how long for. I was told afterwards that while there were no actual bust-ups, there was definitely a toxic vibe in the air.

A reality check also came when we were passed by a Japanese man, probably in his mid sixties, who was looking distinctly unwell. He was showing the now easily recognisable symptoms of AMS, stumbling like he was drunk and seemingly unable to focus on what was in front of him. His face was almost purple in places and those he was with were trying to give him oxygen. By the time the second group saw him he looked in real trouble, and this cannot have helped the mood they were in. By the time they arrived it was the first thing most of them mentioned. I tried to find out more information on this man, but have not been able to find anything, so I can only assume that he was taken safely to a lower altitude, as had he not made it the news would have been reported. I have no doubt this is a surprise to many in our groups who saw him struggling and even to our medics who tried to help.

Gareth Lewis takes evasive action against the dust

Alan and Kirt arrive at Gorak Shep

CHAPTER NINETEEN

I t was shortly after midday when the team of people on the first flight
saw what they had waited almost 12 months to see. Just as Kirt had
described in a hundred press conferences and talks, we came over a
ridge and looked down on Gorak Shep, and finally understood what he
had been banging on about for all this time. I whipped out my camera
and grabbed a couple of shots but was soon overcome with a feeling of
real elation. All around me the guys were jumping up and down, forget-
ting their headaches, blisters and general aches and pains, as they looked
down on the arena where we would play our match. There was a pretty
steep descent in front of us but we covered it in no time and were soon
standing on what in just a couple of days would become the world's
highest official outfield. Glen in particular, totally lost it. He was whooping and hollering like a man possessed and had launched down the slope
to the ground high fiving anyone he saw, sometimes complete strangers,
and threw his rucksack down when he got there, just standing in the
centre taking in the surroundings.

It was not long before we were all there, having a look around what
is essentially just a giant frozen lake covered in sand and large rocks.
Assuming the people already in the tea houses did not know we were
coming, we must have made a very odd sight. Most people roll into
Gorak Shep tired and grumpy and use it purely as a stop-off point for
climbing Kala Patthar to get views of Everest, or on their way to Base
Camp. Of course, Gorak Shep was Base Camp for the expedition led by
John Hunt in 1953 when Hillary and Tenzing first reached the summit,
so this place had a history all of its own already, but now it was about
to get a whole new one. Kirt and I took a moment and embraced in a
very manly way, not quite able to comprehend that we were finally here,
and once that happened there were suddenly people hugging all over the
place. It was such a huge relief, especially for me after the night before
and all the negative thoughts I had going through my head. I was here
now and had 36 hours before the match was due to start, so if I wanted

I could simply sit back and rest, making sure I was fully acclimatised by April 21st. My aim before the trip, as I was not playing, was to get up to Kala Patthar at around 5,600 metres, as well as take in Base Camp, but I would have to wait and see if I would still do that, for now I was just happy to be here.

Eventually we meandered into our tea house and sat down for lunch. The handful of people already there were quick to discover who we were, and yes they had indeed heard of us. In fact, they had just returned from a morning at Base Camp and apparently we were the talk of the town up there as well, something we really wanted to be but were not sure if it would even register. People who attempt Everest often spend months acclimatising at Base Camp and from what I am told it can get pretty dull, so we hoped that a break to see something as unusual as what we were putting on would be welcomed by many of them, plus it would give us a chance to chat to people who were actually going up the mountain, real life heroes to some of us.

That afternoon however, we had some work to do: the outfield was full of rocks, plenty of them pretty large, and we needed to clear as many of them as possible, then work out where we were going to lay the pitch, which in turn would determine where we placed the boundary markers. It took a while, and many conversations between myself, the two captains and a few of the more experienced cricketers to eventually decide on the optimum position, and then it was time to lay out the wicket. Flicx had specially designed this pitch for us, making it slightly lighter than normal wickets and having slightly more sections to be easier to carry. The guys in charge - Jamo, BJ, Nick Mullineux and Mike Preston - set about rolling it out and flattening the ground underneath, while Kinsey took up the role of Head Groundsman.

I have mentioned already how much kit we had and what a great job these guys had done in packing it all up and transporting it. Quartermaster Nick deserves immense credit as we arrived at Gorak Shep with every single item that had left Heathrow with us. I had asked him several times during the trek how much of a burden it was and he continually played it down which is a credit to his nature. He had to make sure everything arrived each day and then at Gorak Shep go through the lot and make sure it was all ticked off. I was struggling to deal with the contents of my own rucksack, half of which was just strapped to the back of it by this stage as every time I closed it up I found something else I had left out.

Out on the field everyone was quick to help out and before long we had virtually all of us out there trying to shift rocks and level the playing field, as it were. Perhaps the best part of it was seeing the enthusiasm the guides and porters for our teams had, and it was here for the first time that I became aware how proud they were to be involved in this event. I had sought out Nir when we arrived at Gorak Shep and said a few words of thanks to him, but in typical fashion he said he would not be happy until everyone was with us, but he remained sure the others would make it. For now though, the guys he had employed to work for him were setting about the removal of rocks with a vigour that could not be matched by any of us, despite our best efforts. At various stages we thought we had done the best we could and that it was time to leave the field alone, but time and again the Nepalis were having none of it. Shovels appeared, as did pick-axes as they continued to shift some of the larger rocks – which we had dismissed as immovable - out of the way, sometimes digging holes and then moving the rocks into them. It was great to watch, and so typical of these guys who wanted to play any part they could and were once again using their considerable strength and initiative to help us out.

After the initial adrenaline rush had worn off I discovered my head was throbbing again and after removing rocks from around the edge, I had to sit down. I looked up to see my sister strapping one of the porter sacks to her head and having it filled up with rocks to be carried off to the side. Not to be out-done Markby did the same and before long both these two had headaches of their own, which was hardly surprising. Medic Breck was at the side on the verge of a complete meltdown and had some pretty strong words to say to everyone, along the lines of "Slow the Hell down."

We also got news that Will had reached Lobuche and joined up with Joe and Zooby, which was good as it meant he was clearly faring better again, and we hoped they would all be joining us the following day. There was one slightly strange episode that took place however. After Christmas when Kirt and I returned from Nepal and had the whole schedule put in place, the idea to have two and a half days at Gorak Shep was for several reasons. The main one was obviously to give everyone as much time to acclimatise as possible, but we also had in mind that while we intended to play the match on Tuesday 21st - if we heard reports that bad weather was on the way, we could shift the match forward a day. Playing on the 20th was actually something that the Lord's Taverners were quite keen for us to do as they were having their big annual dinner that day and we would be able to do a live broadcast to them, possibly during the match if not immediately afterwards (the time difference was going to be an issue there considering Nepal are four and a three-quarter hours ahead of the UK). However, since the weather was nothing but wonderful all the way up, there was not a chance of this happening. Somehow though, a rumour went round that we would be playing the match a day early. It was pretty easy to put this straight among the people at Gorak Shep, it just involved walking up to the Tenzing tea house, which was slightly higher than our own, and explaining this was not the case. It was not so simple for the guys a day behind however.

The news that the game was being brought forward a day had reached Joe, Will and Zooby at Lobuche but they were unable to get clarification. All they had heard was that there was a chance it might be moved because of the weather. Once Will reached Lobuche he was in no real condition to carry on to Gorak Shep so the other two were spending a second night there, hardly a joyous experience, before getting up early the next morning and doing what we had just done. Halfway through their walk they were told the game was definitely happening the following day and they were hugely relieved, but there was still time for them to panic one last time.

As their small group came over the crest and looked down upon Gorak Shep they did not see the empty space we had seen the day before, but instead two teams playing cricket, fully kitted out in the respective outfits, with the umpires standing. Joe particularly was devastated and admitted to shedding a few very lonely tears. The walk had been very tough for him all the way up, but the dream of playing in the cricket match was what kept him going – to see it taking place without him was a hammer blow. As they walked closer however they noticed that a few things did not quite look right: there was no scoreboard, and very few spectators. Why was George Powell standing at first slip with his camera? Suddenly it dawned that they were actually watching the practice match and photo shoot that they had all forgotten about. With a spring in his step Joe bounded the last few yards and was soon out in the middle with his pads on belting the ball to all parts.

That first evening was marked by two events. In the Tenzing tea house a Norwegian trekker had returned from doing both Base Camp and Kala Patthar in the same day and collapsed almost as soon as he walked in the door. Fortunately for him he went down right in front of Breck and Nick, the two medics, who were on to him immediately, hooking him up to an IV and giving him some of our meds. Many people were talking about heading off to either Base Camp or Kala Patthar the next day, after the practice was done, but this event put serious doubt into the minds of many people who did not want to put themselves at risk before the match. Of course, selection had not yet taken place, and while Haydn said he would be picking his team the following day, ie: the night before the match, Glen was sticking to his decision of announcing it a couple of hours before play was due to start in order to give everyone the chance to be fit and healthy and be given the all-clear by the medical staff.

The other event was a bit of a shame. There was a bit of bad feeling out there about our match, mainly from people who were jealous they had not thought of the idea themselves. As I explained earlier, many people have played cricket at Gorak Shep, and even higher, but nobody has played a proper match there, with full playing kit, proper cricket balls, a wicket, qualified umpires and strict rules on overs and fielding positions. Even the professionals who had gone up 18 months earlier had only played an eight over game with a plastic bat and soft ball. Word had reached us that there might be 'bandits' around willing to sabotage the match. It was thus decided that we would not leave the pitch out overnight but instead go through the rather painstaking process of rolling it up and bringing it in, which we would do again the following day. There were other concerns such as the cold freezing the pitch or passing yaks having a nibble on it, but it was the fear of sabotage that made the decision for us.

That night I was rooming with George Powell who planned to get up at dawn and have a go at Kala Patthar. This peak is around 5,640 metres high (18,500 ft), so another significant climb on what we were already at, but George wanted to get his photos of Everest and there is no doubt that this is the best place to get them. As I went into another fitful night's sleep, full of coughing and toilet breaks, George was planning to be up before 6am and reckoned he would be back for breakfast. On my part I intended to get up when I wanted and have a pretty easy day. I would do some umpiring in the morning to get a feel of what it was like in the middle, and then decide on whether or not I would go to Base Camp, probably taking the advice of the medics and see what other people were doing. It was the target I had set myself before leaving the UK, but I was certainly not prepared to jeopardise my participation in the match by exhausting myself the day before.

Hillary were due to practise first and were on at 10am, so it made sense for me to umpire and monitor proceedings and Helen did so as well in case either Hillsy or I got sick between now and the following morning, which was not beyond the realms of possibility. In fact, Hillsy was struggling terribly and spent most of the day lying in a very dark room; I took him water and visited him whenever I was free but he was really not in a good way and I was genuinely concerned for him.

It was a beautiful day however and the pitch men were once again out there at the crack of dawn making sure it was laid down correctly and all fitted together. By now they were definitely getting the hang of it and had a decent idea of how long it would take to get everything ready the following morning. This session, though, was highly anticipated by everyone as we had no idea what the pitch was going to play like. In Trafalgar Square at the Press Launch the ball had bounced like a tennis ball because of the concrete underneath, but here with it being laid essentially on sand, there were concerns that it might just die completely and roll along the ground. Fortunately those fears were soon allayed as the bowlers managed to cause the batsmen some difficulty; but not enough to lend strength to our other main concern, that everyone would be too weak to play cricket and both teams would be all out in a handful of overs for some pathetic score. The signs were good, Hillary had a session where each batsman faced eight balls from two different bowlers at each end; not a long session but it meant Glen got to have a final look at everyone (except Will who arrived just as they were finishing) and it confirmed his desire to bat first.

What happened next was as surreal as it was exciting to behold. As we turned to leave the field, with Tenzing now gathered and waiting for their session, we saw a group of people walking towards us in two lines. It looked immediately to me like they were dressed as cricket teams and my initial thought was, 'What the Hell is going on here?' We wandered across to meet them, some people thinking they were either coming to challenge us or wanted to play a game there and then. Needless to say, with the rumours of sabotage floating around, the effects of altitude getting to most and the concerns about not getting picked to play, the reaction of a few was at first slightly hostile, although not directly to this group, more in the chat between themselves. We then discovered who the man leading them towards us was, none other than Kiwi climbing legend Russell Brice, CEO of the hugely respected climbing company Himalayan Experience (Himex). While most climbers will take any client who shows a vague level of competence when it comes to climbing mountains, and more importantly is willing to pay, Himex will generally only take those who already have an 8,000-metre peak to their name, making them an elite group.

They walked into camp and asked for Kirt, who fortunately knew exactly who Russell was, as did Glen who shot over there like a bullet from a gun. Russell has worked on Everest for more than a decade, and says that around 80% of his mates have died climbing, one example being Rob Hall. Russell is mostly known now for the series filmed by the Discovery Channel called 'Everest: Beyond the Limit' of which there had been two seasons already and as we looked around there was actually a camera man present filming for the third. This year Russell was in charge of all safety on the mountain for the season, not a job he takes lightly and not something that is just handed to anyone, his experience and know how is unparalleled and for him to come and see us was a huge honour indeed.

They were not going to be able to see the match because of climbing commitments they had as part of that year's Everest preparations and the previous day had actually climbed the 6,145-metre Lobuche Peak as part of their acclimatisation, but were pleased to at least be able to watch us practise. Of course, that was not the reason they had come down. One of their guys, Valerio, would later that day post his version of events on his blog:

"Today's 'rest day' involved one of the largest practical jokes I've ever been part of. Many of you in the UK will be aware, given there are nightly reports on ITV news, of a group of cricket-playing Brits known as the 'Everest Test' who are attempting to play the 'Highest game of cricket in the world'. Their plan was to hold the highest game of cricket ever and claim the record for the Guinness Book of Records, playing at Gorak Shep, at a height of 5,165 metres. That was until Russell found out about it two months ago on a trip to London and made plans for some serious one-upmanship.

So this morning Russell announced his little wheeze. We would form two teams of 10 players, dressed in uniform, with two umpires, and, oh, of course he had had a set of professional cricket equipment brought up for the joke. But the sting in the tail is that we would hold our cricket match at Camp 2 on Everest itself, on the flat ground of the Western Cwm, at 6,400 metres on the 28th April. This is a full 1,235 metres higher, which would of course set a new world record, and mean that their record would be held for....only 7 days. Naturally, the winners of the Everest Test match were invited to join us in a 'Mini knock out tournament', but they would never make it to that altitude given the look of them.

I've never seen Russ as animated as he was after breakfast this morning, marshalling everyone. There were to be two teams of 10 – one Sherpa (the Khumjung Tigers, headed by Sirdar Phurba Tashi), and one Western (the Icefall Warriors, headed by Senior Guide Mark 'Woody' Woodward). Each was to have its own uniform, Sherpas in orange, the Westerners in red, and all with the Himex black down vest and matching black trousers. He was such a perfectionist that everyone had to be dressed exactly the same – no scarves, matching caps – I was even issued with the same trousers as all the others because my black ones were a different fabric! Russell was manager, and given the Everest Test is sponsored by Nokia, Russell decided we needed sponsors too, so he nominated me as the 'sponsor' or money man, representing the MCC (Mountain Corrupt Corporation). I was duly decked out in the only shirt we could find, a piece of black climbing tape as a tie, and a cap on which we scrawled 'MCC' in huge letters.

Once everyone was ready the full team of around 30 proceeded down to Gorak Shep. We had sent a scout ahead to find out who the captains were and to make sure the players were on the pitch. As we approached the players, like children, we all hid behind a rock to get in uniform before the final 200-metre march onto the pitch in military formation. We could see the ITV cameras trained on the pitch and our Discovery film team were ready and waiting as well.

So Russell made the call and we marched out from behind the rock, with Russell and the money man (me) each leading the teams in full uniform and in perfect line formation with the captains carrying bats and stumps, and towards the dumbfounded cricketers. Some of our 'civilian spies' heard the captains say 'What the f**k is going on?' They were taken completely by surprise. By the time Russell got to the pitch he called the captains and they came over, and the challenge was duly handed over.

To be fair by the time the captains came over they realised that a) it would be bad sportsmanship to be anything but gracious, and b) someone recognised Russell. Soon their whole two teams surrounded us and Russell and the captains exchanged signed caps. It was all in good humour, although one of the captains, conscious that they could never take up the challenge at that altitude, wryly remarked that 'We had hoped to hold the world record for more than 7 days....'

Anyway all very funny, with plenty of good humour, and given the amount of effort they had put in, they took it well. After handing each captain a bottle of whisky, Russell was interviewed for ITV, and then we all sat in the sun to watch them practise before returning to Base Camp. The captains and some of the players even came up to our Base Camp for tea and beers later on."

The whole episode was very surreal and when the challenge was handed over to Kirt he simply burst out laughing. When I came home I did a little research on the web and actually found an article on this event on the 'Outside' website. The person reporting the story actually thought Russell was serious about breaking our record and did not realise it was just a big joke.

Of course Russell knew that we were playing an official match and that he was not going to drag a pitch all the way to Camp Two, really it was just an excuse to get his guys out of Base Camp and do something a little different. I loved his commitment to a practical joke and we all signed a couple of bats for him as well as giving him one of our branded cricket balls, while Glen swapped caps with him. Glen would later have his Scotch taken from him by some rather harsh customs officials at Doha airport, he had not wanted to pack it in his main bag in case it was damaged so had it in his hand luggage. He was absolutely devastated.

The ball and cap would later reach the summit of Everest, something that made us all very proud. As Valerio mentioned, Russell extended an invitation to any who wanted to come and visit them later that day at Base Camp before settling in to watch the Tenzing guys have their training session. Russell later sent us a few photos of a couple of his sherpas posing with the signed bat and ball in front of some stumps on the Western Cwm, quite a sight!

Tenzing then took the field to practise. One thing that both sets of players agreed on was how quickly they were out of breath after bowling just a couple of deliveries, which would make things interesting the following day. While most people now had a feed and settled down for the afternoon into the usual routine of card playing or diary writing, ten of the group and three guides, headed off to Base Camp to take Russell up on his kind offer. Of the ten who went only Glen, Kirt, Charlie Campbell and Russell De Beer were in the playing squads, I very much wanted to go but still felt pretty iffy and with Hillsy down as well it would have been nothing short of a disaster if I had gone and then both of us had come down sick, so I chose to stay back. It was a disappointment, but I would not go as far as to say I regret not going, because I made the right call at the time and I have every intention of going back there another time.

I was surprised that these guys went however. Kirt had been before so felt confident he would be OK, and was feeling much better now that he was taking Diamox twice a day, and he also felt it would be rude to not take up Russell on his offer. Glen had doubts about whether he should, thinking it might set a bad example to the guys on his team, and would be awful if he did get ill, but the temptation simply got the better of him and he very nearly paid the price. He foolishly didn't eat anything before heading off and before long he was becoming increasingly dizzy and had a splitting headache, once he reached Base Camp an immediate visit to the bakery there was a smart move and after a considerable amount of water he began to feel better and the fear that had hit him subsided.

Kirt describes the trip to Base Camp best:

"We had a good wander. We had tea at the HRA hospital tent, met some climbers. I got invited to meet 'The Colonel' at the Indian Army Expedition tent. Nice bloke. Wanted to send his boys down for a game of cricket! Told him no, as we only have a licence for one game and I didn't want to get arrested! After a pastry at the bakery (Yes they even have a bakery there now!) we left the main camp and popped in to see Russell at his separate camp. At the entrance to his camp there is a sign that reads 'Trekkers − F**k Off!' (Like I say he doesn't like visitors since they can bring illnesses). However, we ignored this as we are in fact cricketers!

Once in the camp we were given a warm welcome by Russell and the others. We were given a tour and then lead into his 'lounge tent'. This guy doesn't do anything by halves. Compared to the squalid conditions the climbers at main Base Camp endure, this camp was 6 Star! The cooking and dining facilities amazing, toilets amazing, looking at the supplies going to the upper camps, amazing. You are able to see how he has such a phenomenal record when it comes to getting his clients to the top and back safely.

However, it was the lounge tent that was the ultimate. High ceilings, full walled windows, plasma screen, DVD player, stereo, Scalectrix and most importantly bar with beer fridge! Russell was quick to offer up a beer to us all. I know we're not supposed to drink up here, but you can't refuse Russell Brice, that would just be rude. So we enjoyed a Tuborg and had a good old chat – awesome! However, we needed to get back as it was getting late and the clouds were coming in, so we didn't hang around."

It was gone 6pm before I saw the group, by which time all sorts was taking place up in the Tenzing camp. That day was also Victoria Staveley's birthday so a few people had mentioned doing a quiz or something along those lines to make the evening slightly different and we spent much of the afternoon thinking up random trivia, but then we found out that Tenzing had wanted to do their team selection.

None of them had trekked to Base Camp as they were still on the field and so had spent the whole afternoon together mulling over the prospect of not playing and wanted to get it out of the way. In our hut however, we had our own problems as George, who had already gone up to Kala Patthar that morning, was now slumped in the corner looking in a terrible state. I went across to speak to him or the medics but he was totally out of it, cross-eyed and unable to get any words out. He was hooked up to an IV and looked like he would not be going anywhere for a while. Isla said there was a spare bed in her room on the ground floor so she was going to put him in that to keep an eye on him so all I could really do was get some of his stuff out of our room and cross my fingers. He had come a long way and taken an absurd amount of photos, if he was denied the chance to get shots of the match because of over-exerting himself the day before it would seem very cruel.

I also needed to have a meeting with the captains to talk through with them the various rules and regulations we would have to adhere to in order to make the game official, and to ensure that they were happy to agree on certain aspects of the Twenty Over format we would be playing. I wanted to get the two guys in the same room but that was starting to look difficult with Glen out all day and Haydn busy in the evening. I had managed to speak to Hillsy about it and have a brief chat with him that afternoon to iron out a few things and make sure we were both on the same page as it were. News had filtered down that selection was going on but I had no idea how long it would take, or even how they were doing it, so Glen, Helen and I decided to go up to the other building and try to pin Haydn down. It was pitch black now so we strapped on our head torches and walked up there, even this short walk on a fairly easy gradient had me gasping for breath so I could only imagine how I would have coped on either of the other walks. We walked into the main room of the tea house and encountered a scene that I really did not enjoy.

The atmosphere was awful and not a single person in the room looked happy: everyone was being called into a room one at a time and told if they had made it or not, and the only people still in the room were those who had not yet been called in, with the exception of Blinky and James Butler. Neither were looking overly happy, Butler especially, so I was convinced he had not made it, while Tooves looked positively petrified. Turns out Haydn had given a big speech to everyone to get them stirred up, the usual kind of thing; play for pride, each other and all that. There were four guys who were going to have to miss out but would still have a role to play and it was important to remember that.

The second part of the chat perhaps explained why nobody apart from the girls had paid us any attention whatsoever since we walked in. Haydn had directed the team to take it ultra-seriously and that started now. There was to be no talking to the opposition on game day and no mucking around in view of anyone else. This reminded me of the final net session that took place at Lord's shortly before departure. Both teams had two nets each and started at the same time, about ten minutes into the session Haydn called his team into a circle. Hillary carried on regardless and thought little of it, but I was told later that the directive was to stop messing around and to remain focussed and committed to every delivery, especially with the opposition there watching. This struck me as extreme; we were all friends and had got to know one another very well, often complimenting each other on a good ball or good shot, while also taking the piss out of the bad ones. We are not professionals, or even close to it, and yet Haydn was clearly trying to create that feel among his team. I have no doubt it was an attempt to make Tenzing a tighter unit, something he admitted later that he wished they were, but personally I thought this was a step too far.

I finally found out where Haydn was and how the whole thing was panning out. Blinky and Butler were the first two who were called in since it was being done in alphabetical order, and had gone back into the area where everyone was afterwards, so when James Carrington did not come back everyone assumed he was the first casualty. Then David Christie did not return and it was discovered that they had now been asked not to go back in and celebrate in front of the others. Another aspect to all this was that Wes was also in the room, not as part of the selection team, but to film each person being told of their situation. Many people were really upset by this, it was not an episode of X-Factor, ITV were not filming, so as gritty as Wes wanted his film to be it seemed harsh to have a camera there during what was a very difficult time for some of the guys. What did not help was that the process was constantly being stopped to reload film cartridges or make sure the light was right, which was all a bit of a farce from what I can gather. Haydn played it down when I spoke to him saying that he was not all that bothered by the camera, the selection was part of the trip and was no big secret, but a few of the guys admitted they reacted differently because they did not want to be seen as angry on camera when they heard the bad news.

As we went to find them and see when they would be done I saw Gareth coming out of a room and asked him how it was going, his response was pretty telling. 'I feel like the most hated man on earth,' and with that he walked on, not allowed to exchange many more words. A brief talk with Haydn before Gareth came back with the next person and it was clear that we would not be able to speak with him that night. They were only halfway through and he wanted to do another talk to the guys after the team was named, so Hillsy would have to brief him on everything later, so the three of us and Hillsy simply found a room and ran through everything then. The basic laws of the game say that provided the two captains agree before a match you can essentially have whatever laws you want, so not having Haydn there to discuss anything made it difficult. He had simply said that he would accept anything we said and he trusted Glen enough to agree with what he was happy with. Once we were done with that we walked out and again bumped into Gareth, but Haydn was with him this time and they had now finished.

After some pressing I found out who was left out, and was both surprised and disappointed, but that would have been the case whoever had missed the cut.

James Markby virtually knew his fate already, but that did not ease his disappointment. Nick Mullineux was the next to hear he had not made it. Coming in late had made it difficult for Nick to really make a mark on the group, and even more so because he lived outside of London. Like Markby he is not a natural cricketer and while Glen had said he would pick his team purely on how much people had contributed to the cause, Haydn had decided on 75% contribution with 25% playing ability as a split, so that did not help his cause either. It was a little harsh after his duties as Quartermaster, but unfortunately that was deemed not quite enough.

The next to miss out was Neil Sharland. Neil had fallen ill and been left behind, so a part of him was just grateful to be at Gorak Shep at all, but he had a decent case for inclusion. Along with his brother he had led the Trim Trail sessions for more than nine months, had been part of the Events Committee and had done a considerable amount of work involving the newsletters and many other documents we needed put on headed paper. He is also a reasonable player and Haydn admitted it was agonising leaving him out, unfortunately Haydn had chosen to train on his own so had not seen Neil putting everyone through their paces. One school of thought is that Neil had not played well in the practice session that day, which might just have done enough to tip the balance against him.

The last man to find out he had not made it was Joe Williams. This was incredibly tough for Joe to take, especially after what he had gone through during the past 24 hours thinking that he had missed the match altogether before then finding out they hadn't. He admitted he walked into the room totally confident he was going to be picked, especially having batted so well in the practice, and was utterly shell-shocked when told he was not going to be in the starting line-up. Joe was one of the most popular people on the trip, and had done his bit as well by bringing Bulldog on board and making many of the weekends away and all of the Tuesday net sessions at the Oval, despite living and working on the other side of London. He had battled his way up the mountain and would battle back down again too, and had done all he could to get into shape for the event. He was understandably crushed and that would soon turn into enormous resentment for the next few days. Once back in the UK he admitted that he had perhaps been a little too caught up in the disappointment and that the whole trip was still a terrific experience, but I think he felt it more than most.

I could easily sit and give a reason why everyone in the Tenzing squad should have made the starting XI, but sadly four people simply had to miss out. We never expected to have a full complement of people for the match and it is a huge credit to everyone for making it, but that is little consolation. I was relieved I had not had to go through this ordeal, and once again felt my choice to umpire was vindicated. I had a quick chat with Blinky; while delighted at being picked (only in his own head was he ever not going to be), the whole experience had drained him considerably and by the time he went to bed he was shattered. They did however, have their team and on paper it looked a pretty decent outfit to me. I had seen the majority of them play and knew who their big players were. I also had a good idea by now who Glen was going to select, but had kept it to myself since he was waiting on a final medical check-up in the morning, so there were going to be some very interesting battles on the field the next day.

There was however, still a bit of controversy to come. After the team was named one person felt a little uncomfortable with the selection, and that was Mike Preston. He was very aware that his skills as a cricketer were well below those of Joe Williams, and he was worried that he might have made the side because he was a friend of Haydn's from before the trip started, and he wanted to make sure that was not the case. After agonising about what he was going to do he sought some advice from a few of the guys, specifically Wes and Gareth. Neither of them really said anything either way, the decision had been made but Mike was still feeling uneasy about it so he went and spoke to Joe. He told him he was not sure he should be playing and that he would speak to Haydn about seeing if they could swap. Joe could have jumped all over this but instead told Mike that while he would of course love to play, he was not going to pressure someone else into giving up their spot. I asked Mike and Haydn about this when we returned and Mike said:

"*I was uncomfortable knowing that there was a much better player than me being left out. Yeah it was a charity match, but we were all there to win and I knew we would have a better chance of that with Joe in the team. I did not sleep well that night and even after speaking to Gareth and Wes was not sure what I was going to do, so mentioned to Joe what I was thinking and he was really good about it, saying he was not going to pressure me either way.*

I was worried about speaking to Haydn, I did not want it to look like I was undermining his decision; it had been a tough call to make and he had made it, so for the players to then reverse it among themselves would not have been good for him. At the same time though, I was even more worried that he was picking me because of our friendship, which would have been inexcusable. I spoke to him just before the match started and outlined my concerns, and he explained why I was picked and I eventually left it how it was, but knowing there was a guy there who could have more of an impact than me made it pretty hard."

Haydn's take was that Mike was worried he did not deserve his place in the side, so he needed to convince him that he did. He had already explained that Mike would be batting at number 11 and was not going to bowl, so there was a chance he would only be fielding anyway, but making the starting line-up was an honour in itself and Haydn felt Mike deserved that, and explained as much. This episode is what riled Joe, and left him pretty angry at the whole thing for a time.

As I walked back to my tea house, behind Glen and Helen, I was unsure whether it was my place to tell the other guys about the selection, but I decided that they would find out eventually so it was not that big a deal and as it turned out by the time I got there Glen had mentioned it to a few already. Tom understandably wanted to go and see his brother but decided it was best to stay put for now, and for the first time I think some of the Hillary guys really started to think about the final line-up. Up until now the Hillary camp was always incredibly relaxed, but for the first time I sensed a bit of tension starting to grow. A few of the guys, Glen and Kirt particularly, were involved with interviews over the telephone and after a light dinner most people decided to retire to bed early, knowing that the next 24 hours would be the culmination of 12 months' incredibly hard work.

The pitch on match day

Match day

CHAPTER TWENTY

Being in a room on my own with George downstairs I had no alarm to set so was mildly nervous about oversleeping and missing the whole thing, so after repeatedly telling myself not to be such an idiot I eventually fell asleep. It was another standard night of coughing and visits to the toilet, but I was used to this now, although I was constantly surprised by the sight of a dog wandering up and down the corridor during the night and trying to come into the bathroom with me. I woke with the sound of others moving up and down the hallway; clearly everyone else felt like it was Christmas so were up at dawn. It was around 06:15 and as Jamo was heading out to put the pitch together people were beginning to stir. It quickly transpired that the other guys on my floor had even taken to wearing ear plugs so they could not hear me through the walls, one person mentioned that they heard snoring and it kept them up for hours, at which point I decided to go downstairs before I gave myself away.

Upon walking into the front of the tea house the first thing that struck me was that I could not see out of the window. This had nothing to do with the hordes of bearded trekkers sitting and eating breakfast - we had put in place a no-shaving on the mountain rule since landing in Kathmandu, so we really were looking like adventurers by now - but because there was a thick fog that had settled on top of Gorak Shep making visibility practically zero. It was around 7am by the time I reached the room and it was bustling already. Jamo came in after a little while saying that the pitch was all laid out but that it was bitterly cold out there. The day before I had made an off-the-cuff remark about how ironic it would be if the weather did change suddenly and we had passed up the chance to play the game in near perfect conditions. Now I was worried that this comment was coming back to haunt me, still, nobody else seemed all that bothered, or had not really noticed so I decided to keep quiet and hope for the best.

After breakfast we all had to line up for our medicals, including myself, in order to be given the all–clear, and then Glen called everyone together to announce the team. I was not aware at the time but he had already spoken individually to the three people who would not be playing and explained his reasoning to them so they at least were not finding out in the same painstaking way that the Tenzing guys had to go through, while those who were in the team did not know they were until they heard their name. He read the names out in the order which he had written them on the official Team Card that we had to fill out, which was written in no particular order. Tom Sharland, whose name was written last, must have been having palpitations the longer Glen went on without saying his name.

Of the guys who missed out, Russell De Beer was no surprise. In fact, it was so inevitable that he actually approached Glen on the morning of the match and said he had no expectations of making the starting XI but had every intention of being a team man and would be happy to be a substitute fielder and hopefully contribute in that way. Russell is another who had suffered from living outside of London, being based in Norwich, so it was harder for him to get to team meetings and socials, but he really had not been seen at all. In fact, the first time that I, or many of the others, actually met him was the team weekend in Dartmoor at the end of January. He was good to have around and I have to admit he changed the opinion I had rather unfairly created in my mind since I had heard so little of him, and the way he behaved that morning was a real credit to him. I spoke with him shortly before the start and he said he always knew he was going to make Glen's life a little easier and had just enjoyed the trek and getting to know a few new people.

The other two people to miss out were both part of the Drovers Cricket Club, and this was hard to take for both of them. The first was Jonathan Woods, which was tough on him but he would admit to me once we were back in Kathmandu that he was not overly surprised and accepted the decision. He understood that 14 did not go into 11 and that while he was the man who sorted out the insurance for everyone on the trip, quite a big task in itself, he was not as involved as he would have liked to have been. The main reason for this was a change of jobs in the New Year and a few weeks before the trip he had actually said to Kirt that he was thinking about pulling out altogether due to the pressure he was under. Fortunately he was talked round as Woodsy was one of the characters you need on a trip like this and had kept people entertained on the way up with his own very individual brand of humour. I was stood just in front of him after Glen finished reading out the names and asked him if he was all right, with the rather obvious answer being, 'No, not really, but I'll get on with it.'

The last man to miss out was John Richards. Glen admitted that this was the hardest of the lot, and that when he left the UK he would have put John in his starting line-up, but over the course of the trek someone else had put in such an effort that he deserved the place instead. That person was Ben Jarman (BJ). To be honest he was someone who I was surprised to learn had ever been a doubt, he was the only person to be at every single weekend away in January and February, and drove to all of them as well, always giving people lifts. On the mountain his efforts with the kit were probably what swayed Glen's thought process, as I would say there is not a great deal between them in terms of cricket ability. The big thing in John's favour was the amount he had raised for charity; he was the highest fundraiser on the entire trip having almost reached £5,000, a considerable amount more than everyone else bar David Kirtley. Glen spent 15 minutes talking him through his rationale and hoping he would understand, but I am not sure he ever did.

As we walked outside and began preparing I went over and said a few words to John, the sunglasses were well and truly on. I asked how he was and he said he was devastated but was not about to throw a hissy fit and would do all he could to help the team win. Just like with the Tenzing group the night before, it was tough on those left out but they would still have a part to play as substitute fielders would form an important part of the match and I tried to convince John that I could just picture him taking a vital or even the winning catch, sadly that never happened.

It was evident that both teams were fired up now and while Haydn very much had his serious face on, and was making his team stick to the no talking to Team Hillary rule, Glen was certainly not joking around either. Both teams were incredibly determined, how could they not be after what they had gone through to get there? There was a significant crowd gathering as well, which certainly served to spur the guys on, and all that was left now was to get the ball rolling, and that was down to us umpires.

Agreeing to opt out of a world record, in order to officiate it instead, was never an easy choice. As I have said throughout this book, it is a decision I have not come to regret and am actually quite proud of, but that was not always the case. There were times, especially when I was being interviewed by the occasional journalist, that I would have to reply to their questions about what it would be like to play by telling them I was simply standing at one end. One guy even said, 'Well you'll get to signal the first six on Everest then, I guess that's your aim is it?' It was a valiant effort by the chap, but again hammered home the fact that nobody really gives a damn about the umpires (incidentally, I did not signal the first six on Everest!) the interest was always going to be in the players. Considering the amount of hard work and suffering we put ourselves through to become qualified, this was always a bit disappointing, but then we were hardly in it for the glory.

Despite our troubles of the previous few days, both Hillsy and I were able to take the field, and all the players from both sides were deemed fit. George had thankfully recovered from his exertions the day before, a great lesson to anyone not to take on too much at altitude, even things that you would do with consummate ease at sea level can cause serious problems higher up.

We quickly set about putting the boundary markers in place, as well as those for the 30-yard circle, and then getting ready for the toss. Both teams were also warming up, although not doing anything too strenuous, and it was the first time we had seen both teams in full playing kit and the strips looked fantastic, like genuine cricket teams! There was a lot of other kit to sort out; finding the match balls and a coin for the toss (paper currency only in the mountains, fortunately Vicks had a 10 pence on her for some reason), getting the scoreboard set up and assigning responsibility to look after it to someone; finding the scorebooks and making sure they were filled out, etc. These sorts of tasks are a pain for every club every weekend of the summer, but for once I was actually enjoying this stuff. We even used a couple of rucksack covers to put over some of the larger stones that we were unable to move, thus making them stand out more so hopefully making it a bit safer for the fielders.

While this was going on somebody, I forget who, came over to Kirt and I and said that there was talk of singing the national anthem before the start, given that it was the Queen's birthday, and since we had been lucky enough to receive a letter from her chief aide wishing us luck on her behalf it might be a nice way to pay homage. Kirt and I agreed that despite being proud Englishmen, this was a bit naff. Both sides had antipodeans in them and this event was never supposed to be nationalistic so we said no, although Mark Jordan would later get a small group to sing 'God Save The Queen' and put that into his report for ITN, which annoyed me a little. We were then told that James Markby wanted to say a few words to everyone before the match started, and the anthem was his idea. His secondary idea however, was a considerably better one.

Whenever The Drovers went on tour in the past we always had a 'Tour Bible,' something that I am sure many sports teams are familiar with. These involve a profile of all the players, accompanied by an embarrassing photo, along with some information about where we are going and some useful phrases in the local language. I asked Jules and Jamo to put together one for everyone on the first flight while Gareth and Tooves put together one for the second. The only request I made was to include the famous snippet from the speech known as 'The Man in the Arena' by Theodore Roosevelt in 1910. Nearly everyone had commented on it and Markby was particularly keen on it, like me believing that it encompassed what our trip was all about. He requested that he dedicate the match to the Her Royal Highness, and then read the words aloud.

By now the toss had already taken place, with Glen calling correctly and opting to bat, and so with the game due to start at 09:30, the two teams stood in a line, with the umpires in the middle separating them, and Markby began his speech. This was to be his moment, and one that was shown on most of the news pieces of the day after Mark Jordan filmed the whole thing. 'The Man in the Arena' served its purpose magnificently, stirring up a bit of emotion among the guys and looking at the photo taken of the teams in a line you can tell by the facial expressions how pumped up everyone was. This was the extract:

"It is not the critic who counts; not the man who points out how the strong man stumbles, or where the doer of deeds could have done them better. The credit belongs to the man who is actually in the arena, whose face is marred by dust and sweat and blood; who strives valiantly; who errs, who comes short again and again, because there is no effort without error and shortcoming; but who does actually strive to do the deeds; who knows great enthusiasms, the great devotions; who spends himself in a worthy cause; who at the best knows in the end the triumph of high achievement, and who at the worst, if he fails, at least fails while daring greatly, so that his place shall never be with those cold and timid souls who neither know victory nor defeat."

I would have to say that this was a particularly proud moment for me, having really wanted that speech to be in the Tour Bible I was glad that it had struck a chord with so many of the people on the expedition and had to hold back a few tears myself when Markby read it out and all I could focus on was the peak of Everest just over his right shoulder. Once he finished the two teams walked past each other shaking hands and exchanging the odd hug and wishing good luck, while Hillsy and I turned to walk into the middle and take our positions.

Of course, we had not yet decided who would have which end and who would be in charge of the first ball. We discussed it shortly before the toss and I suggested that we just pick our ends and ask the opening bowler to let us know where he wanted to bowl the first over from, thus taking it out of our hands. Honestly, I really wanted the first ball at my end. The idea of standing with arm out and having the chance to say the word 'Play' and get the match underway was what I had been thinking about since the moment I knew I would not be playing myself. I knew Hillsy wanted it too and it would have been unfair for me to just demand it because I had invested more in the trip than he had. As luck would have it however, Blinky was opening the bowling for Tenzing and chose to bowl from my end, so my wish was granted and as things panned out Hillsy was standing at the bowler's end when the match reached its conclusion, so we each had our moments.

I had no idea who would be opening the batting or bowling for either side so was a little surprised to see Glen walking out to bat alongside David Kirtley. As I have mentioned, David is a quality cricketer and the thinking among Tenzing was that if they could use the early nerves and prise him out cheaply it could have a demoralising effect on Hillary and so Tenzing could really get stuck in. There was logic to this thought process, and why Haydn would have chosen to bowl first anyway even if he had won the toss, especially since they had dismissed Hillary so cheaply in the warm-up game having bowled first. With David facing first it meant Glen could stand at the non-striker's end and size up the bowler, a bloke he has known all his adult life.

Blinky took the new ball and David dismissed any thoughts of nerves by crashing his first ball through the covers for four, which did nothing for the bowler who struggled throughout his overs to find his rhythm. Despite that, towards the end of the over Glen came very close to giving him bragging rights over his mate for eternity. Having kept out his first ball, he flicked the next one off his pads, the ball absolutely shot through the air, never going much higher than waist height, and Mark Waters dived valiantly forward to try and claim the catch at deep square-leg, just missing it and instead stopping the boundary with his stomach. Everyone was amazed at how quickly the ball flew in the thin air, particularly Mark who was left with a rather colourful bruise to remind him of the missed chance. Nobody in the field was wearing gloves so hands were pretty cold, which to his credit Mark did not use as an excuse.

From the other end Dave Christie began beautifully. The oldest player on either side, his performance in the practice the day before was enough to persuade Haydn that he was a good choice to open and so it proved, hitting the spot immediately. I should also point out that what struck me most about Dave was what a total gentleman he is, I knew this already from rooming with him at Namche Bazaar, but often these quiet chaps become total lunatics on a sports field - not Dave. Before every delivery he raised his arm to make sure the batsman was ready and in he would come. A small gesture, but a noticeable one, and his actions throughout the day only served to heighten my opinion of him. He also never lost his temper when things went against him, which was just as well when Gareth dropped the simplest of chances in the gully in his first over, Glen once again the man reprieved. At our level of cricket such catches often go down, and to be fair to Gareth it came off the edge pretty quickly, but had either of these chances been taken Hillary would have been pushed onto the back foot very quickly.

For the next few overs David and Glen cashed in with David hitting the first six on Everest before Glen joined the fun by taking 16 off the first three balls bowled by Tenzing's best bowler Mark Waters. It took until the ninth over of the innings for a wicket to fall, in a manner that nobody quite expected. We had agreed to have breaks after seven and 14 overs in order to make sure both batsmen and fielders were keeping hydrated. They were short stops but it was clear by this time that people were puffing a little, not least the batsmen. David looked exhausted, and they had not yet done a huge amount of running thanks to the big hitting but the low oxygen was clearly beginning to have an effect. We had also agreed that at this stage the pitch could be flattened out again if the batting side wanted it to be, but a miscommunication meant Glen thought it was up to the umpires rather than him and so it was left alone. This was an issue I would have to deal with later and was a bit uncomfortable with, but showed that we were all struggling to take in certain things that we would normally have no problem with.

Tooves came on to bowl from my end and after two deliveries he was complaining of being knackered already. Considering he bowls little twirlers off a few strides I wondered how the other guys were feeling coming in off several paces, but I have to admit I was having trouble concentrating properly as well, even counting to six was hard work and Hillsy and I had agreed to signal to each other after four legal deliveries in every over. As usual I had my head down as Tooves came in to bowl and saw his foot land in front of the line; I looked up knowing I needed to shout 'No-ball' but for some inexplicable reason the words did not come out and I watched with horror as David Kirtley took an enormous, tired swipe at the ball, missing it completely and the ball hitting halfway up middle stump. Oh dear, my first mistake and it was rather costly. Glen immediately said he thought it was a no-ball and I muttered some kind of feeble excuse before walking away pretending to see who the new batsman was. Up until this point I had not had very much to do either, there were a couple of LBW appeals but I had already decided that to give anyone out I needed to be 100% sure, and neither were close enough to give.

David had scored a 34-ball 45 and Glen departed shortly afterwards for a run-a-ball 28 when Gareth came on to bowl and clearly wanted to make up for the dropped catch earlier, knocking over his off stump. Will Simmons and Kiwi Palmer were now at the crease, Will not looking himself and I think probably still feeling a bit under the weather, but he stuck around for a few overs in support of Kiwi who was going well at the other end. Tenzing however, had their tails up at this point and the run-rate slowed considerably as Tooves finished his four over spell with highly respectable figures of 1/21. There was also a considerable amount of chirp from the sidelines, much of which I could not quite hear but I was told about later. One bit that did bother me was people trying to claim that Tooves was bowling no-balls and hassling Helen to say something to me. I was paying clear attention to his front foot now and it defied belief that people sat behind the point boundary were claiming they could see where his foot was landing better than I could.

At the 14th over there was another break and I saw for the first time how fired up the Hillary boys were. This time they came on to flatten out the pitch. The reason this needed doing was because when it was first rolled out in the morning it was still bitterly cold, now at around 11am it was warmer and so was expanding. When it was flattened out by the non-batting members of Hillary it was clear it had expanded a lot. I doubt this had any real effect on the run-rate, but it caused a few of the guys, particularly Kirt, to be pretty irate as well as downright rude about it not being flattened at the seven-over break and blaming me for it. This annoyed me immensely considering none of them had been present when Glen and the umpires had talked through the rules the previous evening, but was just another example of how the lack of oxygen was messing with people.

Still, it was not an especially big deal, but showed that the guys on the field were coping better with the pressures than the guys waiting to come in. This was highlighted with the dismissal of Kiwi a few overs later when he top edged a ball from Mark Waters, now bowling from the other end, high towards mid-wicket where Haydn stood in front of the crowd. As the ball came down Kirt shouted 'Drop it' from the side, which was as out of character as it was out of place. Haydn took the catch before throwing the ball to the ground and turning towards the crowd while snorting and kicking the turf like an angry bull while Tooves jumped on his back and started bellowing at the crowd as well. I was not particularly far away at square leg and saw directly how much it fired up not only Haydn, but the whole of his team. Everyone passionately wanted to win and while it was threatening to boil over slightly, I was actually pleased to see how much it meant to everyone. Before play re-started I called Glen over to have a word and keep control of his guys, he was actually in the toilet when it happened so had no idea what I was talking about, but Jules, much to his credit, as next man in and vice captain, apologised immediately and the matter was put aside.

By now Tooves had taken over wicket-keeping duties and promptly taken a stumping off the bowling of James Butler to remove Will and gone totally ballistic in doing so, while Mark Waters bowled Charlie Campbell for a rapid 14 and finished with 2/32. Hillary had registered a decent score of 152/5 but nobody really knew what a good score was so the Tenzing guys felt they were in with a good chance. Each of the teams went to their respective tea houses for a one-hour break that we had agreed the day before. I found out later that Haydn was badgering Hillsy up in the Tenzing camp because they wanted to get out there as quickly as possible, but we had agreed on an hour mainly for safety reasons. I was particularly worried about James Butler who looked exhausted when he walked off and said his head had been pounding from the first ball. I knew he was likely to bat high up the order so mentioned to one of the medics to quickly check him out during the interval; of course his state of mind was actually called into question before the match started when he accidentally mistook his tube of Savlon for toothpaste and was left gagging.

I also had to deal with this pitch situation. Glen had come up to me during the break and said he thought it was my call as to whether the pitch was tended to or not, while I said it was his; but he now felt it would be unfair if Tenzing were allowed to roll the pitch after seven overs. It was being done in between innings anyway but it was still with some trepidation that I approached Haydn with the matter. To his eternal credit he said he did not mind and that they would just roll it at the 14-over mark; he did not have to do this and I made it clear that he was totally within his rights to say no, and it would not have surprised me given the chat he had received from beyond the boundary and the general competitive attitude that was swirling around. It made my life considerably easier that he accepted it, and when we in fact came to roll the pitch on 14 overs it barely moved, showing that by now it was fully thawed out and would not be expanding any more anyway.

There was a good amount of support out now too. The Trektators had obviously spent the first innings cheering everything. A few of them had allegiances but generally they were not that fussed about the result, but wanted to enjoy the spectacle. Zooby wandered around and took some photos, a few of the girls went over to the other side to sit with the medics and look back across the pitch and see Everest looming over us, while we had also picked up a couple of random people from Base Camp who were still acclimatising in preparation for climbing the mountain in a few weeks' time. Other trekkers were there as well and the guys who worked in the surrounding tea houses were all out watching too – in total there were probably close to 75 people outside of the pitch all watching the game. Included in that number of course were those who missed out on selection, but each had an opportunity to go on and field for at least a few overs and say they played a part.

Before the start of the second innings the Tenzing team lined up to give Kirt a guard of honour as he ran out to field, a brilliant gesture from those boys showing that despite how much they wanted to win that they were still aware of the sacrifices everyone, especially Kirt, had made to get us to this point. If that helped boost the mood, it did little for Tenzing's fortunes. James Butler was opening up the batting and is a decent cricketer as he had already proved with his performance in the field, but if anything he considers himself a batsman. Charlie Campbell came steaming in from Hillsy's end and after his first ball wide, his second legal delivery struck Butler on the pad and Hillsy raised the finger. Butler walked off stamping his feet and swearing profusely while muttering something along the lines of 'Umpire just wants to get in the game.' Everyone knew he was plumb LBW and he eventually apologised for his rage afterwards.

Mark was then promoted up the order from ten to three and his first two scoring shots were a six and a four, but Blinky was not having as much joy and was cleaned up by BJ in the fourth over. Wes was next man in and batted as well as I have seen him. He was not as fired up as he usually is and when he was stood at my end he turned to me and said 'Check this out man, look around you. Can you believe we're actually doing this?' It was great to see him enjoying it and soaking it up, and that perhaps helped his batting. These two put on a healthy partnership and at the seven-over break Tenzing were 48/2 and looking pretty good. As had happened in the first innings however, the break brought a wicket shortly afterwards when Mark called for a run but Wes sent him back and a sharp bit of work by Jules and Will behind the stumps meant that Hillsy was once again raising his finger. Kinsey was next in and the runs were starting to dry up as Haydn struggled to deal with Kiwi Palmer and batted out the first maiden of the day and his next over became a wicket-maiden when it ended with Kinsey scooping a full-toss to Jamo at point.

Wes responded by hitting one of the biggest sixes I have seen outside of the professional game but tried to repeat the dose the following over and Tom Sharland pinned back his middle stump. This dismissal was significant for several reasons, the first was that it was one of the only shots of the actual match that Mark Jordan filmed and was used in every news story nationwide, much to the delight of Tom and chagrin of Wes. It was also great for Tom who had not batted and had spent a considerable amount of time working on his bowling so it was good to get some reward. Perhaps the most significant aspect was what took place in the build-up. Haydn was batting with Wes at the time and the two had argued when Haydn first came in as he wanted to use the bat Wes had, which riled him slightly. When Wes was out he gave the bat to Haydn but was pretty annoyed, I think both with the timing and manner of the dismissal as much as anything else, but I was a bit worried at the time that they might have a full-scale argument right there in the middle.

Charlie Campbell returned and swung the match decisively by bowling Haydn before two balls later removing Dave Christie with an absolute gem. With wickets tumbling regularly it looked like the match was only going one way, the last hope was James Carrington who came in at number seven, surprisingly low for someone of his ability although he could not have come in any higher having been off the field during most of the Hillary innings. A great pick-up over midwicket for six signalled his intentions but Chris Martin bowled one that cut back in a mile and knocked over his stumps, leaving the bowler to do an Eric Cantona-style celebration (posing that is, not kung-fu-kicking a spectator). Gareth was next in and drove his first delivery over cover for six and there was a brief thought that he and Tooves might be able to put a partnership together but by now they needed 68 from 30 deliveries.

Gareth then came forward to a ball from Kiwi and was stumped by Will bringing in last man Mike Preston. Batting in the only manner he knows how, aggressively, Mike struck a couple of boundaries and they needed 37 from the final two overs. Glen brought himself back on to bowl his final over having helped slow the rate but not yet collected any reward, and it looked like he would remain wicketless when Mike smeared him for six, but two balls later Glen had his revenge. Mike, like Wes earlier, tried to repeat the shot and like any classic tail end batsman heard the death rattle as the ball hit halfway up middle stump.

The match had really been over as a contest for some time, something Tooves had admitted several times while standing at the non-striker's end, but the release of tension was palpable. I was at square leg and simply made my way across to collect the bails and shake hands with the players and other umpire. It was around 14:30 when the match concluded so there was plenty of time to soak up the occasion, and everyone did just that. Team Hillary went totally nuts, as you would expect, and there was a part of me that really wanted to join in. Of course, I was pleased they had won, they were the side I had trained with and been a part of and I was always made to feel part of their team, but strangely my thoughts went immediately to the losing side. I looked across and, with Everest immediately behind them, I saw a circle of pink shirts, in a huddle, and assumed Haydn was saying some words. I have deliberately not asked anyone what was said in that circle, it is between those guys, but I think they should be proud of the way they performed and unfortunately one team had to lose, that's the nature of sport.

The match may have finished, but there were still a few formalities to do and I for one wanted to make the event last for as long as possible. I was given the opportunity to do that when I was asked if Hillsy and I wanted to run the presentation ceremony, which we most definitely did. There were a couple of awards to be given out, Stick Cricket had donated a trophy for the most sixes in an innings which went to David Kirtley for striking four, while The 'Charlie BN Man of the Match Award' had to be decided by Hillsy and I. After much deliberation and several honourable mentions, we gave the award to Charlie Campbell for his 14 quick runs and for taking 3/23 from his four overs. Kiwi Palmer was a close challenger having scored 27 and taken 2/7 from three overs, but while we expected such performances from him and David Kirtley, we felt Charlie had really excelled himself. Tooves and Mark Waters also received mentions, as did Glen and Wes. It was a good thing for Charlie as well, having been one of the three expedition leaders at the start before drifting out of it when he lost his job, to come and perform well must have meant a lot.

I called up both captains and the contrast between the two guys could not have been bigger. I spoke to Haydn first and he was holding back some tears, he admitted to maybe taking it too seriously in parts, which I thought was pretty big of him, and said he was proud of his guys. When I spoke to him back in London he opened up a bit more about how he felt:

"*It pained me that, at times, I felt that the captaincy placed a certain inherent distance between me and the rest of the team, largely I suppose because of the power I had to make decisions on selection. This distance I sensed turned into full-blown feelings of isolation on the day before the game, where I felt like the loneliest guy in the camp. Selection was a horrible experience and, in the weeks following our return to England, and often since, I would think about the decisions I made that day, hoping to find certainty of logic or principle justifying my actions, where there is none. That is a difficult thing to deal with.*

All that said; the honour of leading this team of heroes onto the pitch made up for the occasional feelings of detachment and stresses of leadership. This would be one of the big challenges of my life and I was intent on doing everything in my power to help these guys win that match. It was adrenalin like nothing else and the responsibility of captaincy heightened the experience greatly. The "Man in the Arena" sentiment, relayed to us all on the day of the game, was something I had etched into my consciousness from the start of the trip and I simply decided that my team needed strong leadership and that's what I would provide.

Losing the match was devastating. I was crushed, especially having played poorly myself. But there was no point in going up a mountain, for a world record, if we didn't take the cricket seriously. Better to tell your grandkids that you went up there to play your hearts out, competed for everything, and admit to tears in the aftermath, having played like men. So yes, there were tears, and I struggled hugely with that defeat in the days afterwards, blaming myself for the loss, but I took great comfort in the overall success of the expedition and in the fact that we had simply tried our hardest and had nothing more to give."

Glen on the other hand was smiling from ear to ear. He was quick to thank pretty much everyone involved and talk of how proud he was of his guys, especially those who had not made the starting line-up. I often wonder how different things may have been had the result gone the other way. I think the person it mattered to most was Kirt, despite not being a cricketer of any special ability - he neither batted nor bowled in the match itself - his passion for his team had grown stronger every day, and even more so once in Nepal. After all the time and effort he had put in it would have been tough to finish on the losing side, and I think in part his team felt that as well, and raised their game accordingly. I spoke to him afterwards and was glad he had taken a moment out while in the field to just soak the whole thing up, as Wes had done and no doubt most others did too. The whole thing went pretty quickly, a 09:30 start all over just five hours later, but there's no doubt it will stick in the minds of everyone who was there for as long as they live. Glen wrote:

"For something to be such a huge part of your life for 12 months, a real focus of every day, and then be over, is simply surreal. Never before had any of us done something quite so magnificent - ordinary people doing extraordinary things - it was an amazing achievement. While Team Hillary celebrated, I took a moment to think about the people who had got me where I was and who had inspired me to throw everything at this. I know that they were with me all the way up the mountain and played a part on game day. I also thought for Haydn and Team Tenzing, who had invested as much as my boys had, but had not had the result go their way. Some took it harder than others.

In the end, all of the Zingers (Hillary's nickname for Tenzing) came down to our teahouse, and joined in the celebrations - after all, the result was less important than the achievement. In particular, I was impressed with two of the most competitive Zingers being the first to walk through the door and congratulate us. Vice Captain Gareth 'G-Man' Lewis, and abrasive Australian Nick Toovey. For the duration of the expedition, these two were always there to keep morale up, and the post-match was no different. We drank into the night, champagne, beers, Scotch - 50 friends celebrating taking their place in history. It tasted pretty good."

Watching Kirt and Wes take a knife to the wooden box containing the Mumm Champagne was quite a sight, but not as good as watching Kirt pop it straight into Wes's face before Wes himself grabbed it and sprayed it all over the guys nearby, something he had promised himself long before that he would do at the end of the match whatever the result. It was great to see, and Wes clearly was not all that bothered about coming out on the losing side. This was all about the bigger picture and we spent a fair while outside supping champagne before gradually moving back to our tea houses.

The teams split and went back to their respective buildings, but as Glen mentions above it was not long before the Tenzing guys came down to join us. Tooves said later that he had got over the result from 'the moment the bails hit the floor' which was pretty big of the little man. Gareth had said to me back in Tengboche that the thought of losing had simply never entered his mind; he was utterly convinced they would win and would be devastated if they didn't. So devastated he was, and said as much, but he was also able to appreciate what we had all achieved as a group of 50, not just the one team of 11. As the evening went on more and more of the guys came down and most people were gathered in the one place celebrating in the only manner we know how.

While we were celebrating several of the guys, mainly Kirt and Glen, were constantly being called outside to talk on the satellite phones to various news agencies in the UK, Kirt being quoted on the BBC as it being the 'Proudest day of his life' and that it was an 'Amazing spectacle that none of us will ever forget.' It was at this time that I was called in to do my match report by Marcus and desperately thrashed something together as quickly as I could; from speaking to him it was evident that people wanted to know what had happened and that the story was making waves back in the UK, which only served to heighten spirits further.

It remains the most significant day of my life so far, a watershed moment that proved I can be part of something great.

Winning captain lifts the trophy

CHAPTER TWENTY-ONE

A ll of us woke up on April 22nd thinking the same thing: it was over, the match was done and to the victor the spoils, while we were all able to celebrate our contribution to a world record. Except that was not quite true, it was not yet over, we still had to get back to Lukla and catch our flights to Kathmandu. We all figured the hard part was done, and as we started packing our bags that morning and preparing to head off, we acted like that as well: complacency crept in and our normal rigid procedures were all of a sudden not being adhered to, and that's where the problems first started.

When you have spent a year of your life planning and training for something, and it is then completed, you immediately let your guard down. For example, after completing my marathon in September I went for one run in the next nine weeks, I felt I had earned my respite from training and as a result was not in the best physical shape I could be for the expedition. In the Himalayas you need to be at your best all the time, we may not have been at the top of Everest, but the same rules applied - save some strength for the way back down. James Cracknell talks about this in 'The Crossing' when he writes:

"To the emergency services you are only considered a survivor when you get home. The theory is that the human body is incredibly tough and will force itself to survive in situations that don't seem possible, but that when your eyes tell your brain that help has arrived, the body seems to stop looking after itself, expecting someone else to do it for you. Apparently, this is why so many people relapse when the emergency services finally reach them."

OK, so we were not quite at that stage, but I think this is relevant to what we were experiencing. Not only that but I think many of us were acutely aware that it was not long now before we all returned to the real world, went back to sitting in an office and doing all the mundane things that we had so enjoyed being away from. The sound of the mobile phone ringing would replace the stillness I had so enjoyed in Sagarmatha National Park, while our means of transport would go back to being the cramped London Underground just as summer is starting, rather than our trusty walking boots in the open air.

One person who had definitely completed his job was Mark Jordan, and I did not see him again until we were back in Kathmandu. I think his expectations of the trip differed slightly from what transpired, and I also think he missed a trick by not filming the trek back down, when drama did start to unfold, but I guess by then the interest was over back home due to the match having been completed. I had the chance to chat with him when we were back in the city before flying home and while he was aware that some people did not take particularly well to how he did his job, he knew there was a conflict of interests.

This was something we had invested significant time in and were very passionate about, while for him it was simply another assignment. He did feel he had got something out of the trip and that it was certainly worth his while being part of it, which I was pleased about, and I also saw in him the commitment and dedication it requires to achieve what he has in his career so far. For example, the evening after the match when we were sat in the tea house drinking beer and champagne, Mark was in the corner trying to edit all his footage with his headphones on, totally focussed on the gear in front of him.

Marcus then asked me for the match report. For me this was quite a big deal and with the effects of alcohol combining with the altitude I quickly developed a nasty headache and was also aware that quite a lot of people would be reading what I was about to write. I whipped up something pretty quickly and as I was sitting next to Mark I asked him if he would mind reading through it given he was a professional journalist. It was only around 500 words so would have taken about two minutes to read, but I received a flat 'No' and he didn't even turn his head, in fact he hadn't since I sat down. At the time I found this incredibly rude and this kind of situation was very common throughout the trek with him, but as with the case involving Lucy and Miles on the way to Namche Bazaar, he was actually working and under pressure to do something to a very tight deadline. In retrospect, I probably would have dismissed me as well.

First thing that morning a handful of people rose and walked up to Kala Patthar, including the Kirtley cousins, which meant that people were not quite sure what time we were supposed to be leaving and so we were just moseying around the tea house not doing very much, and were in no real hurry to either. It says a lot for the leadership Kirt had shown up until this point that the first time he was not around to tell everyone exactly what to do, nothing happened.

We were on a tight schedule now and were supposed to leave at around 8am, with the people who had gone to Kala Patthar catching us up, most likely at lunch or quite possibly not even until Pheriche where we would be spending the night. We heard that the top tea house would be leaving first, so all of Tenzing, and that the second group would leave at 08:30, but we ended up waiting for Kirt and the others to arrive and left at around 08:45, and then discovered that the other guys were leaving at the same time, so we were all in one big group, which was far from ideal. For some reason they thought they were due to leave at 9am. Still, this was not the end of the world, but nobody was exactly on top form and we were all slipping in certain aspects of trekking life, some metaphorical and others in a more literal sense! We had up until now always been very strict with using our alcohol spray to keep our hands clean and were pretty liberal with the stuff, but I think that is one of the things that we started to slack on and it caused us problems later on.

Personally, I was tired and a little hungover, and not feeling all that great, plus we were now back to carrying our full packs for the first time since leaving Dingboche and since the ground underfoot was particularly loose I was finding it hard to keep my balance. This became abundantly clear after about 20 minutes of walking when I managed to slip forward and hit the deck hard, which was swiftly followed by a barrage of verbal abuse directed at the rocks beneath me. I was picked up and found I had Helen and Alex F immediately behind me checking if I was OK. I had been pretty lazy that morning and rather than packing my sleeping bag into my rucksack had strapped it to the back and it was hanging pretty loose. For some reason everyone was convinced that this was what was throwing me off balance so one of the guides, Prakash, pretending he was making some adjustments to the straps just look it off me altogether, along with my jacket and fleece that were also hanging off the back. I was being particularly grumpy and stubborn at the time and just wanted to be left to carry on at my own, admittedly rather slow, pace. This mood was not helped later when we began to walk in an area totally in the shade from the sun where the temperature dropped considerably, but as I now had no fleece I was freezing.

A couple of hours later Helen herself had a bad fall and had me utterly petrified. We were on the slope below Chukpo Lare heading towards Dhukla when she suddenly flew past me and landed on her back. Fortunately she was also carrying her pack and that completely cushioned the blow, but for a moment those of us who were there were pretty damn worried. After that I made a point not to be such a grouch when she asked if I was all right as clearly people needed to be looking out for each other. We stopped for lunch at Dhukla, where we had left Will behind on the way up, before pushing on to Pheriche. This meant we would be on a part of the trail we had not seen before, which was great as I think part of the tedium and lapses in concentration on the way down were due to going over old ground that we felt over-confident about.

At lunch I found out that a few other people were struggling as well, but the main person was Markby. Just as Will had done on the way up, he slumped behind the giant dish for heating water and looked in a bad way. I was concerned about him but there was not a lot we could do other than try to get him back down as fast as possible. The walk to Pheriche was relatively flat, but still felt incredibly long. I was now walking with Hillsy and Joe and spent a lot of time picking over the previous 48 hours with them. Joe was still upset about missing out on selection and there was little that either of us could say that would make him feel any better. As we carried on we soon caught up with David Kirtley and Jules and while Hillsy joined another group it was with these guys that I walked into camp.

I was surprised David was with us; on the way up he was nearly always at the front of whichever group he was in and was clearly one of the fitter guys in the group. Still, he had climbed to Kala Patthar that morning, and had probably not had a whole lot of sleep the night before so was taking it slowly. Thinking back on it I am surprised that I made the same mistake twice, having experienced the same thing with Neil Sharland two weeks earlier on the steep walk into Namche Bazaar, here was a guy struggling and I failed to spot the symptoms, instead thinking it was the excellent quality of my company that prompted him to walk at the back of the group. It was beginning to get dark as we approached the cluster of tea houses; we were able to see the settlement from quite a distance and seemed to have been walking towards it for an eternity without it getting any closer. We were still around ten minutes away when we saw a group of people walking towards us and I suddenly recognised they were guides from our group and both Nir and Dharma were there. I asked them what they were doing as they approached and they said they were worried about the condition of James Markby who was still around 30 minutes behind us, so they were taking out a stretcher to carry him if he needed it. Breck and Wes were still with him, but it was really quite dark by now and I did not envy those guys going back out to help. They thought he was suffering with exhaustion, and turned out to be right, although I discovered later that all three of these guys were suffering from diarrhoea and vomiting and Markby was indeed carried into camp that night.

Being in the camp was a relief, but again I was far more spaced out than I thought I was. I shared with Woodsy in a different building to where the tea house was and decided to have my first shower since Namche Bazaar nine days previously, which was once again colder than the driven snow, but served its purpose. When I went back into the main building I sought out the medics and found Ian and Isla, I was still coughing almost non-stop and it was driving me, and plenty of others, up the wall. My headache had not yet subsided either so the guys gave me a few tablets and told me to keep on the fluids. When I went in for dinner I was pretty lightheaded and unable to make much conversation. Nick Walker came over and told me he did not want me to carry my pack the following day, which I did not take overly kindly to. I tried to put up a fight by saying that I was sure I'd feel better in the morning. He decided to massage my ego by saying that Wes was ill and Kirt was having stomach issues too and so he did not want me, as next in charge, to get ill (his words not mine!) which made me feel rather important and so I let it go. I was not happy about it, with everyone else carrying their packs I simply felt like I was not playing my part if I did not take mine. I found out later that Kirt had told Nick I would put up a fight and not to have any of it, so at least it was known that I was not going lightly!

I took what I was given by the doctors and had my best night's sleep for what seemed like a month, when I went to the dining room of the other building the next morning it was only then I realised what kind of state I was in the night before. Just like in Lobuche my stuff was scattered all over the place, trekking poles on opposite sides of the room, my hat, fleece and water bottle in one corner and my sunglasses in another. Clearly I was far worse off than I had realised and decided not to argue any more about my pack and just put together a tiny day sack that I had borrowed from Helen. I did feel like a bit of a letdown, heading off sans backpack with everyone else still ploughing on with theirs, but ultimately it was the right call by whoever made it, as had I carried it that day I would have had a terrible time. Fortunately for me that did not happen, but almost half of the group were not so lucky as we were about to experience the lowest point on the entire expedition.

After the match was finished Kirt decided to change our schedule slightly, it was not an easy call to make, but he had heard reports that the unseasonably good weather we had experienced up to this point was not going to last much longer. This created new problems, he needed to get everyone back to Kathmandu in time to connect with their flights home, but the flights from Lukla only run if the weather is fit for flying, it is too dangerous otherwise. With this in mind the call was made to walk down in three days rather than four; we always knew the descent would be tough and now it was going to be even tougher. What it meant though, was that we would have an extra day in Lukla should we need it if no flights left on our day.

That morning we set off slightly later than intended once again because more people had fallen sick in the night; David Kirtley was one of them and I went to see him as soon as I heard. Going into his room, shortly before we were all due to leave, I quickly realised that things were pretty serious; he did not look well and was barely speaking. All the same, we had to go and for the first time we were splitting into three groups with the sick guys being the third, including David, Wes and Markby, as well as Breck, who was also now sick, meaning they needed another medic with them so Nick Walker stayed back too. The first part of the walk was easy going and quite pleasant. We were flanking Ama Dablam and I once more marvelled at how that mountain looked totally different depending on what angle you looked at it from. I had some good conversations as well with the guys I was with, including one person I did not know; Dane Cunningham is a friend of both Kirt's and Zooby's and in a rather weird small-world twist is Glen's step-brother-in-law. He was travelling on his way back home to Australia and upon hearing about our trip asked if he could tag along. For the first few nights he stayed in separate tea houses and ate his own food, but after a while we agreed a fee with Nir that he would pay and just join the trip as one of us. He certainly looked the part with his giant beard and general Yeti-like appearance and turned out to be a pretty good lad as well.

As we came in to our lunch stop the sun was shining and everyone was in good spirits, particularly after a more flavoursome meal than what we had become accustomed to during the last week or so. As was normal the second group caught up and went and sat inside and eventually the last guys arrived as well, proving to us all that they were still alive. The first group of us had spent too long there, and this was where the problems started; Dane had shot off ahead because he needed to reach Namche in order to change his flight out of Lukla so he could go in with us and wanted to get there before everything closed, I should have realised that this was an indication of how long we had sat there for. The next indication was when Jamo came out and asked if he could leave with our group since he had eaten his lunch and wanted to get going. I was not keen on the idea and said as much, thinking that we needed to stick to our original groups, but he was not particularly happy with that and I caved and told him to check if it was all right with Kirt.

As I left with the first group I noticed that Jamo was with us, as was Kiwi, Russell and Mike Preston who had not been there before, and a couple of others as well. After we had been walking for around half an hour I heard Kirt on the radio confused as to where the hell half his people were and why they had all just buggered off. This was where the problems started as now the front group had more like 25 people with the two behind having 15 and ten respectively. Not only that, but nobody was quite sure who was in what group and as people began to stride ahead this became even harder to ascertain. I did not concern myself too much with it at first, but when we reached our scheduled place for an afternoon stop things began to come to a head.

By the time I arrived, although not quite last man in, the people at the front had been waiting for around 45 minutes and wanted to get a move on since they were beginning to get cold. I was adamant that we should be staying as a group and since people were still arriving they were just going to have to stay put. The situation was then compounded when Joe Williams began to get seriously sick. After lying down for around ten minutes he promptly threw up and things were getting pretty bad. By this time the people at the front of the next group were arriving so I went to meet Kirt as he came in so I could have a quiet word with him and explain the situation. Despite insisting that I should speak to him alone, as soon as he arrived around four other people jumped on his case and told him what they thought we should do. Kirt, who was not feeling great himself and trying to hide it as best he could, got a bit irritated with everyone crowding him and so I never actually spoke to him at all. The call was made to carry on but leave Joe with the second group for another 30 minutes or so in the hope that he might improve while one of the guides took his pack, the poor bloke was probably not helped by the fact that he had to have an injection into his backside to try and help quell the nausea, and that Chris Martin found this utterly hilarious.

We pushed on and in no time the group was spread out too far to be able to keep track of. We were now back to paths that undulated constantly and there seemed to be no respite. I was in a group with Gareth, Zooby, James Carrington, Glen, Blinky, Jen and Sugar and as the sun began to fall behind the mountains so people began to struggle. It was like watching people crack on the Alp D'Huez of the Tour De France as they would suddenly lose the ability to keep up the walking speed we were going. Zooby was the first to go and Gareth and I split what stuff he was carrying to try and make his life easier. Then Glen began to struggle, and in a way I was deeply disturbed about this. We were walking, as we often were, on the edge of a mountain with a path just wide enough for two people side-by-side. If the person on the left slipped, he would tumble to an inevitable death, so when Glen began to swagger all over the path I became very worried about him. I was incredibly grateful to not be carrying my pack now, and Gareth had already pointed out more than once how much more talkative I was compared to everyone else. When I realised how badly people were struggling I took it upon myself to try and keep them going, so I made sure Glen walked on the inside of me as I was terrified he was going to tumble down the side of the mountain.

The walk seemed to go on forever. Every time we came round a corner hoping to see the end we were just greeted with another long and winding pathway as far as the eye could see; it was spirit-crushing. Soon we were caught up by Haydn and Tooves who were in the other group, Haydn shot passed but Tooves stayed and walked the rest of the way with us, and we had also picked up Woodsy somewhere along the way. When we finally reached the top of the hill that would take us into Namche Bazaar the whole group was virtually broken. We were talking only to encourage each other on and convince ourselves that it could not be too much further. Everyone held it together, just about, but it was incredibly tough. It was very dark by the time we reached the village, and we were in the first group so there were still a good 20 or so people behind us. Tooves was practically walking on one leg by this point having rolled his ankle earlier and we had also been joined at the last stages by Lucy whose knee had just about given up altogether. We stumbled into the tea house like we were returning from a war.

When I entered the tea house, my sense of humour really failed me. As we came in one of the guides was out on the path saying to follow the road down and go into the first building we saw, these were not the easiest instructions to follow but we made it without any real difficulties, but upon walking into the dining hall the first thing I saw was a group of around seven of our guys having a beer and eating steaks. That in itself is no bad thing, but these guys had come in ages ago, they were the quickest walkers and the strongest guys and while the lesser lights were coming in behind them, in dire need of help, their first thought was to have a beer and order themselves some food. To be honest, I was livid, and so were several others.

It was not long before the rest of the second group caught us up as well and reports were coming in about who was struggling. I heard Will was in trouble again and that Jules was as well so I set about ordering as many bottles of fresh water I could to hand them out to people as they arrived. Then I heard that Jules had collapsed on the trail and was having chronic problems with his back. Having slipped a disk during the lead-up to the event this got me particularly worried so I sought out someone who could get a room sorted for as soon as he came in. He arrived with his wife Victoria and while she seemed OK, he was worse than I imagined. Green as anything and totally unable to speak, he said afterwards that he had no recollection of arriving, only of passing out and waking up in the night, our guide Shambu had virtually carried him in. Joe had also been throwing up throughout the afternoon and evening and was in desperate need of help, being put straight to bed on arrival. Kirt had arrived by now, as had Hillsy who was perhaps the angriest of all that there were no people out helping and said as much too. Alex F also pointed out that hardly anyone had asked her how she was in the previous two days, and that it seemed nobody really gave a damn about anyone other than themselves now that the match was over.

In fairness, a couple of people first in went round apologising that night for splitting the groups and not helping the others in, they did not realise how bad the situation was because they had gone so far ahead that nobody among them had a radio. Isla was also quite irate as with Ian in the second group and Breck and Nick at the very back, she was effectively left dealing with somewhere between 25-30 people and had no idea if these people were in front or behind her. If someone had fallen ill then they simply would have to wait until she got there. For the first time we had really come apart as an expedition and tempers were fraying. The guys in the final group made it in eventually, in almost total darkness, and by the time they arrived food was waiting for them. Despite this low point, and all that it involved, everyone came through it, and when I sent my questionnaire round after the trip, I asked the question 'What was your favourite day of the trek?' Inevitably most people answered with the day of the match, but one person wrote this:

"My favourite day was the descent to Namche Bazaar, when I had the warmest feeling of team spirit on the trip, albeit in a tiny group. I will never forget the support, optimism and sense of humour of a small number in the face of adversity. A brilliantly exciting day / evening, arriving in the most extraordinary of towns well past night fall, having done 22km."

So despite the overall break-up of the expedition that day, once again the small pockets of people were helping each other on. It was just like when we had arrived in Namche on Day Two of the trek, but even more extreme.

Kirt was a bit all over the place, at one point suggesting that we might need to go out and find somewhere to charge the satellite phones. That never happened and before long he was putting himself to bed, a wise move as his resolve and decision making was really being tested. He knew it would be tough on the way back down, but had not bargained on everyone getting sick. Things seemed to be calming down however, despite someone who was not even part of the trip throwing up in the middle of the dining area and us discovering there were not enough rooms at the inn so Mark Waters and Dane volunteered to be moved (a selfless act I think they both regretted after seeing the state of their alternative accommodation!), and while Hillsy and a couple of others tried to persuade me to sit up with them for a while I opted to crash since it was another hefty trek in the morning. My day was still not complete however, as I walked down the stairs to my room where Tooves was already asleep.

It was colder than I was used to so I wrapped up fairly warm and switched off the light. I was desperately trying to sleep and as I began to doze off I suddenly felt a wave of nausea hit me. I tried to belch but only managed to throw up in my mouth. I rolled over and tried to ignore it, that along with the fact that now around half the group were suffering from D&V. Moments later I could ignore it no more, fortunately the bathroom was next door, but unfortunately I had done my sleeping bag up so tight I was struggling to get out. Finally I was free and I grabbed my head torch and loo roll as I had earlier found that the light in the bathroom was broken. This delay was crucial however, as I threw up all over the bathroom, except in the toilet. It was a truly upsetting experience and as I stood there heaving I heard someone stirring outside in the corridor, fortunately it was Helen and she came to see who was making such disturbing noises, all I could mutter was the word 'Medic' and she went running off to bang on some doors since she had no idea where the guys were sleeping. Eventually Isla appeared and by now I had done a vague clean-up job on the bathroom and was sat in the corridor. Nir arrived as well and looked utterly horrified at what was going on, not being able to help at all. When Chris Martin was laughing about Joe getting an injection in his butt I genuinely thought it was a joke, but soon discovered it wasn't when Isla instructed me to drop my shorts and inserted the needle in the 'fleshy part' of my body. I was pretty miserable as I climbed into my sleeping bag, having thought I had gotten away without having as bad a day as everyone else. Isla's parting words were 'Keep the loo roll handy, you're going to be doing a lot of sweating and pooing during the next 24 hours or so.' Well that's just splendid I thought.

The following morning I was wary about the day ahead, but I had got through the rest of the night without any further problems and so I took a few painkillers and said a quiet prayer before heading out to join the others. We were all gathering outside and surprisingly spirits seemed pretty high, Wes was certainly very talkative and I think everyone was just happy that this, after exactly two weeks actually on the mountain, was going to be the final day of trekking and by the end of the day we could finally relax. If only that was the case for everyone.

As we set off, this time going down the huge slope that we had all struggled up, I decided right away that I was going to stick at the back with Joe, who had Ian keeping him company to make sure he was OK. The walk itself was not overly strenuous, but it was pretty slow going. Mr & Mrs Staveley came past and I was glad that he was back to his normal self. It did not take long for us to fall quite a way behind everyone despite Ian being the only one carrying a backpack. Surprisingly I actually felt all right, but Joe clearly did not and we were stopping regularly. The scheduled lunch stop was at Phakding, where we had spent our first night on the trail, and we wanted to get there to have lunch with everyone else. This was when I really lost my rag with the workings of 'Nepal time,' while I was used to the odd time estimate being ten or 20 minutes out, once it became two hours out I really started to lose it. As we reached the bottom of the steep climb we spotted Hillsy, Will and Wes not too far away in the distance, but they moved ahead as Joe stopped to throw up and Ian administered another injection. We did catch them up a short while later and felt pleased that we were not too far behind the others, but it would be several hours before we saw them again.

By midday Kirt came on the radio to ask how we were and we said we were making steady progress, he did not think we were that far behind and said they would be stopping for lunch soon and was confident we would reach them. By 13:00 the guides said we were around 45 minutes away from lunch and asked if we wanted to stop and eat now instead. We figured that 45 minutes was not beyond us and so would push on, they must have asked us every 20 minutes from then on if we wanted to break for lunch but as we were convinced that Phakding was just around the corner we carried on. Had we known that at 13:00 we were in fact still more than two hours away we would have stopped, as it was we got to Phakding at 15:15 and Joe simply collapsed inside. The others were still there but had been waiting for us for quite a while, Kirt asked how I felt and I was surprisingly OK. He said they had to get a move on and one or two others offered to wait with me for 30 minutes if I wanted to get some food down before pushing on. I said I was happy to crack on right away as I felt good but Nir was adamant that I eat something. When I went and looked at Joe it was clear he was going nowhere and that he and Ian would have to catch up the following morning. I was really torn, I so wanted to finish the trek with everyone and enjoy the inevitable celebrations that would take place in Lukla, but I also felt a responsibility to Joe. The guy had been through a hell of a lot on this trip and I wanted to help him out if I could. He was totally unable to focus and even though we got some water into him he was unable to keep it down. We found him a room and hooked him up to an IV drip once again and I watched as the others departed without us.

As it turned out, a lot of people were struggling in the group in front but were keeping it to themselves. Hillsy admitted later that he should have stayed with us such was the state he was in, and David Kirtley and Lucy were much the same. David fortunately had a packet of jelly babies with him which he had brought from the UK and he gave them to us as a means of getting some sugar into Joe; I think that packet of sugary goodness may just have saved him! Ian and I took the opportunity to chill out during the afternoon, and the radio was constantly buzzing into life with jokes and those at the front offering to help those behind, the lessons of the previous day clearly learnt and once again things were back as they should be. Ian and I discussed this at length and said how great it was that all the bad feeling from yesterday had vanished with the dawn of a new day; it really proved how close this bunch of near total strangers had become during all the build up and how important that was. Had we been strangers when arriving on the mountain I think it would have been very easy for bad feeling to fester and cause problems, but there was no chance of that with these guys.

Ian and I took the opportunity to check our emails and surf the internet for the first time since leaving the UK, it was the first time I was able to contact home and let them know we were all OK and the trip was a success, although once I went onto the net to see what coverage our match had received I need not have worried about people knowing. There were reports all over the place about what we had done, the BBC and CNN websites both had reports as did most major newspapers not to mention a whole load of smaller ones. It felt good finding this out and Ian and I had a couple of beers that night in quiet celebration. We were worried about Joe though and he was still unable to keep his food down that night. We knew we needed to be on the trail early the next day if we were going to catch our flights, and with me being on the first flight out of Kathmandu had I got stuck in Lukla for a day then things would have become a bit nervy. The alarms were set for 5am and we crashed hoping that Joe would be all right.

Meanwhile the others were steadily making their way into Lukla. The way from Phakding is deceptively long with a bit of a climb at the end, but on they went and fittingly it was Kirt and Wes who came up the slope and rounded the corner into the village together. When the people drinking in the local bars realised that this was the group of cricketers spontaneous cheering broke out and before the guys knew it they were being showered with beer. It did not take long for Kirt to join in and within minutes he had a beer in his hand and spent much of the evening exchanging words of thanks and congratulations to virtually everyone involved. There were high-fives being thrown out all over the place and the majority of people had a great feeling of elation. Sadly it was not quite everyone as Hillsy was sick shortly after stumbling in while Lucy was in pieces as well. Those who could celebrated into the night while those who couldn't forced down a beer or two before collapsing into a well deserved sleep.

The three of us still had this last section to cover the following morning. I had wanted more than anything to finish the trip as a group, now that I could not do that I was determined that we would at least get to Kathmandu together, hence the early start. The guide that stayed with us, Shambu, was up at 5am and we were on the trail by a little after 05:45, deciding to have breakfast somewhere on the way. By the time we reached that point we were within range for the radios again and Kirt came through to say that they were all at the airport and waiting to depart but they would leave a guide behind for us and there would be no problem getting back to Kathmandu. Again I was disappointed and every plane I saw flying out of the airport that was now in sight away to our right I assumed was carrying some of our group. We finished breakfast and continued on, coming into Lukla a little after 08:30 having spent an hour over breakfast. I heard a cheering and at first thought it was Prem, the guide who Kirt said was staying behind, since he is such an excitable chap, but as I squinted through the fence I suddenly made out Kirt, Gareth and a few others. Down we dashed and we had made it in time to join with them. There were seven guys left at the desks and I hugged each of them just being so happy to have met up with some of the group again. Meanwhile Joe was once again dropping his trousers to have a fifth injection in his ass, this time immediately behind a girl who was sat at a desk checking people's tickets. We dropped our bags and walked through 'security' where I discovered all but nine of the expedition, and felt even better.

Returning to Kathmandu and checking into the Kathmandu Guest House, this time without any issues, felt great. People were beginning to recover and it did not take long for the beers to be cracked open and the varieties of food to be ordered. That night we drank in Tom & Jerry's, the well known watering hole in Thamel, while the following day many of us recovered by paying a visit to the Yak & Yeti Hotel. There we were able to use the swimming pool after some negotiations with the staff and thankfully Joe was finally restored to a degree of health. This was the day Kirt had cut from the trek to ensure we got off the mountain in time and, while we had not needed it in the end, an extra 24 hours in the relative comforts of a city were incredibly welcome. Not everyone was though as people continued to come down with the same illness the guys had on the mountain, but that night we all reconvened at Rum Doodle, the restaurant all of the guys on Flight One visited that first night.

There we gave out gifts to Kirt and Wes by way of thanks while Vicks Nicholson and I also received a token of appreciation, which was touching. Before cracking on to the booze once again and racing rickshaws through the streets, we paid a visit to the Central Bank of Nepal which bizarrely has a bar on the top floor where we were able to see a small video. Alex Rayner back at Captive Minds had put to music a collection of footage and images of our whole trip and it had taken Marcus 18 hours to download it in Kathmandu. After it was shown everyone went nuts, so much so that we had to watch it three times. After that we took the disc off to Tom & Jerry's and got them to put it on every TV screen in the bar, and run it on repeat. It was a little self-indulgent, but we really did not give a damn. We had done it, the expedition was a success and we were going to celebrate it in every possible way we could.

EPILOGUE

EPILOGUE

_____

The flight home was relatively uneventful for my group. We had around five hours in Doha airport and numerous people were still falling ill, Helen having to stop the mini-bus on the way to the airport to throw up in the street. Landing back at Heathrow we were greeted by a few friends and family, including Alex Rayner whose bear-like figure I was never more pleased to see. Again an Addison Lee coach was waiting to take us back to Clapham Junction where we arrived some time after midnight and I hopped in a taxi home. I discovered later that Jules and Victoria Staveley were to have another moment similar to that in Doha on the way out when Jules left the house keys on the coach and they ended up tracking it down to a depot in east London at 3am.

The Tenzing group however, had a miserable flight. They were due to arrive the next day and a number of them were going straight to the office, but they were re-directed to Gatwick because of bad weather and sat on the tarmac there for four hours, which cannot have been any fun at all.

Getting back to the real world was a strange feeling. Thankfully the following Monday was a bank holiday so we had a short week followed by a long weekend. I was not able to enjoy this as I finally fell foul of the virus that had gone around and on Friday afternoon was sent home from work and remained on the sofa for the next 48 hours. I was reminded by Wes however, that he would have happily swapped places with me if it meant not getting ill coming down the mountain, so I stopped grumbling. Team spirit saved my bacon though, as Glen and Jules heard I was suffering and phoned round everyone to track down some leftover antibiotics and James Carrington duly delivered them to my flat on the Sunday night.

Getting better was particularly important for one incredibly strange reason. While we were on the trek Gareth Lewis had received a text message from his girlfriend saying that we had a fan in Chris De Burgh and that he wanted to invite us to a concert of his to give us an Easter

Egg. When we returned the full story was unveiled as it turned out he was a guest on *London Tonight* and saw one of their daily updates about how we were getting on over the Easter Weekend. He had been given this enormous Easter Egg by the *One Show* and wanted to pass it on to us by way of congratulations.

And so it was that a week after we returned Wes, myself, George Powell, Jules Staveley, Blinky and Marcus Chidgey took to the stage in front of a full house at the Royal Albert Hall and were ceremonially presented with an Easter Egg by Chris De Burgh's daughter, Rosanna Davison who was Miss World 2003. Chris regaled the crowd with tales of who we were and how much he loved the British Adventurous spirit before asking Wes a few questions. Mark Jordan was there to film and was in super spirits, clearly enjoying having real power to run his camera, plus warm surroundings and an even footing. To complete the strangeness of the evening Marcus and I convinced Wes it was a good idea to ask the former Miss World on a date, which he duly did and they went off to watch the Polo together some weeks later. Much as we have all come to love Wes, I think if the relationship had been any more than this single outing it would have been too much for most of us to bear!

After that things began to settle down and everyone moved back into their normal lives. Not all of us did though; I quit my job and went home to Cornwall to write this before disappearing off travelling, which did not really end until July 2010 when I took a new job with the Adventure Travel Company Wild Frontiers and in July 2011 spent five weeks trekking through the Wakhan Corridor in Afghanistan and another month going up to K2 Base Camp in Pakistan. Kirt and Vicks signed up for a six-week mountaineering course in Patagonia the following January. This has enabled Kirt to lead around 200 people to the summit of Mount Kilimanjaro in 2010 as well as take a group around Nepal's Annapurna Circuit while next year he hopes to climb his first Himalayan Mountain when he leads a group up the 6,476 metre (21,245 ft) Mera Peak, as well as doing the Inca Trail at the time of writing. Vicks meanwhile went on to work for both Russell Brice and extreme sailor Olly Hicks and spent time living the dream in Chamonix. Ben Jarman completed the Mongol

Rally in 2010 while Will Wintercross continues to photograph extreme parts of the planet. Kirt and Wes continue to talk about the next project, but as yet nothing has unfolded. Having toyed with the idea of repeating the cricket, Kirt and I decided that it was simply too much for the two of us to run alone, with no funds and no help from the Nepal Tourist Board who had previously appeared so keen to make it happen again.

We were both left penniless by The Everest Test, Kirt himself ended up swallowing around £3,000 after various outstanding debts were called in. Captive Minds were paid less than they felt they were owed, The Lord's Taverners were unhappy with the amount of money they received so turned down our pleas for help and Mission, the PR company for Nokia, continued to refuse to pay bills for branding and shipping of kit. All that was a disappointment and has taken more than a year to conclude, but it is done now and the biggest lesson we have learned is never to stretch ourselves so far again. We aimed high, and in the end raised around £100,000 in total for the Lord's Taverners, Himalayan Trust UK, Sport Relief and The Himalayan Rescue Association. That's one hell of an achievement no matter which way you look at it. Surrey County Cricket Club lent us the use of one of their function rooms to hold a photo exhibition of George Powell's shots.

Once we returned a few people were reined in by their partners, which is entirely fair. As a group we had been incredibly self-involved for the previous 12 months and were lucky that family, friends and partners had been so supportive and accepted our absences at Christmas, weddings, birthdays and Easter to name but a few. Now they wanted their loved ones back.

We recently heard that the money we raised for the Himalayan Trust UK was put to use in the Kanchenjunga area of Nepal. George Band, their President, was the first man to climb this mountain, at 8,586 metres (28,168 ft) the third highest on Earth, and has always wanted to give something back to that region. The money we raised has gone to providing teachers, uniforms and other essential items for schools throughout the region, which is something we can all feel proud of. The Himalayan Trust were always incredibly grateful to us and we were invited to the Royal Geographical Society for a talk given by Chris Bonington on his Everest Experiences where afterwards they showed the four-minute video that Captive Minds put together which has become a real reminder for all of us of that very special time.

I can happily say that I am still in touch with most people from the trip. A few have dropped off the radar, but the occasional email still goes around and most of us managed to make a One Year Reunion party and the premiere of Wes's movie. I think our biggest achievement was forming the relationships we did with a bunch of people who knew precious little about each other but all shared a common goal. It seems only right to give the final words to Richard 'Kirt' Kirtley:

"An immense amount of hard work went into The Everest Test 2009 and there were so many highlights, both in the build-up and on the expedition itself. One thing that amazes me is how 50 almost perfect strangers can bond so completely in a common cause and pull together to achieve something truly special. It was watching these bonds form during the whole trip that form my highlights.

On the expedition itself I really felt in my element. Of all the many things I have done in my life few match the satisfaction that leading everyone up the mountain brought me. We were blessed with the weather, but it was the willingness of everyone to pull together that was great to see. Highlights must include coaching the children of Shangri-La Cricket Academy and Khumjung School, seeing the locals help us prepare the pitch at Gorak Shep, sharing a beer with mountaineering legend Russell Brice at Base Camp and working with Nir Lama of Peace Nepal Treks and all his amazing guides and porters.

However, nothing will bring a smile to my face quicker than remembering taking time out from the match to look at the amazing scene before me. Something that I had imagined three years previously was actually happening before my very eyes and I was sharing it with 50 people who I have come to hold in the highest possible regard. That was a very special moment indeed."

EVEREST TEST PEOPLE

B elow is a list and brief description of everyone who came along on The Everest Test 2009, split into their respective teams and put in alphabetical order within those teams. Any nickname they may go by during the book is in brackets.

TEAM HILLARY

Charlie Bathurst Norman (BN)

A friend of the Drovers through a long running rivalry with his own club, the Maladroits, Charlie BN really came into our group in 2007 when meeting Alan Curr and Jonathan Hill in Barbados during the Cricket World Cup, and wanted to be part of the expedition from the off. He batted in Trafalgar Square at the January Press Launch, hitting a six into a fountain, became a qualified umpire and was our main link to Surrey County Cricket Club. He was a genuine contender for the Team Hillary captaincy and organised several team get-togethers. Ultimately he was unable to travel, dropping out in the final weeks due to a serious illness. In recognition of his contribution, he had the MOM award named in his honour.

Charlie Campbell

A founding member of the Drovers, Charlie Campbell played a key role in the early planning stages and was instrumental in motivating Kirt to kick start his dream of the Everest Test. Redundancy in 2008 left him struggling to stay involved to the level he wished, but he remained a committed fundraiser and went on to win the MOM award in the match itself, taking 3/24 from his four overs.

Russell De Beer

Being a former Royal Marine Fitness trainer could not prevent

Russell De Beer from succumbing to altitude sickness early on. He heard about the trip through Charlie Campbell but was hamstrung by living outside London, thus being unable to attend many of the events and, although he was named in the squad, he had no illusions of making the final XI.

Ben Jarman (BJ)

The trip's youngest participant, Ben Jarman, along with his friends Chris Martin and Joe Williams, was often one to provide comic relief when needed. All three met Kirt while travelling in New Zealand in 2005 and BJ was more committed than most when it came to giving his time, taking part in every single weekend away and driving people to each of them. While on the trip he assisted Nick Mullineaux with monitoring the central kit and these contributions earned him a starting place in the final XI ahead of John Richards. He now works at the Royal Geographical Society and in 2010 completed the Mongol Rally.

David Kirtley

As Kirt's cousin, David Kirtley was one of the few people who knew hardly anybody when the trip began. One of the leading fundraisers, collecting more than £4,000, David was only able to commit fully to the trip once the cricket season was over due to his commitments captaining Cardiff CC. Upon doing so he used his contacts to provide much of the medical equipment as well as the team clothing. His brother is former international James Kirtley who helped publicise the event. On the mountain David took part in the porter race at Namche Bazaar, opened the batting and top scored with 45, also winning the Stick Cricket trophy for the most sixes.

Richard Kirtley-Wright (Kirt)

The man with the idea. Kirt first visited Nepal in 2006 and that is when the idea began to grow. He started playing for the Drovers two years previously as he was at Cheltenham College with several other people on the trip. Following on from The Everest Test he has worked tirelessly with the Walking with the Wounded charity campaign, led numerous people to the top of Mount Kilimanjaro and continues to make his name as an expedition leader, while also managing events closer to home such as Polo in the Park.

Glen Lowis

One of many who found out about the trip through friends of friends, Glen Lowis would go on to play a key role in the trip by earning the captaincy of Team Hillary. A New Zealander, his motto in life is 'Live for the Lost' after losing a friend a decade ago, and he spent several months living in Venezuela where he claims to have carved a cricket bat with a machete out of a tree trunk. This story on his application got him selected in the first place. In the match itself he opened the batting and took the final wicket to seal victory for his team.

Chris Martin

Our resident comedian, Chris Martin helped organise the comedy night in March which was a huge fundraiser, as well as providing Team Hillary with a place to have net sessions through connections at his old school. On the mountain he also took charge of the comedy night at Dingboche, where he was the butt of several jokes for his sunburnt ears. Another who met Kirt while travelling in 2005, he was a constant source of amusement throughout.

Chris Palmer (Kiwi)

Another original member of the Drovers, Chris Palmer missed out on the early planning stages because he was living in New York. A talented cricketer, once he returned he quickly took on the role of cricket coach for Team Hillary and also instigated extra training nights during the week. He married his long-term girlfriend Rebecca Demery on New Year's Eve 2009 and now lives in the Cayman Islands.

James Peterson (Jamo)

Standing 6ft 8" tall Jamo Peterson is an easy man to spot. He was the sole player from Team Hillary to emerge with any credit from the practice match in September and organised several get-togethers for the team, including the trip to Dartmoor. He was closely considered for the vice-captaincy but narrowly missed out, and fell foul of food poisoning on just day two of the trip. He was well enough to participate in 'The Everest Factor' which was an idea he remains very proud of.

John Richards

Another Drover and Cheltenham College boy, John Richards would finish as the top fundraiser on the trip totalling around £5,000. Unfortunately this was not enough to push him into the starting XI on match day, although his good humour and boisterous personality was invaluable throughout the trek. He married his long-term girlfriend, Eve, in Dublin during October 2010.

Tom Sharland

Often referred to as 'The Terminator', Tom Sharland ran the Trim Trails and is widely thanked by those who attended for toughening them up for the task ahead. He also wrote up the Environmental Policy which was vital in gaining permission from several Ministries in Nepal to play the match. He knew Kirt through their time together at Roehampton University and persuaded his fiancée Uju to delay their wedding to September 2009 in order to come on the trip.

Will Simmons

Another Cheltenham old boy, Will Simmons captains the cricket club there and is an excellent wicketkeeper. Living away from London made it difficult for him to be as involved in the team building as he would have liked but he still managed to raise the profile of the trip through the local media. Was struck down with illness on day eight of the trip and arrived at Gorak Shep a day after the group.

Jules Staveley

Ever the man with a film quote when you need one, Jules Staveley earned the duty of Vice Captain after bringing a lot to the expedition early on. His contacts help source the pitch itself, plenty of cricket equipment as well as training products. Travelling with his wife Victoria, they were the only married couple on the expedition and had a frightful row when she thought she had left her passport on the plane in Doha. He was at University with Gareth Lewis and Lucy Brooks in Bristol and suffers from a terrible fear of heights and suffered on occasion during the trek, collapsing on the penultimate day back down and having to be almost carried into Namche Bazaar.

Jonathan Woods (Woodsy)

Joining the Drovers in 2005, Jonathan Woods sourced the insurance policy that would cover a trip as unique as ours. On the mountain he won the beard growing competition but was one of the three unlucky ones to miss out on selection. He married his long-suffering partner Emily in March 2010 and as of December that year is the proud father of Alexander.

TEAM TENZING

Chris Beale (Blinky)

Another New Zealander and close friend of Glen Lowis, Chris Beale went on to get the 'Man of the Expedition' award as chosen by Kirt and Wes for his extraordinary work with the website and various technologies that enabled us to send back reports and images throughout the trip. He opened the batting and the bowling on match day with limited success.

James Butler

A latecomer to the expedition, James Butler is good friends with Nick Toovey and as more of an indoors type, was perhaps further out of his comfort zone than most during the trip. He met everyone for the first time during the freeze mobs in December and contributed by visiting schools as in the UK to pass on the message of what we were doing and collected prayer flags which were later hung up in view of Everest. He was with the group at the back with on the way to Namche Bazaar but reached Gorak Shep without any major setbacks, apart from mistaking Savlon Antiseptic cream for toothpaste. He also made me promise not to use the word 'duck' anywhere near his name.

James Carrington

Like Charlie BN, James Carrington plays for the Maladroits and was in Barbados in 2007 when the idea of cricket on Everest was first floated to him. His largest contribution was putting Wes in a room with the CEO of Qatar Airlines leading to us being given 50 free flights to Kathmandu and 450kgs of excess luggage allowance. He represented Tenzing's last real hope of success in the match but was unable to do much damage coming in at number seven.

Dave Christie

Another late addition to the squad, Dave Christie was able to negotiate significant discounts on trekking gear with the North Face and Ellis Brigham. Like James Butler he too registered a duck on match day but bowled well with the new ball. Dave also raised more than £2,500 for the Lord's Taverners.

Kinsey Hern

A committed Drover who has served as treasurer for almost a decade, Kinsey Hern is a charismatic personality who celebrated his 29th birthday with the comedy night at Dingboche. Prior to the trip he hosted a fitness training weekend on his farm in Hereford and did the bowling in Trafalgar Square during the press launch in January. Another active fundraiser, he has collected nearly £3,000 at the time of writing and continues to raise funds for the Taverners today.

Gareth Lewis

Policeman Gareth Lewis has played for the Drovers since 2004 and knew Jules Staveley and Lucy Brooks from his time at Bristol University;

and Alan Curr from their schooldays. His all round enthusiasm and constant suggestions earned him the job as Vice Captain of Team Tenzing. He took charge of events on Ben Nevis when the weather turned bad during his team's aborted attempt on the three peaks in October 2008.

Haydn Main

One of the few people unconnected to anyone else on the trip at the beginning, Haydn Main quickly proved to Wes that he was captaincy material and was given the job in September. He was a close advisor to Wes during the early stages and had plenty of ideas when it came to planning events and marketing the expedition. He fell sick during the trek as he struggled with the local food but recovered sufficiently to lead his team on match day.

James Markby

An irregular Drover, James Markby was at Reading University with many on the trip and due to his long working hours was unable to involve himself in the planning of the trip as he would have liked, but was still able to contribute. He batted in Trafalgar Square and despite missing out on selection for the final XI he read aloud 'The Man in the Arena' extract before the start of play.

Nicholas Mullineux

Joining the expedition late, and living in Oxford, made it difficult for Nick Mullineux to get to know the group before departure. As another from Reading University and a man for a challenge he was recognised by Wes as a valuable part of the squad. He climbed Kilimanjaro on his honeymoon some years earlier and had also participated in the entire Round the World Clipper race. Given the role of Quartermaster, he monitored all the central kit throughout the climb while his wife Philippa was the 24-hour emergency contact back in the UK while we were in Nepal.

Michael Preston

Another of the Kiwi contingent, man-mountain Mike Preston was introduced to the Everest Test by friend Haydn Main. Admits he was unable to play much of a role prior to departure, although he did host a team weekend for Tenzing at his home, and so took part in the porter race at Namche Bazaar. Made the final XI and then offered his place to Joe Williams on the morning of the match, but he played and was the last man out.

Neil Sharland

Brother of Tom, Neil Sharland worked with Glen Lowis and helped run the trim trail sessions through the winter. On the mountain he fell ill on day three which acted as a wake up to everyone that fitness was not relevant when it came to altitude sickness. He ultimately did not make the final XI.

Nick Toovey (Tooves)

Friends with Glen Lowis and Chris Beale; Nick Toovey is an avid fan of Australian cricket. He made nearly every training weekend and brought Stick Cricket to us which proved an excellent way of driving traffic to the website while we were away. He proved to be one of the characters on the trip and took the first wicket of the match on route to being his team's most economic bowler.

Mark Waters (The Ginger Rocky)

The only man who knew nobody on the trip at the start, Mark Waters also left his wife and two daughters at home to come and participate in the Everest Test. Kept an excellent blog including such gems as the Bath Half and Umpiring Course descriptions, which helped people get to know him since he lives in Hertfordshire. On match day he was the leading wicket-taker for Tenzing and joint top scorer for them as well.

Gareth Wesley (Wes)

The man with the motivation, Gareth Wesley was the spark that ignited the Everest Test. Despite suffering from undiagnosed chronic fatigue Wes was able to grow the project to the scale it became and went on to make an hour-long documentary on it. On the mountain he suffered more from drinking water laced with Kerosene but recovered enough to joint top score in Team Tenzing's run chase.

Joe Williams (MC Shark)

Arguably the best player on Team Tenzing, Joe Williams has scored a hundred at Lord's in his days as a Middlesex age group player. Another who met Kirt out in New Zealand in 2005; his rap on the comedy night at Dingboche remains one of the enduring images for those present. Unfortunately left out of the starting XI and suffered continually during the trek itself, staying behind one day at Lobuche and reaching Gorak Shep a day late and staying behind again at Phakding on the way back down.

UMPIRES

Alan Curr

Having been at Reading University between 1999-2002, Alan Curr was one of the original XI Drovers in 2003 and was Club Secretary in 2008, going on to become Expedition Secretary to the Everest Test. Before departure he completed the Berlin Marathon in September and the Umpires Course in February. Was joined to Team Hillary throughout the planning stages and brother of Helen, he stayed behind at Phakding when Joe Williams was struggling, and thus finished the trek a day later than the group.

Helen Curr

Before the trip Helen Curr passed the Umpiring course and completed the Berlin Marathon. One of the few girls who attended Trim Trail from the very start, Helen embraced everything about the Everest Test from day one. Sister of Alan, come match day she acted as third umpire.

Jonathan Hill (Hillsy)

Drovers Chairman in 2008, Jonathan Hill is another from Reading University and Cheltenham College. He failed the umpire exam at the first attempt, passing only days before departure and was attached to Team Tenzing. Another who excelled in the fundraising department, collecting around £3,000 for the Himalayan Trust. A new career as a teacher meant he was unable to be as involved as much as he would have liked in the planning stages, but was a valuable part of the teams on the mountain.

TREKTATORS

Lucy Brooks

Unofficial leader of the Trektators, Lucy Brooks came up with the idea that a group of others not playing cricket should be involved in the expedition. Friends from University with Jules Staveley and Gareth Lewis, prior to departure she was fundamental in organising several of the social events, not least the launch party in September. Once on the mountain bad knees caused her plenty of grief but she soldiered on regardless.

Marcus Chidgey

Founder of Captive Minds, Marcus Chidgey was a big supporter of the Cricket on Everest idea from the moment he heard about it and worked tirelessly to help find sponsors and drum up media coverage. While on the mountain he was often up late sending reports and images back to the UK in order to keep the story in the news.

Rebecca Demery (Sugar)

Now the wife of Chris Palmer, Rebecca Demery was unable to involve herself much before departure due to living in New York for much of the early planning stages and working long hours once back in London. Happy to give advice with event organising, she knew most of the group from Reading University.

Alexandra Fudakowska

Since becoming friends with Wes, Alex Fudakowska was keen to help out in any way she could from an early stage. She initially acted as a general organiser gathering the required information from people before passing on those responsibilities. She but remained on hand to help with event planning and returned to Nepal in 2011 to do voluntary work.

Paola Fudakowska

Sister of Alexandra Fudakowska, Paola was another of the leading fundraisers gathering almost £4,000 for the Himalayan Trust. Helped out significantly with the organising of various events and also provided professional advice when it came to certain laws and customs of which the Expedition Leaders needed to be aware.

Jennifer Gladstone

Friends with Charlie Campbell and Jamo Peterson; Jen Gladstone was the chief lawyer on the trip. She moved to Dubai in November 2008 but still made it back to several of the group meetings. On the mountain she was one of the few who were rarely in any difficulty.

Mark Jordan

The cameraman for ITN, Mark Jordan did not meet the bulk of the group until day one of the trek at Lukla. His reports were sent back to London Tonight every day and the footage and interviews he did on match day were carried on the national news.

Miles Nathan

Miles Nathan knew Kirt and Tom Sharland from Roehampton University, Miles came as an extra cameraman and producer. He spent much of his time with Team Hillary early on and came a cropper on day one of the trek when he wanted to carry his own pack like everyone else and also do the required filming. He changed his mind about that from day two onwards.

Victoria Nicholson (Vicks)

Having heard about the expedition through both Paola Fudakowska and the sister of Will Simmons, Vicks Nicholson was immediately keen and ended up taking over many of the responsibilities that Alex Fudakowska passed on. She obtained the letter from the Queen's aide wishing us good luck and was instrumental in writing up the sponsorship proposals as well as dealing with charities and organising events.

George Powell

George Powell was another who attended Reading University and as a professional photographer he became involved in the trip for the obvious photo opportunities. Also a trained fitness instructor, the early bleep tests were his domain and he took many of the images that now hang on the walls of those on the trip. He married his partner Weenie in June 2010 and became a father for the first time a year later.

Victoria Staveley

Half of the only married couple on the trip; Victoria Staveley lost her passport in Doha airport and also celebrated her 28th birthday in Gorak Shep the day before the match took place. She had her first child in May 2011 and is due again in late 2012.

William Wintercross

A friend of Kirt's, Will Wintercross is another professional photographer and his image of Ben Jarman in front of Everest made the front page of the Independent on the Tuesday after Easter. A keen climber, Will has climbed several peaks in Europe and is now setting his sights on Central Asia while continuing to freelance – largely for the Daily Telegraph.

Jamie Zubairi (Zooby)

Initially invited onto the trip as an amateur photographer, Jamie Zubairi became a victim to the sheer size of the trip and the need for professionals. His largest contribution was unquestionably designing the

Everest Test logo which went on every item of clothing, letterhead and web page that was produced throughout the trip. A keen artist as well, he often sketched while on the mountain but also fell ill in Lobuche and stayed back one day.

MEDICS

Isla Cox

Closet cricket fan Isla Cox had plenty of experience in Expedition Medicine and saw The Everest Test advertising on the wall of her hospital. Expecting it to be a paid job she called up only to discover that she would in fact have to pay £1,500 to be involved, but signed up anyway. She actively involved herself with the Trektators and stayed behind in Dhukla with Will Simmons when he became sick, catching up with Jamie Zubairi and Joe Williams the following day at Lobuche and arriving at Gorak Shep one day after the group.

Ian Ditchburn

Geordie Ian Ditchburn heard about the expedition from Jamo Peterson and having done some work at altitude in Bolivia was keen to do some more. He stayed behind with Neil and Tom Sharland on day three when the former became ill, and again with Joe Williams and Alan Curr on day 14 in Phakding meaning he finished the trek one day later than the group. Although not obliged to raise funds as travelling in a professional capacity, he did his best to contribute towards the Himalayan Trust.

Breck Lord

The last of the Antipodeans in this list, Australian Breck Lord is both loud and highly enthusiastic. He was terrified throughout the trip that someone was going to get seriously ill and made sure the group always knew the risks they were facing. He often featured heavily in the ITN reports sent back by Mark Jordan.

Nick Walker

A doctor in the army, Nick Walker was the most experienced of the medics on the expedition who heard about the trip via word of mouth. Biggest contribution on the mountain was perhaps his joke-telling on the radios while he was also swift to warn people of the dangers of trekking too quickly.

OTHER SIGNIFICANT PEOPLE

Alex Rayner & Lara Roussel– Captive Minds PR team who took leading roles in the January Press Launch.

Nir Lama – Head of Peace Nepal Treks, Nir organised everything that happened in Nepal and got all the permissions we required.

Dharma Maharajan– A self employed guide, he took Kirt to Everest in 2006 and came with us as an additional guide.

Jim White – Employed by Cricket World, Jim had huge belief in the expedition as soon as he heard about it and put us in contact with any number of suppliers of equipment and kit as well as giving plenty of coverage on the Cricket World website and magazine.

Shona Langridge – Lord's Taverners Employee who was on the mountain at the same time, she handed over the trophies in the post match ceremony.

Neil Laughton - Everest summiter and expedition patron. Neil spoke at several of our events and was a great source of support throughout.